A Scottish
Childhood

A Scottish Childhood

COMPILED AND EDITED
BY
ANTONY KAMM AND ANNE LEAN

COLLINS
IN ASSOCIATION WITH
THE SAVE THE CHILDREN FUND

First published 1985
Reprinted 1985, 1986 (twice)

Copyright © The Scottish Council of
The Save the Children Fund 1985

ISBN 0 00 435696 9
Printed by Collins, Glasgow

Photoset in Great Britain by
Rowland Phototypesetting Limited
Bury St Edmunds, Suffolk

Contents

Preface

BY H.R.H. THE PRINCESS ANNE, MRS MARK PHILLIPS, GCVO
PRESIDENT OF THE SAVE THE CHILDREN FUND

BUCKINGHAM PALACE

"A Scottish Childhood" offers fascinating memories of days gone by. This is an age of gas lights, tramcars, coal fires in the bedrooms (for the lucky ones) and poaching salmon for the Moderator. Some of the anecdotes are happy, some are sad. Between them they paint a vivid picture of life as it once was in households stretching from the rolling Border hills to the far north and the Outer Hebrides.

Thanks to the generosity of the contributors, The Save the Children Fund will benefit from every copy sold. This means that many of the world's most deprived children will get a chance to grow up - and remember.

Anne

Foreword

BY THE RT HON. THE EARL OF DALHOUSIE, KT, GVCO, GBE, MC
PRESIDENT OF THE SCOTTISH COUNCIL OF THE SAVE THE CHILDREN FUND

BRÉCHIN CASTLE
BRECHIN
ANGUS
DD9 6SH
TEL. 2176

The compilers of this volume, Antony Kamm and Anne Lean, have combined in a novel and ambitious enterprise to raise money for The Save The Children Fund in Scotland and their efforts have resulted in *A Scottish Childhood*. No less than seventy-two distinguished Scots have contributed a few lines about their earliest memories and it can be said that never before has a collection of such a nature appeared in print. This in itself is some achievement; but it is not just for its novelty, it is for its charm, in the highest sense of worldly values, that we must thank and congratulate the compilers. They have given us a book of great worth in which to delight.

I read the proofs first in two sessions and then I read them again over the course of a week and, in fact, have been dipping into them on and off ever since. There is no doubt that the two-session reading was a mistake. If the ordinary reader is to share in the emotions and childhood impressions of the individual authors and fully savour what mattered to them so greatly at that vital period of their lives, I can recommend the 'dipping in' system. The long-session one is sheer gluttony and makes savouring the various delicacies an impossibility.

The contributors come from every walk in life. As I say, all are distinguished and together they give a balanced blend of town and country unbringings. Their ages range across no less than 76 years and the compilers have been clever in arranging the pieces so that the scenery changes from Edwardian times to recent days. This parade through the years, as it were, serves to enhance the individual work of the writers.

I did find a temptation to extract points of interest from the book as a whole. This I have resisted for it is the treasured thoughts of each individual that gave me so much pleasure and I am sure you will find the same.

Dalhousie

Introduction

BY PROFESSOR A. NORMAN JEFFARES

Childhood is something that we have all experienced, in the normal even texture of its days, in its ecstatic joys and in its anguished sorrows. But if we ask whether a Scottish childhood is different from any other kind of childhood some inhibition about generalizations may stop us in our tracks. Can we dodge that obstacle? We can certainly approach it with some generalized expectations after a quick reconnaissance – and here we discover that in this book we find not only accounts of childhood in Scotland, but of the childhood of Scots (and in one case of a half Scot) outside Scotland as well. So there is more than Highland and Lowland, croft and castle, house and tenement; there is the Scottish character and its shaping, its ethos and values, its vitality and variety.

This vitality and variety come across clearly in these recollections, in their accounts of rich or poor, comfortable or cautious families, of varied background and social position, religion and education. They record a profusion of interest: in the arts, reading and writing, painting and visiting art galleries, making and listening to music, acting and attending the theatre, going to the cinema and listening to the radio. And there is the creative art of conversation, as well as argument, discussion and debate. Gardening, too, affects individuals as well as places, while recollections of sport reflect the richness of Scotland's space: shooting, stalking, fishing (poaching salmon and tickling trout included), rowing, riding, bicycling, and walking. There are organized games as well, football, cricket, rugby, ice hockey, tennis and, of course, golf, not to mention motor racing and those intricate games children play in the streets.

Life for children is not, however, always pleasant – one essayist may strike a chord in readers' minds with his recollections of the horrors of children's parties. Embarrassments and, worse, fighting, bullying, thrashings and beltings are recorded here. The darker side of adult life emerges as war, strikes and deaths caused by the savagery of the sea impinge upon children's consciousness.

Against this are balanced joys and wonders, delights and delectations: the haven-happiness of home, the protection of parents, the sunshine of seaside holidays, the occasional ridiculousness of relatives, the poignancy of youthful passion.

Some of Scotland's particular imagery naturally recurs in these pages: pipes, kilts, tartans, tatties, neaps, haggises, stags, glens, lochs, firths, peats, manses, sabbaths, sermons, psalms, maukins, gullions and drams jostle in a rich kaleidoscope. And echoes of the Enlightenment blend with the oral traditions of Gaelic speakers; they remind us of the richness and complexity of Scottish customs, institutions and intellectual life. Sometimes some of this life is seen by the contributors from windows in those trains that still traverse tracks of romantically spectacular countryside, sometimes through the smoke of black houses on the isles, sometimes from the windows of stone houses in the cities, or sometimes imagined by Scottish children far away in Africa, India, Japan, New Zealand or Russia – or even exiled in England!

The pattern that has been chosen for these recollections is one that arranges them roughly in the order in which incidents, or some main incident described in the piece, occurred. Thus we have a spread of social, political and economic history as backdrop, and become aware of the many different Scotlands these varied contributors have recreated for us, out of which a living picture of a rich and complex country emerges. It is one where the individual still matters, in Burnsian terms, where a sense of history prevails as in Scott, and where adventure echoes in Stevensonian energy. A lad or lass looks to a larger than local community; the persons and personages they have become, playing and having played their notable roles in it, look back on their youth with a sharpened awareness of ancestry, of the presence of parents, of the events – intense, isolated, accidental, or, at times, blessedly funny – that accentuate their individual development, crystallize the complex nature of their particular Scottish childhood.

A. NORMAN JEFFARES FRSL FRSE FAHA, PROFESSOR OF ENGLISH AT THE UNIVERSITY OF STIRLING, IS CHAIRMAN OF THE NATIONAL BOOK LEAGUE IN SCOTLAND AND A BIOGRAPHER, POET, EDITOR AND CRITIC.

Naomi Mitchison

AGAINST THE COLD

Both Edinburgh and Cloan were always cold. Central heating was still in the distant future (after a period of being disapproved of as unhealthy and unnatural – look at the Ancient Britons!) and double glazing even more so. Nor is it entirely simple to put central heating into solidly stone-built Scottish houses. In thousands and thousands of these houses the under servants carried the full coal scuttles upstairs and the empty ones down to the cellars and often had coal-smudged faces. I think my parents worried a bit about them, but probably not the older generation. It was after all their place. They were fortunate to be in 'good service' with security and respectability and the chance to move up.

At the beginning of the century the unders still only got a few pounds a year, but the wages of the senior servants were beginning to creep up. All of course wore long aprons over stuff dresses, ankle length, and white caps, but an upper, especially a parlourmaid, might have becoming streamers and her afternoon apron at least would be starched and tucked muslin. I think there must have been a butler in the Edinburgh house who probably among other things warmed *The Scotsman* – and *Times*? – for Grandpapa (my mother's father) who was fussy about his health. There must have been one at Cloan for there was certainly a butler's pantry where the silver was cleaned and I seem to remember green baize aprons, though I am much clearer about the head ploughman who came from the Mearns, as indeed most of the best farm servants did. I think perhaps the butler came up from London with Uncle Richard, while Granniema and Aunt Bay only had women servants.

A fishwife from Cockenzie called at Grandpapa's house, 10 Randolph Crescent, once or perhaps twice a week, splendid in her kilted skirt and striped petticoat, the creel of fish on her back. Of course the horse vans from the shops with which we dealt called every day, not yet having been partly replaced by the telephone. With luck one might be there when the orders were handed in and might find oneself in the way of sugared almonds, biscuits, cookies or French bread. One after another, the 'good' Edinburgh shops disappear and the supermarkets take over now. It isn't even easy to buy really fresh fish. But in those days people rarely ate out; today's coffee houses and cheerful students make up for a lot.

10 Randolph Crescent towered five storeys up in front, but, as it was built on the edge of a cliff above the Water of Leith, dropped down for countless storeys on the west side, past all of which one must climb to get to the gardens; this was a distinctly alarming process which just appears in my six-year-old diary: 'I went down to the cellars where I saw some things that looked like ghosts. The cellars are covered with Stalagtites; under them are stalagmites which are like bumps of India rubber on the floor. Stalagtites are long thin dark black things caused by water with lime in it driping between the stones in the roof.' Thus scientific interest is allowed to mask the terror. Jack describes it in greater detail with a plan and mention of an old well and pipe which I have forgotten. All this was below the kitchens and the wine cellar, far below Grandpapa's study where gentlemen were allowed to smoke, the dining-room, and above it the great double drawing-room and 'boudoir' where there was a singularly horrid picture on an easel of Boy looking good with long ringlets and a hockey stick. The Edinburgh drawing-room must have been beautiful; there was the long, glass-fronted bookcase topped with china, the very best of it in the centre cupboard, pictures, flowers, the gorgeous Worcester tea set and electric light. But, somehow or another, the bulbs were done up in yellow silk bags. Why didn't they get burned? Perhaps they did.

Above them again were the best bedrooms, and the narrower stairs to our rooms above. All has been remodelled inside into unrecognizability. Only the wonderful view remains, north to the pools of the Water of Leith between the high green branches, or down river, and the splendid granite cliffs of the rest of the New Town.

But could Edinburgh in winter have been quite as cold as I remember it outside? Perhaps our clothes were inadequate, though I had a muff on a string and of course gaiters with a row of horrible pinching buttons. Most ladies had muffs and fur necklets for winter, often with an animal's head on one end; these replaced the summer 'boas' of short ostrich feathers, white or dyed, but these were garden-party wear and of little practical merit. Next to us we all wore woollen combinations, thick in winter, thinner and short-sleeved in summer. One had clean ones on Sundays. The difficulty was that the edges round the slit at the bottom tended to get a bit sticky and scratchy. Over these one wore serge knickers, buttoning below the knee, but these had linings which could be changed more often. Men and boys had thick woollen vests and long pants in an unattractive 'natural wool' colour. Combinations went on during all my young life until the early twenties when I cast them off in favour of longish chemises of fine linen or printed silk – and of course I mean real silk – man-made fibres were still rather nasty. But I expect my mother's generation stuck to their ladies' combinations until the end.

Anyway, that should have kept me warm in the east wind of Edinburgh but it didn't. I was taken for walks, my hand held firmly, but I was allowed to run in Prince's Street Gardens or in the Randolph Crescent gardens that sloped steeply to the Water of Leith and St Bernard's Well, repaired by one of my forbears but whose water I was wisely not allowed to drink. I often hoped I would see a would-be suicide floating down from the Dean Bridge, parachuted by a petticoat as the story had it. Edinburgh pavements were particularly appropriate for the lines and squares ritual with their huge granite sets. I avoided the lines as, presumably, most right-thinking people do. Yet there must be some who actually step on the lines. It would be interesting to know with what other abnormality this is correlated.

I think we must usually have spent Christmas at Randolph Crescent until such time as Grandpapa died and Granny moved down to Oxford, when I was turned out of the nursery to an upstairs room, but at least then we had our Christmas tree at home. Still, Christmas was good wherever it was. How long the grey Edinburgh light took to seep through until one could see the shape of one's stocking at the foot of the bed. Was it as big as last time? Bigger? That promising bulge? Boy and I had separately helped to fill one another's stockings but had kept firm secrets. Some of the presents were wrapped, anyhow. I can't think I ever believed in Father Christmas coming down the chimney, but I gave the notion lip service to please my elders as my own children have kindly done for me.

There wasn't nearly such a variety of toys and games in the shops, though of course there was a blissful penny drawer in the arcade where I sometimes went: this had divisions each holding different penny toys: small wooden dolls or animals, tops, marbles, puzzles, single lead soldiers. That was the best place of all when it came to shops. But in Prince's Street, which must have been then partly unspoiled, there was Maule's at the corner by Charlotte Square, where Binns is now, which had 'ballies', round shells into which one's bill and money were put to whizz up on to an overhead rail along which they trundled to a central desk and then back. How deplorable if two purchases were made at the same counter so that both went into one 'ballie'! Jenner's, however, had a lift. Duncan and Flockart had blackcurrant jujubes which made a cold into a treat and there was also the hairdresser where my mother, before her time with short hair which indeed became her well, had it brushed with a rotary machine. I would have thought it would have been very bad for the hair but she kept hers much the same well into her nineties.

From *Small Talk* (Bodley Head, 1973)

NAOMI MITCHISON CBE (BORN 1897) HAS WRITTEN OVER SEVENTY BOOKS, INCLUDING HISTORICAL NOVELS, SCIENCE FICTION, TRAVEL AND CHILDREN'S LITERATURE.

Marion Lochhead

EDWARDIAN CHILDHOOD

Edwardian is an accurate adjective. I was born in 1902, the year of the coronation of King Edward VII, and the first public event to impress me was the death of that amiable monarch in 1910. There was a great deal of visible mourning: newspapers heavily bordered with black; token mourning dress at least; black hats and scarves worn by ladies, some even in black dress or coat and skirt (most feminine wardrobes had something black in reserve for possible bereavements). On the day of the royal funeral a service was held in the parish church where pulpit and gallery were draped in purple. This, my mother told me, was royal mourning. As pulpit and gallery were painted yellow, the effect was not dismal. My mother wore more than the decorous minimum of black, I wore a black-and-white striped coat and black-ribboned hat, and as we went into church we were handed purple bows to wear in our coat-lapel. An aunt in London sent me a postcard-photograph of the new Queen Mary, tall and stately in black with a huge hat, the young Princess Mary similarly attired, and between them the little Prince John.

Newspapers and magazines were full of anecdotes (selected and discreet) and of photographs. My father brought home a large, beautifully-produced album, which I wish I had kept. It was a picture gallery of the reign. Two centre pages had small but clear photographs of the King and Queen Alexandra, with their son, daughters and grandchildren, and a quantity of nieces and nephews from all over Europe: Russia, Spain, Roumania, Norway. A few years previously there had been a cult of the little Crown Prince Olaf whose mother, Queen Maud, was the daughter of King Edward.

There were pictures of events: dinners, races, garden-parties. One of the most delightful showed Mark Twain in formal morning dress, holding his top hat and being presented to Their Majesties. He had obviously made a good joke or told a funny story for the King was laughing heartily, while the Queen, afflicted by deafness, smiled sweetly.

Next year came the splendour of the Coronation of King George and Queen Mary, with local celebrations in varying degree. Then things settled down somewhat, and life went on at home and in school. One teacher, whom I greatly liked and remember with affection and gratitude (our friendship was renewed when I grew up) had an excellent habit of ending the afternoon with a story. She introduced me to Grimm. I already knew and loved Hans Andersen, and even then was aware of the difference between them; of the individual genius of Andersen, his unique blending of the magic and the everyday. But the Grimm tales came a close second. They were very well told.

This lady was a graduate of Glasgow University; a distinction still unusual though not startling. The Scottish universities had granted degrees to women since the 1890s. One afternoon she told us her own true tale and memory of the visit to the university by the Prince and Princess of Wales, now King George and Queen Mary. The undergraduates had all turned out, men and women, in their scarlet gowns and black mortar-boards. That sowed a seed which was to grow into my desire to go to college and which, at the end of the First War, I did. This was taken for granted – by my parents as by the parents of many school friends. All we had to do was to pass the necessary examinations, then on to an MA in literature or languages, or a BSc or MB. Most middle-class parents were in favour of higher education for daughters as well as sons. My father was also in favour of votes for women, which were not granted until 1919. The militant suffragettes who made a good deal of trouble before the 1914 War were not approved.

School was neither miserable nor entirely happy. So much depended on the teacher. Later, at High School, it became better. I struggled with mathematics, only just scraped through enough to let me go up to university, but I was willing and able to read any books, to learn French and Latin, both with positive enjoyment. I could make little of geometry, nothing of algebra, was rather dim in chemistry. Latin from the first made sense and it has lasted: the discipline, the structure, the economy in words – and the beauty. French was extremely well taught. We were soundly drilled in grammar, idiom, irregular verbs, an acceptable discipline, like that of Latin. But, besides, we were in our first year introduced to French fairy tales and nursery rhymes, and sang 'Frère Jacques' and 'Sur Le Pont d'Avignon' and other agreeable songs. My French teachers were delightful women with whom my friendship was renewed and continued in later years. One of them looked French, with dark hair and eyes, and a talent for losing her temper without malice or any hurt to us. In fact, we liked to see her in a temper and were not above provoking her. The dark eyes flashed, the hands flew out, the words were eloquent.

An English teacher was equally inspiring. She introduced me to modern fiction from Meredith to Hardy and Conrad, and, during the War, to the poetry of Rupert Brooke.

6

But the love of books began before I could read. My mother had a gift for retelling stories: fairy tales at first, then episodes from Dickens. I knew the small David Copperfield, Florence and Paul Dombey, Oliver Twist. Then I began to read for myself and to read for fun. There were books in the house, there were books in the local library – subscription for one at a time, five shillings (or twenty-five pence); for two, seven and sixpence.

Reading was never a duty and I was never told what to read. We did not have special Sunday books. I was not told to stop reading that rubbish, whatever it might be; good books were tactfully put in my way and were found to be interesting and amusing, while the rubbish drifted away.

We were middle-class, comfortable and secure, but we knew about poverty: children in shabby, even ragged clothes, some-times barefoot, emerging from very poor homes, perhaps eating a 'piece' of bread thinly spread with margarine or a scrape of jam; the piece was their usual meal. Our good, plain food – porridge, fish, eggs, soup, meat and vegetables and pudding, plenty of bread and butter, home baked scones, cookies and jam (and cake on Sunday) – would have appeared a banquet to them.

From about 1912 until 1914 we were aware, however dimly, of black shadows, wars and rumours of wars. In Ireland there was the threat of civil war, in Europe there was war in the Balkans. Until then wars had occurred in history and we took sides. We were of course wholeheartedly Scottish and proud of Bannock-burn, enraged by Flodden. The English Wars of the Roses did not interest me. In the Civil War I was passionately Royalist, through reading *Children of the New Forest*; about the French Revolution, again Royalist, led by the Scarlet Pimpernel; and in the Napoleonic war, entirely British. But all these were history.

Then came 1914 and talk of Germany and Austria; then the fourth of August. It came very close to us. My brothers both served, the younger only for a year, and both came safely home. But of some of their friends, my elder brother was to say thereafter: 'He didn't come back.'

Peace came and an easy way of life; many more comforts, relaxation of rules, college life, work and fun – until again the shadows fell.

Looking back, one profound and happy impression remains –

that we, as children, were not aware of a gulf between our parents and ourselves. There had been changes since their childhood but not drastic. The First War made a gulf, but it was, for a time, bridged; modern improvements came, life for the middle class was easy. But the Second War brought the end of the old world.

MARION LOCHHEAD MBE FRSL (BORN 1902) WAS A NOVELIST, BIOGRAPHER AND WRITER ON SOCIAL HISTORY. SHE DIED ON 19 JANUARY 1985, SHORTLY AFTER WRITING THIS PIECE.

Lord Home

THE POWER OF NATURE

My father was a naturalist, so my brothers and I were early steeped in the love of birds and beasts and fishes. From dawn to dusk we used to derive great excitement from learning their habits and ways. The secret of success is to be neither seen nor heard, which took some learning, as a boy is not naturally still. Once acquire that art, and the animals and the birds will come out of hiding and be your companion.

Nature teaches a boy that life has two sides to it – the beautiful and the cruel. The most beautiful of the birds have claws, and the stoat hypnotizes the rabbit to its death.

Butterflies do not deal in destruction – except that the caterpillars eat the leaves of plants – and they are perhaps the most vivid of all beautiful things.

So nature is an introduction to philosophy.

Schools nowadays take the young boys and girls into the country, so there is a real opportunity to be an amateur naturalist. I commend it. In the presence of nature – and I must include the flowers – life can never be dull.

LORD HOME OF THE HIRSEL (BORN 1903) WAS FOREIGN SECRETARY 1960–63 AND 1970–74, AND PRIME MINISTER 1963–64.

JOCK TAMSON'S BAIRNS

When I was a bairn I lived within sight of enemy territory. Only a stones-throw away lay a strange foreign country. England!

I was told the natives were an unfriendly lot. Indeed, they were our bitterest enemies, waiting for an opportunity to slink across the Border, steal our cattle and sheep, and burn down our abbeys.

The very farm on which I lived had been the scene of many a bloodthirsty battle in the past. There were still many scars to prove it, including the ruins of a look-out tower on the hill where the sheep were now peacefully grazing. It was here I played houses, but never forgot to keep a watchful eye on the frontier, ready to fire the beacon and raise the alarm if the dreaded enemy showed face.

> Fee-Fi-Fo-Fum!
> I smell the blood of an Englishman.

I was a trifle disappointed to see nothing more warlike on the horizon than the baker's horse or the postie on his bicycle. My catapults and bows-and-arrows remained unused, for I never even smelt the blood of one Englishman.

The trouble was there was a kind of No-Man's-Land on the Border: nothing but wild rolling hills that were Scottish one moment and English the next, though they looked exactly the same to me on both sides. Could it be that the human beings were alike, too? But how could the English be human?

I was soon to find out.

I met my first foreigner at the village school where I was a Mixed Infant. *She* was much more mixed than I was. Was she not *English*? Had she not cycled over from that dreaded 'other place', and did she not speak with a strange accent? Her ancestors had killed mine, and I wasn't going to let her get away with it.

I fought the battle bravely, but lost. The result: my first black eye, which I richly deserved. I was quite proud of it for a time, and then a strange thing happened. We became firm friends. Me! – fraternizing with the English!

From then on, I forgot the bloodthirsty tales of the past, and found out for myself what lay across the divide. The people were people, just like us, though they did speak in a different tongue; but it was only an accent. And, looking at Scotland from the other side, I began to wonder if maybe we were not entirely blameless ourselves. Had we not done *our* share of foraging?

There were scars on both sides, but surely they would heal. My black eye did; and soon my English friend and I were sharing the best of both worlds. We became bilingual. She taught me songs about 'The fishy in the little dishy' and 'Keep your feet still, Geordie hinney'; and in return I introduced her to 'Annie Laurie' and 'The lum hat wantin' a croon'. Soon I forgot she was English. She was just a lassie like myself.

It surprised me to find there was heather growing on her side of the Border, looking every bit as Scottish as it did on mine; and that English sheep had four legs, no different from ours. Ah! But the shepherds were. Ours had his own special way of whistling through his fingers to call the collie dogs to heel, and he counted his flock: 'Ane-twae-three-fower'. The English shepherd, on the other hand, had a queer kind of rigmarole: 'Een-teen-tethera-methera'. But it all added up to the same thing, and he came over the Border to help us at clipping-time. And never spilt a drop of our blood.

Gradually I forgot there was a frontier there at all. I still played houses in the ruined tower, but I never bothered about looking for the enemy or firing the beacon. I watched the horizon instead to see if *she* was coming – my English friend who had taught me we're a' Jock Tamson's bairns, no matter on which side of the Border we live.

LAVINIA DERWENT MBE CREATED THE CHARACTER TAMMY TROOT, AND HAS WRITTEN MANY OTHER BOOKS FOR CHILDREN, AS WELL AS BOOKS ABOUT HER CHILDHOOD.

Alastair M. Dunnett

My Mother

My first clear memory of my mother is of her winning the Married Ladies' race at some picnic in a crowded field. She was wearing a white blouse, a long black skirt, with a narrow-waisted black belt, and a huge picture hat. I was three. We were often at these picnics, travelling to the country by special train, the children with tin mugs hung round their necks by ribbon, and you got milk or tea, and sandwiches and cakes that weren't made by your mother. There was great cheering when she came skipping up the straight but I thought it was nothing out of the ordinary, since I knew she could do everything. Her prize was a sewing outfit in a yellow velvet case with embroidered flowers. This was such a treasure it was never used, but she would sometimes take it out and show it to me as a special treat.

Because I remember most of all some of the difficulties there were when she was old, it is pleasant to think back on her amazing agility. George came home once from school – he would have been about eight – claiming that a girl in his class, at playtime, had 'stotted' (bounced) a ball a hundred times. 'A hundred times!' mother exclaimed. 'That's nothing. Get me a ball!' We handed it over, and she stotted it two hundred times, which was more than I could count at the time. Of course there simply couldn't be anybody else's mother who could do this. Or who would even try.

Her great feat, however, was swinging the can full of water. We had this can, a receptacle of chipped blue enamel, which was used when we were sent for extra milk. When she was in the mood she could readily be persuaded to swing it round her head, half full of water, without spilling a drop. Then we would cry 'More water'. She would fill it three-quarters full, and swing away with centrifugal violence. The excitement was intense, as by this time the fevers of performance were in the air, and 'More still' we would demand. 'Make it full.' So, with the old jug brimming, she would set off again, while we watched the miracle. It is a sure winner with children, but if you try it, practise first, making sure that there is nothing in the way like children's heads, and testing that the handle won't come off. The main problem is the slowing down and bringing the receptacle to a stop. I can tell you, there were giantesses in those days.

From *Among Friends* (Century, 1984)

DR ALASTAIR M. DUNNETT (BORN 1908) WAS EDITOR OF *THE DAILY RECORD* 1937–40 AND 1946–55, AND EDITOR OF *THE SCOTSMAN* 1956–72.

William Montgomerie

COALS IN THE BATH

David's mother, scraping the bottom of the white-washed bunker with the coal shovel, decided that there had been too much dross in the coal. She stood the shovel on the scullery floor, beside the bunker, in case it might be buried under the first bagful of new coal, and laid a dozen or so pieces of slate in the ashpan under the fire in the kitchen grate. She would show them to the coalman. He was about due now, she thought, looking at the long grandfather's clock hanging between the inset bed and the mantelpiece. To make sure he would not pass, she folded a newspaper, taken from under the armchair cushion, carried it through the lobby to the Room, and wedged it between the bottom sash of the lefthand window and the sill. The coalman, looking up, would know to bring her two bags.

'It's a windy day,' said David's father to the Boss of the coalcart, who brought the first bag.

'It's aw that,' said Mr Christie, glancing out of the window between the Nottingham-lace curtains, as though the wind might have dropped since he left the street three minutes ago.

Erchie brought the second bag up the three stairs, and tipped it from his back over his right shoulder into the bunker. Then he closed the lid down to keep in the stour. The Boss never thought of doing that when he brought the second bag. He was that kind of man, and for that reason David's father never moved his chair to talk to him, but just turned his head.

But when Erchie came out of the scullery, his father turned his armchair round to face him, and discussed the coalmining situation as if Erchie were an authority on all aspects of coal production, from the number of stones in each bag up to the politics of coal-strikes and lock-outs.

Erchie pushed his cap up off his forehead, and the clean skin, between his black face and his dark hair, was wet like the cold side of the fireplace where the kettle steamed it. On his face there fought fear of his Boss, waiting for him on the coalcart and desire not to offend Mr Eglinton who seemed to value his opinion.

'It gives him a wee rest,' said David's father, after Erchie had gone. 'Of course, he doesn't know any more about the pits than I do.' And he told the coalman, each time the Boss was discussed, that the man would never go so far as to discharge Erchie.

'He knows he's got an honest workman,' he would say, and then, 'You'll be having your own cart someday yourself.'

'Aye,' said Erchie doubtfully, and thought it over for nearly twenty years.

David's father came each evening by tramcar from the centre of Glasgow, from the big work-a-day world, where David had seldom been, into the street that David and his mother lived in all day, for school and house were on opposite sides of the street. Even on visits to the seaside, neither parents nor children stayed long enough anywhere – one week at the most – ever to transfer all their luggage from their cases to the drawers and clothes-hooks of their lodging, or to unpack their Glasgow street from their minds. Maybe it was something David's father never knew, for, packed like camphor against moths, was his own country childhood at the bottom of his mind.

One Friday evening, no different from any other Friday, David's father was wiping his black boots on the bass outside his own door, and knocking rat-a-tat-tat-tat, rat-a-tat-tat-tat, on the right-hand panel of the dark-stained varnished door. There was more delay than usual before the door was opened.

'Didn't you recognize my knock?' asked his father, for the family all knocked on the door in a special rhythm, 'the Eglinton knock', they called it.

'Aye, but A wiz jist pittin coal on the fire for the boys' bath. A hid tae wash ma hauns first,' explained his mother, just a little bit apologetically, to explain the delay in opening the door.

In the early evening, David stood naked in a few inches of warm water, in the frosted-zinc bath, rubbing his chest and neck slowly with a dripping sponge. The big cast-iron kettle had been filled with cold water at the well in the scullery, and put by his mother on the hob of the black-leaded Carron grate, for his brother's bath. She was now sewing a tear in the seat of his short, navy-blue trousers, ready for tomorrow morning, and he felt the heat from the fire on his wet belly, for he had turned his back to her. His father was also behind him, writing a letter at the table, and Iain was playing at the other end of the same table with a Meccano crane, raising a half-pencil – a huge tree-trunk – six inches from the well-scrubbed table-top, then swinging the crane out over the edge of the ravine, so that the pencil reached almost to the floor, at the end of a yellow thread, the wire handle spinning round and round.

Friday night was bath-night, and his mother's hard hands, painfully hacked and rough, so that the skin clung to silk and satin, like sticky Willies from a hedge, grew soft, white, and wrinkled at the fingertips. He had first of all objected to her sponging him in front. He said it tickled him, though that did not exactly describe the sensation. Then he had turned his back to her and the kitchen with a new shyness, and had begun to imagine that his parents and Iain were glancing at him. Actually this was not true of Iain, and his parents had a greater understanding of him than he imagined. His mother still bathed Iain all over, but he was two years younger.

Actually this was the last time he would bath himself in that house, for next Friday his father told him that he was now grown too big to sit down in the zinc bath, which was true; there was too much splashing of soapy water on the hearthrug, and its colour was fading, which was also true, though neither was the real reason, and that it would be more convenient if he and Iain went on Saturday morning to the public baths, round the corner at the Cross, when most men were still at work, and the boys wouldn't have to wait.

The girl in the glass-fronted paybox at the Corporation Baths took the coppers from David, gave the boys a ticket each, and pointed to the door.

'Right through there!'

Through there was very dark and cold, and smelt damp. An old man in thigh-boots and grey shirt, sleeves rolled up over his biceps, took their tickets, and led them along another corridor with doors. There were sounds of splashing behind a few of the doors, and water ran along a shallow channel in the corridor floor.

'Here we are, sonny!' said the old man, pushing an open door wider, and going in first. He gave the big bath a quick wipe along a greasy tide-mark, and turned on the hot water with a brass key. The pale green water rushed down, and hissed and spluttered and gushed, as if alive, and the bath began to fill with swirling water, the bubbles rising from the hole made in the water by the thick jet.

David felt the old man looking at him, just like his grandfather.

'Ye keep yer coals in a bath tae, A see,' he said.

'We don't have a bath,' said David, 'not that kind,' very puzzled, and pointing to the big bath, that was bigger than any bath he had ever seen.

'Richt, first time,' said the old man. 'Ye're an intelligent laddy. Hoo can ye keep coals in a bath, gin ye dinna hae a bath, eh! It fair beats me.'

He looked at the hot jet, turned on the cold water with his brass key, and half-turned off the hot water. It had been difficult hearing his voice in the rush of the hot jet. He stirred the water with his wrinkled hand, like David's mother with the zinc bath at home, quickly turned off both jets, and picked up a very hard bristle scrubbing-brush.

'Dae ye ken whit that's fur? No, ye dinna. It's for scrapin the skin aff ye, like a new spud, an whan ye're scrapit clean, ye bile yersel in that hoat watter. A'll come in wi butter, an oatmeal, an syboes. That's the wey A like ma tatties.'

He grinned at David, as if they were old friends.

'Aff wi yer claes, sonny, an in ye get!'

He went out, closing the door, and taking Iain, who had waited in the corridor peering in, into the next cubicle. David could hear him joking with his young brother, but with the sound of rushing water beyond the partition, he could hear nothing of the sense of the conversation. He looked for a place to put his paper parcel of clean combinations and stockings. The only place that was dry enough was the corner of the grated board, lying in front of the bath, so he laid it there, and carefully piled his discarded clothing on top of his boots on the cement floor.

It was a completely new experience to lie stretched out in the bath, half floating in the water. He forgot for a long time to soap himself, but lay there looking up at the single electric bulb on the ceiling. He noticed that the partitions between the two cubicles on either side, and his own, did not reach to the ceiling, so that he could clearly hear the man in the next bath, grunting and scrubbing and snorting, with every now and then a splash and a gasp. He saw that he could stand on the end of the bath and look over, but decided not to do so.

The door of his brother's cubicle shut with a bang. Almost immediately, his brother's head appeared at the top of the partition.

'Ha, ha!' said Iain, with a knowing look, and his head vanished.

'Don't do that again, or I'll punch you black and blue, when we get out,' shouted David, sitting up, and reached for the soap, which was like a square of very crusty white cheese.

'Ha, ha!' said Iain, and began splashing as if he were lying on his back too, and thrashing with his legs.

When they were outside again in the corridor, each with his parcel of soiled underclothing wrapped in brown paper under his arm, the old man came along, swabbing the corridor. He grinned at them.

'So, ye haenae droont yersels ava!'

Just as they turned into their own street, they met the son of Mr Skilling, the school janitor, and told him where they had been. Iain was almost exploding with the message he had to give him.

'David's got hair between his legs,' he said excitedly.

David found it very difficult to restrain himself till they both entered their own close, where he punched Iain in the ribs till he grat.

WILLIAM MONTGOMERIE (BORN 1904) IS A POET AND FOLKLORIST, AND WAS EDITOR OF *LINES REVIEW* 1978–82.

First Love

The Big Boy took me into a lonely corner of The Field and told me the awful things that fathers and mothers did together. It was several years before I discovered that he was quite wrong. He was just about as innocent as we were, and wasn't in the class of the boys at school who carried around a marked copy of the Bible, so that they could turn to the dirty bits at a moment's notice.

At the time, however, I just disbelieved this Big Boy. I had a great talent for believing what I was told by my parents, and I had already fought a friend of mine who said that Father Christmas was really just your father. I am the eldest of nine children, so that I had quite a lot of experience of babies arriving in our family. And I knew perfectly well that Dr Mackinlay brought each new baby along in that black bag he carried when he visited my mother.

But I have strayed somewhat from the pavement, which we all preferred to The Field. The pavement was in front of the four closes which made up the odd side of Kennyhill Square. A close, in case you don't know, is an entry to a tenement building. On each floor there were two facing flats, eight in all since it was a three-storey tenement. The numbers were 1, 3, 5, and 7, so that we were on the odd side of the Square. My family lived at 7 Kennyhill Square, looking straight at the entrance to the bowling green which separated the odd and even sides.

I have said that it was a respectable place. It certainly was. The tenements were solidly built of bright red sandstone and the closes were proudly described as 'wally'. That meant that the entrance and the stairs up to the first landing were tiled. After that the scheme of decoration petered out into paint. To have a wally close right up to the top landing was rich indeed.

There were a great many boys and girls in Kennyhill Square – at least, there were on the odd side; we hardly knew anybody on the even side. And on the warm summer evenings we'd all be out there playing games or talking or chasing the girls. We played Leave-O (called by the lesser breeds 'Relieve-O'), Run a Mile; Kick the Can; Hopping Charlie; and Robinson Crusoe.

Robinson Crusoe was a good game, but it could be played only when a new boy arrived in the Square. The new boy was designated Robinson Crusoe and posted on the top landing of one of the closes. He was instructed that, when the leader shouted from the foot of the close, 'Robinson Crusoe, give us a call, please give us an answer', he would reply 'Cooee!' and then run down the stairs shouting, 'It was me! It was me!'

Below him, on each landing, stood a boy at the ready. When the leader shouted his Robinson Crusoe call, each boy pulled the bells of the two flats on the landing and ran downstairs. And then the unsuspecting Robinson Crusoe descended, just as people were opening their doors to the summons, shouting 'It was me! It was me!'

It was on that pavement in Kennyhill Square that I first fell in love. I was ten at the time and my inamorata was a girl of twelve. She had an exotic attraction for me, because she was English and knowledgeable. Her name was Viva Pringle, and she was the daughter of the proprietor of Pringle's Palladium, a picture house in Dennistoun which became a dance hall. But it wasn't her superior status in life which impressed me. I just thought she was beautiful.

The Pringles lived in Alexandra Park Gardens, and that meant that I could look from our kitchen window up at Viva's kitchen window. How full was my heart when, after gazing at that magic casement for quarter of an hour or so, I would see Viva actually appear and even give me a wave. She was the queen of our circle and decided that we all should have a nickname, which she herself would bestow. I can't remember anybody else's nickname, but the one she chose for me was 'Tusks', because of my protruding front teeth. Strange to say, it never caught on.

Alexandra Park Gardens overlooked Alexandra Park, and every summer we went into the park to listen to the band or watch the concert parties. Naturally, I couldn't afford the tuppence to get into the enclosure, nor could Viva. So we stood outside the railings and watched from there. Once or twice, when I was really in the money, I bought a penny programme and so became acquainted with the works of the masters – at least, those masters whose works were suitable for brass or military bands.

I was not only younger than Viva, but also slightly smaller. So I stood nearest the railings and she stood just behind me. It seemed fair enough. On one such occasion Viva suddenly said, 'Jack, may I ask you a personal question?' I said certainly she could. 'Well,' she said, 'when did you wash your neck last?'

This, coming from the woman I loved, had a great effect on me. I started washing my neck the very next morning, and kept on doing it until the parting of the ways.

That came when Kennyhill Square learned one day that Viva had disappeared. She had not only disappeared, but her coat had been found on the bank of the Monkland Canal. The police were called in, dragging operations were started, and Viva's younger sister told us with every sign of enjoyment that one of the detectives had explained that, even if dragging was not successful, the body would float within a few days.

However, Viva had left her coat on the canal bank just to worry her family. She had actually gone to her grannie's home in some strange place like Hamilton. Her father, the motion picture entrepreneur, went to collect her. Back in town, he told her to wait outside a tobacconist's while he bought some cigarettes. When he came out, she had disappeared again. This time she went to her auntie's on the South side of Glasgow. And there she was once again discovered and her father brought her back.

I can still recall standing at the parlour window of our house in 7 Kennyhill Square, and hiding behind the muslin curtain as Mr Pringle brought his errant daughter home, holding her firmly by the hand this time.

I never saw Viva again. First of all, my respectable soul was outraged at such carryings-on. Secondly, I realized she was not the girl for me. And at the age of ten I had surely time to look around once again. In any case, Mr Pringle moved the whole family from Alexandra Park Gardens, and shortly after that gave up the Palladium Picture House.

I have often wondered what became of Viva. Such a femme fatale must have had a wonderful life. I'd never have been worthy of her anyway.

From *Pavement in the Sun* (Hutchinson, 1967)

Dr Jack House is the doyen of Glasgow journalists. He has written many books, particularly about the city and its history.

George Bruce

ON THE SHORELINE

And even if you were in a prison whose walls allowed none of the sounds of the world to reach your senses – would you not still have always your childhood, that precious, royal richness, that treasure house of memories?

Rilke, *Letters to a Young Poet*

Very occasionally I would wake in the night and there was no sound of the sea. I think that was why I awoke. All its continual sounding was so integrated into the experience of living in Fraserburgh – the sea-town on a broad promontory of the northeast of Scotland – that its absence was strange. I had no fear of the stillness, and enjoyed the strangeness until the security of sleep once again possessed me. I did not know that the sense of security was due, ultimately, to the mental environment created by parents who loved each other and who extended that love to their children. I could not know that the feeling of unconstricted freedom, which was mine, was the outcome of this environment. The running boy, the diving boy, the boy challenging the currents and cold of the North Sea was its product. So the 'royal richness' of childhood was mine.

Yet never for a moment, when I began to write poetry responsibly, did I think of my childhood experiences as appropriate subject matter. That would have been treason to the poet's responsibilities. The experience of adulthood in the thirties was the reverse of a condition of security. In a society which educated us and then threw our abilities on the scrap-heap of unemployment we were the dispossessed; in a minimal measure, it is true, compared to the disposal of the Jewish people in Germany, but the social and political direction of events pointed to a decivilization of which the barbarity of the War was an inevitable culmination. With this background I found myself putting pen to paper in a train as it was crossing the Tay Bridge on a stormy December evening in 1940. The immediate motivation was the falling across my path of a drunk man out of a recess, followed by a woman offering herself, as I made my way to the station in Dundee from the High School, where I taught, my home being in Wormit-on-Tay. These images for my Waste Land disintegration poem got no further than a few lines, and in their stead, matter and style of a wholly different character took over. I wrote 'My House'.

My house
Is granite
It fronts
North,

Where the Firth flows,
East the sea.
My room
Holds the first

Blow from the North,
The first from East,
Salt upon
The pane.

In the dark
I, a child,
Did not know
The consuming night

And heard
The wind,
Unworried and
Warm – secure.

Re-reading these words written nearly forty-five years ago, I see they suggest a structure in total isolation – and so I felt it to be, sleeping on the top floor at the northeast corner of the house – and no growth about it, but there was a back garden, mainly grass, as large as a tennis court, though as I saw it, good for football. As I write these words I recollect an episode, whose meaning I can get to, only by thinking myself into the persona of the boy, as I do now, first reviving the original experience.

Our granite house
by the sea – never
out of its roaring or
shushing or hacking cough –
stood steady as any rock.

A good house with good people
in it: who looked after it,
and us. Everything there
was in its right place,
except us boys, of course,
though we knew where
we ought to be.

The way to the back green
was through the big trellised
gate. It wobbled open
when pushed or kicked
which we did. We would

rush into the back garden
to kick a ball on my father's
lawn, a whole football team
of us. We kicked it to pieces.
Father watched us kick his
green grass to pieces – from the
window – which he had watered
and cut, and got just right.

He did not stop our game,
Just watched from the window.
I went into the house. He said:
'My poor lawn.' Then laughed.
He patted my head. No grudge.

When I was Dad I went back.
No gate: no way: concrete lock-up:
could never be kicked down.
The folk knew nowt of sea.

'No grudge' – and no grudge held against our preserver and
destroyer, the sea. When a boy or girl wore a black armband at

school during winter the chance was the sea had claimed a relative. Our solidarity with the grief of the schoolmate was shown in silence. There was nothing to be said. It was the occasional price of the sea's harvest, and it knit the community closer together. But the plenitude of the harvest could on occasion be destructive of community.

I do not know when I first heard the word 'dumping', but despondency fell on the house and on the town like a fog when word went round that the boats had turned about from the harbour without unloading their catch, had gone back to sea, dumped their catch of herring into the water, and set off again for the fishing grounds. Expressions of indignation at the prodigal waste of the staff of life were rife, but what could be done about it when 'the bottom had fallen out of the market', that is to say when there had ceased to be a consequential demand for cured herring on the Continent, so that the price offered to the fishermen for their catch was not enough to cover the cost of their fuel to the grounds and back. You could not keep the fish: it would rot. It was possible that the artificial scarcity created might stimulate demand on the following day. That was the logic of the events. My own feelings about this 'logic' were crystallized on a sunny June morning about 1925 when I arrived at the harbour in time to see a fishwife bend to pick up a herring from a pile that had been dumped on the quay. 'No lass, not the day,' the skipper said, as the engine of the boat was put into reverse to return to sea. I watched it still laden to the gunwale, along with other boats all gleaming with herring deck-high in the hold, leave the port. It was the custom for the fishwife to top up her creel, which contained white fish of various kinds, with herring, before setting out to sell her fish in the country. The lunacy of what was happening struck me like a blow. 'Why', I, a schoolboy of fifteen years, argued, 'could the herring not have been loaded on to lorries and taken to Glasgow where the children suffered from rickets due to malnutrition?'

Some fifty years later the scene projected itself in my mind's eye as I took account of two pieces of information on the same page of *The Scotsman*. Two starving, refugee children on a road in southeast Asia looked out at me. Less prominently a paragraph stated that owing to the depletion of herring stocks in the North

23

Sea, all fishing for herring must cease. The threat of the destruction of the species was foreseen fifty years previously, when small-mesh nets caught immature herring, and caught them not for human consumption. The starving children exiled from their homes and the new necessary restriction on the harvest of the sea witnessed to man's folly and greed and inhumanity. To which knowledge all I could offer was the uselessness of a poem:

On the Roads

Little children
walk
in their bones
on the roads.

Hump backed
wi her creel
the auld wife cried:
'Herrin. Herrin.'

And the skipper said
tae the auld wife:
'There's ower mony herrin
in the warl. Pit them

back til the ocean.'
And she did.
. . . .

And the deid herrin floatit
on the watter.
Says the man that kens:
'Stop huntin thae herrin.

There's nae eneuch herrin
in a' the seas
tae feed thae folk
on the roads.'

'That precious, royal richness' – no road leads them to that inheritance.

GEORGE BRUCE (BORN 1909), POET AND CRITIC, WAS A BBC PRODUCER WITH SPECIAL RESPONSIBILITY FOR THE ARTS 1946–70. 'MY HOUSE' IS FROM HIS COLLECTED POEMS (EDINBURGH UNIVERSITY PRESS, 1970).

AFTERMATH OF REVOLUTION

In schools the old order was replaced by a new system. Prayers in the halls and classrooms were abolished. The priests, in their flowing black robes, who used to flit from one classroom to another imparting religious instruction to the young, were seen no more.

On account of the overcrowding in the city, the girls' school was requisitioned and its pupils moved to the boys' school. We girls commenced work at eight o'clock in the morning and after a short break, when we were provided with a small roll, continued until one p.m. The boys arrived fifteen minutes later and studied until six p.m. We were growing up now and this arrangement was a source of intriguing conversations, especially about the boys in the top form. We got to know the names of those we imagined were more outstanding than the others.

My attention was focused on a handsome, rather sophisticated boy in the top form named Alexei Anisyev, who was not even aware of my existence nor yet of any of my classmates. At the same time I caught the eye of a bear-like youth in the same top form called Sanka Chekayevsky. Sanka excited only antipathy. The silly poetry and notes left inside my desk, I found repulsive. Having once introduced himself he continued to pursue me on the slightest pretext, trailing alongside like a sad-eyed old St Bernard, but not so pleasing.

In normal times a literary evening used to take place each year in March. Our headmistress, undaunted by the prevailing troubles, decided to repeat the custom. The boys and girls gathered together in the hall and sat divided by a centre passage. The evening commenced with an ardent boy reciting the famous poem by Lermontov, *The Battle of Borodino*. This he did with great style, accompanied by emotional gestures, the rising and falling of his voice much appreciated by an audience who already knew it all by heart. A senior girl climbed on to the stage and sang a moving song all about love and white acacias. This was followed by a short comedy presented by boys only.

When all the performances were over and the chairs cleared away, the boys and girls, joining hands, started a Khorovod – the chanting circle moving round a single figure. After a little while I was chosen by some boy and stepped into the centre. As I danced, I noticed Alexei Anisyev circling with the others. This was a chance I could not miss and, as soon as the chanting stopped, I rushed up to my wonder boy and kissed him on the cheek. He laughed and took my place. The Khorovod began again but next time whom did he choose, but my best friend Shura. After this I lost all interest in the Khorovod and sauntered over to a long table where refreshments were being served. In days gone by we used to be offered hot sweetened chocolate with foaming cream, open sandwiches of various kinds, cookies full of raisins and spices – now there was only watery cocoa to be had and a single roll per head, which, being young and hungry, we still relished.

The moon was high when we were winding our way home. A fresh fall of snow blanketed the sooty snowdrifts and lay thick on the pavements, crunching pleasantly under our feet. In the groups was my faithful friend Valya, Nina Duletova and her father Duletov, the headmaster of the boys' school, who were our close neighbours. Soon, hurrying to join us, was Sanka, who lived in the street before ours. I chose to ignore him and continued my conversation with Valya, who unfortunately soon left us to turn into her own street. When we arrived at the point where Sanka should have turned towards his own home he, instead, continued with us down Olonetskaya Street. I became apprehensive. At the entrance to their house the Duletovs said their goodbyes and disappeared inside, leaving me alone with Sanka. Between the Duletovs' gate and our own was the long length of wall. For a few seconds we walked in silence, and then, deciding on the only course left for me, I took to my heels and ran. I had almost reached the gates when he caught me. There ensued a struggle during which we fell and landed in a snowdrift. The scuffling continued with Sanka determined to kiss me and I, like a wildcat, kicking, scratching, spitting, until suddenly out of the blue came a loud gruff voice saying, 'What the devil are you playing at?' Standing above us, holding his rifle, was a soldier. Thankful for my deliverance I scrambled up. 'I was only seeing her home,' began Sanka. 'And a fine way that was,' the man interrupted.

'Get,' he added, pointing his rifle. The last I saw of my brave cavalier was him scurrying like a scalded cat to the top of the street.

'Where do you live?' The soldier turned to me and on being told, pointed to the gates saying, 'They will allow you through.' I looked up at the house. Every window was ablaze with lights. I realized that a search was taking place.

Soldiers guarding the gates and back entrance allowed me to pass. Upstairs in the hall were more men guarding the door leading to the nursery. I was ordered to go inside where all the members of the family were congregated as well as Katinka and Sashenka. Only Mother was missing. She, it transpired, was going round the house with the men, unlocking presses and drawers, and was now in the garret.

No one knew what the men wanted, but suspected they were looking for arms. Yura's gun, which he used for shooting game, was hidden somewhere, but only he knew where it was.

In a few minutes came the footsteps of the men stamping down the stairs from the garret. We were shepherded into the dining-room. The soldiers carried in a large wicker basket containing a bundle of flags. They were big flags which in days gone by were hung outside the gates during celebrations of royal birthdays. There were also flags of our allies which had been flown on special occasions during the war.

The basket was turned out, the flags spread on the table. The leader of the group, in his sheepskin jacket, sat down and after careful scrutiny of each flag laboriously marked something on a sheet of paper. We stood around wondering idly what the strange purpose behind this confiscation. There they were. The old Imperial Russian flag, French, British, Belgian, Italian and finally one with the faded Lion Rampant. The man stared curiously at it.

Fifteen years ago on a bright winter's morning that flag had fluttered its welcome to a happy Scottish bride driving through the gates to begin a new life in a strange country. And now here it was again spread out before her. This royal flag of Scotland – her Scotland.

She moved closer to the table. 'This flag,' she began, calmly placing her hand on it, 'is the flag of Scotland. It is the flag of my country – you cannot have it.' There was no reply. The man raised his head and stared. He saw no sign of fear in the eyes gazing serenely back – no trembling of the hand. In the oppressive silence, even his men were tensely watching.

He was the first to drop his eyes. Bursting into loud laughter he turned to his men. 'Here's a wench for you, lads,' he called, and, pushing the flag towards Mother, added in a tone that was insolent and yet admiring, 'You can keep your flag.' She did keep it. Many years later I found it amongst the few things she treasured.

The basket was carried down the staircase. I ran to the window and watched the soldiers in the moonlight dragging it through the snow on the river front.

Later, when we were sitting around the samovar, I heard Babushka say, 'Nelly, you were foolish.' And I who had always leant heavily on the Russian side, for once was on my Mother's. Foolish perhaps – but how magnificent!

From *The House by the Dvina* (Mainstream, 1984)

EUGENIE FRASER (BORN 1905 OF A SCOTTISH MOTHER AND A RUSSIAN FATHER) ESCAPED FROM RUSSIA WITH HER MOTHER IN 1920, AND WENT TO LIVE WITH HER GRANDPARENTS IN BROUGHTY FERRY.

Alastair Phillips

FAMILY WORSHIP

Although I never pretended to understand Uncle George's sermons, I was at least word perfect in his prayers. It is possible that I took his allusions, and interpreted the snatches of Biblical quotation on which they were built up, too literally. While praying at family worship he referred at least once a day to the 'well that has been opened for sin and for uncleanness', and of this I had the clearest architectural picture, even down to the bucket and the rope and the winding gear. The equally frequent appeal to be 'tied up in the bundle of life', which I later, in the course of reading verse about, discovered were the words of the Prophet Samuel, evoked only a picture of Bessie the servant gathering faggots in the wood for the kitchen fire.

This was an incitement to inattention, for, with the possible exception of Aunt Maggie who had always something serious and domestic to concentrate on, we had the habit of letting our minds wander during the longer prayers. Thus the bundle of life suggested sticks, and sticks the kitchen fire, and the kitchen fire was always smoking and from that point on the drone of Uncle George's voice might well be no more than a soporific accompaniment to a step by step reconstruction of the sweeping of a chimney.

My complete familiarity with the prayers was only to be expected for we took the Books twice a day, immediately after breakfast and before bedtime, and I accompanied him on most of his pastoral visits, when he would put up a word in as many as a dozen houses in the course of an afternoon. He fell inevitably into habits of expression so that I just needed to hear one familiar word to be able to fill in for myself the dozen which would follow it.

The grace, too, was stereotyped, varying in length according to the presence of visitors, and the extent and quality of the repast. It could, indeed, be extremely curt on those washing days when the midday meal might be something frugal, like boiled potatoes and milk. On such a day Uncle George would say, 'Grant us Thy blessing with these' pause . . . 'mercies. Amen.'

The order of service at worship was unchangeable. We sang our way through the Psalms, indulging to the full our common preference for Barrow, Covenanters, Stroudwater, and Stornoway. Uncle George, having given the lead, resigned the grace-notes to Aunt Maggie, and the rest of us ploughed our way with dogged humility through the tune.

In the evening we read verse about from the New Testament; in the morning from the Old. The only compromise was the skipping of some of the genealogical tables in Genesis, and we pronounced the proper names as they seemed best to us. We probably derived more instruction from the lesson on those rare occasions when there was a train to catch and Uncle George read the whole chapter himself. The servant, always referred to as 'the girl', and those of us who were children were seldom very fluent at the reading, but were expert in the sharp practice of counting ahead, and rehearsing, while the others were reading, the verses that would fall to us. This spared us the humiliation of stumbling too badly, but it left us with little sense of the continuity of the chapter.

Then we turned round and knelt at our chairs while Uncle George said his prayer. This might last anything from five minutes to half an hour, while we weaker vessels drifted into vague reflections, or into secret games of patience. Easy-chairs and high-backed chairs each had their particular advantages. The high-backed chair was not so comfortable, but it was also less secluded, and, peering through the interstices in the woodwork, one could take unobtrusive observations on the room and on the attitudes of the others. Little things which in the ordinary scurry of activity went unnoticed became fascinating and delightful. You watched a coal teetering on the bars of the grate, and waited to see out of the corner of your eye how many would start when it fell. You made little optical tests, like seeing how many titles of books in the bookcase you could read without moving your head. Or there was simple pleasure to be had in seeing that Uncle George knelt with his toes bent back so that his slippers stuck out at an angle exposing the heel of a sock in which there was a big round hole. That was the sort of thing that Aunt Maggie would notice, too, for in the very act of rising from her knees she would be issuing her orders to the maid, and instructing the minister to go straight away and change his socks.

It did not do, however, to catch the eye of any of the fellow-sinners, for Aunt Maggie was watchful, and though she could not identify inattention from a faraway look in an open eye, she was deadly in recognizing intercommunication or collaboration.

The best position was facing an open window on a summer's morning. Then one could watch the pigeons and the crows, and keep an informed eye on the traffic passing on the high road.

The easy-chair called for a different, a more private and personal diversion. Sometimes you just burrowed your head into the three planes of an upholstered corner, and after adjusting it to a position where it was possible to breathe easily, went into a light doze. But that was usually for the evening after a long tiring day.

More often I would be wakeful and in the mood to trace out the pattern of the tapestry and count the blue threads, or to use the design for an intricate mental game resembling snakes and ladders. There were some easy chairs with wide deep arms that provided a complete retreat, and these were most exciting when they had no loose covers. With elbows and arms safely screened from any general view I have had many thrilling and rewarding treasure-hunts down the back and sides of the upholstery. I found pocket-knives, spectacles, screwdrivers, hundreds of pins, dozens of knitting needles, and many trinkets. The difficulty lay in transferring these undetected from the seat of the chair to the pocket.

These adventures in inattention were insignificant compared with the more constructive idleness of two of Aunt Maggie's younger brothers. Once at worship in my grandfather's house, they miscalculated the length of time that a visiting good man would pray, and when the family and guests rose after an unexpected 'Amen' the two boys were discovered, back to back, standing on their heads on the hearth rug. It was Uncle Dan, who was older, and who, I think, envied them their misdemeanour, who told me of that incident, adding, 'By faith, they got an awful lundering for that one.'

The more common embarrassments in a big family were the figures who remained scattered around the room still kneeling asleep at their chairs after the rest had reached their feet.

In the manse, as in my grandfather's house, guests of known eloquence, whether they were ministers or laymen, had the privilege of praying. This worked well where there was but one, or where the status was clear as between an old preacher and a student. It was among contemporaries of equal sanctity that the host had to steer with discretion, working out an acceptable distribution of graces at meal-times and prayers at worship.

Some used to say that Aunt Maggie was more worldly than Uncle George. She certainly took the responsibility of attempting to cut a prayer short if it overran an urgent earthly time-table. I can remember her tugging quietly at Uncle George's coat-tail while a man in a gig sat outside the door looking at his watch and making signs through the window, as he waited to take us and our luggage to the railway station. But she might as well have been trying to stop the tide for all the attention that she commanded.

This suggests in Uncle George a total removal from any awareness of his surroundings, which is not altogether true. One morning before breakfast Aunt Maggie made a milk pudding which she set to cool on the sill of the open dining-room window. After breakfast Uncle George pushed back his plate and called for the Books. Ten minutes later, looking up from the place at which she was kneeling Aunt Maggie saw the cat on the window sill, stalking the pudding.

She said 'Pssst', but nothing happened, and the cat came closer to the bowl. Uncle George prayed on.

Then Aunt Maggie said 'Pssst' again, louder. The cat gave no heed and Uncle George continued to pray.

But when she said 'Pssst' a third time Uncle George, without pausing in his supplication, reached down beside his chair and picked up a book, and, as he pitched it with perfect aim at the cat, he said, 'That's worth a dozen "Psst"s'.'

He then took up the thread where he left it and finished his prayer as though there had been no interruption.

From *My Uncle George* (Richard Drew, 1984)

ALASTAIR PHILLIPS (BORN 1909) HAS FOR OVER 45 YEARS CONTRIBUTED A WEEKLY COLUMN TO *THE GLASGOW HERALD*, OF WHICH HE IS A FORMER ASSISTANT EDITOR.

Robin Orr

MUSICAL OCCASIONS

My parents were both devoted to music. They gave me my first lessons and I grew up in a world where it was considered an essential part of life. I recall occasions in early childhood when I awakened from a dream and was taken downstairs wrapped in a blanket to listen to the music they were making with visiting friends. The 'musical evening' was a familiar feature in countless homes before the days of radio and television. Gramophones of course existed but few people would consider spending an evening listening to one, since quality of sound was very poor.

The first concert I heard on the wireless was around 1922 when I was thirteen; and not until I was approaching sixteen did I attend a symphony concert: Beecham conducting Mozart and Delius in the Caird Hall in Dundee. The impact of this was stunning. There is little doubt that children today miss something – an excitement and freshness – because they are conditioned to music on radio and TV from their earliest years, long before they can begin to comprehend it. Worse still, in many homes it is an almost continuous background noise with no attempt to make of it an event.

My father was a linen manufacturer in Brechin. He designed the family home and much of the furniture, producing all the plans himself and employing only a local builder. He used undressed stone in the native tradition, then quite unfashionable, and was influenced by the style of the old Scots tower houses. An old man walking by whilst the house was building was heard to remark – 'That'll be a recht bugger o' a house.' He might have added to this had he known that my father had also started building an organ (two manuals and pedals with pneumatic action) which was eventually completed in the house itself and proved invaluable to me later as a student.

After a year or two at Brechin High School and a good grounding in Tonic Sol-Fa I was sent to a new preparatory school – Hurst Grange – in Stirling, the very heart of Scotland, with the Castle rock jutting out like the bow of a great ship into the wide plain below and the field of Bannockburn just two miles down the road. Here I enjoyed the inspired teaching of John Kinnear on piano and organ. He had been 'Kapellmeister' to Lord Glentanar who promoted productions of Mozart opera in his house near Aboyne.

From Stirling I went to Loretto, one of the best known Scottish public schools with a formidable reputation for a spartan way of life, considered even tougher than the Royal Naval College at Dartmouth. Unfortunately, facilities for serious practice on the piano were then almost non-existent. I had decided music would be my profession and it became clear that I would have to get away from the school. My parents were entirely sympathetic, but not the Headmaster who quite properly disapproved most strongly. It was evident that no boy had previously left before the appointed time save through death or expulsion. I do not recall an expulsion but there were certainly one or two deaths. I was thankful to leave, but subsequently developed a sense of gratitude and affection for the place. I was simply the wrong type of boy for it.

At about that time Sydney Nicholson, then Organist at Westminster Abbey, invited me to the organ loft for evensong one Sunday. The impressions of that afternoon remain very vivid; the sunlight glinting through the stained glass and excellent music well-performed. A couple of broken down choristers were looking after the books at the organ. Clearly, they did not realize that the proper dress for a Scots boy of my age on Sundays was a kilt. Their scarce-concealed amusement at such an exotic sight was no more than a petty embarrassment, but I wished I could have clouted them over the head. I would have been dumbfounded had I known that more than forty years later a work of mine was to be performed there by the choirs of St John's and King's College, Cambridge, during the celebration of the 900th anniversary of the founding of the Abbey.

My interest in choral singing had been immensely stimulated by occasional performances by the Glasgow Orpheus Choir under Hugh Roberton. I have heard a vast number of mixed voice choirs since those far-off days, but for balance, for quality of sound and purity of enunciation I cannot recall a finer ensemble. There used to be a tale of an old man who went to buy a ticket for one of the Choir's concerts in Glasgow. By some mischance he entered an adjoining (undertaker's) office. To his request for a booking the reply came sombre but clear – 'Aye . . . we can book ye . . . but there are no returns.'

ROBIN ORR CBE (BORN 1909) IS A COMPOSER AND EMERITUS PROFESSOR OF MUSIC AT CAMBRIDGE UNIVERSITY.

Nigel Tranter

How Not to Start a Career

Like others, no doubt, I perpetrated many follies in my youth – and not only in my youth, I fear; but one stands out in my memory where others have been more conveniently forgotten. This because the scars remain to this day – and I mean scars, literally.

I would be thirteen at the time, I think, and as keen then on walking as I am today. I was reared in Edinburgh, and the Pentland Hills, which form such a notable backcloth to the Scots capital, were very much my stamping-ground, even though I lived on the other side of that fair city. One winter Saturday morning, with three of my school-friends, we made as usual for the Pentlands, for a day's scrambling amongst the tops and cliffs of Caerketton, Allermuir and Capelaw, the hills being snow-covered. We had to take the tram-car across town to the Braid Hills terminus and walk the rest of the way, a couple of miles in what was then open country. At the extreme eastern end of the Pentland range, suitably called Hillend, and not far from Robert Louis Stevenson's Swanston, where now there is an artificial ski-slope, there has to be surmounted the first outlier of the greater heights, called then Quarry Hill, a mere pimple compared with the rest – but big enough for what transpired. In those days there was no ski-tow, etcetera, only gorse-bushes dotting the grassy slopes, hopping rabbits and the large quarry which gave the hill its name.

Well, the four of us climbed the quite steep slope on the frozen snow, heading for the dramatic cliff-and-scree heights of Caerketton beyond. And near the summit, we came across the centre-piece of this account – a sheet of rusty corrugated-iron about six feet by two. How it got there I have no idea; perhaps a gale had blown it off the roof of some shack connected with the quarry. At any rate, as we passed it, we kicked it, as boys are prepared to kick anything, and it slid smoothly on the frozen surface – and fate took over. We had been bewailing the fact that we had no sledge, with the snow-slopes just begging to be sledged down. And here was a make-do toboggan. Or so I proposed.

I seem to recollect some doubts on the part of my companions, but nothing sufficient to deter your present hero. I pushed the thing to the beginning of a suitable steep, with a clear run down of perhaps three hundred yards, bar a gorse-bush or two, and sat down at the front of it, legs wide. My friends, Harold, Chogg and Browno, sat in file behind, arms round each other's waists. But despite pushing with our heels, the hitherto mobile corrugated-iron refused to budge, owing to our weight. So I shouted to Browno, at the rear, to get up and give the thing a push, and then jump on again.

Now there was a hole in the iron at the back, no doubt where a nail had once secured it to a roof, and Browno was armed with a stick he had picked up. He stuck his stick into that hole, to serve as lever, and pushed. His effort was entirely effective and the sledge shot away satisfactorily – save only that it went off too quickly for Browno to jump on again. Racing after it, in an effort to delay matters for the moment needed, he dug in his stick at that hole to hold it, with all his strength. His effort again produced results – but not those desired. The would-be sled slewed round in perhaps a forty-five degree angle and again shot off, but in a different direction from that intended, leaving Browno and his stick behind.

We went at an exhilarating speed, for this was a still steeper slope, and we clung to each other – at least the two behind me did – in shouting glee as we hurtled down, the corrugations on the iron as good as any sled-runners. That is until I realized that we were heading straight for the top of the quarry.

It was an off-putting thought, even for a thirteen-year-old. I yelled the news, and the need somehow to stop the thing, or change direction, or something, anything. We had our legs upraised, necessarily, before us. Now we brought them down, to try to dig in our heels. But without the least effect, on the frozen snow. On we sped, at ever-increasing pace, directly for the lip of the quarry.

I suppose that great gouge in the face of the hill had formed a precipice perhaps seventy or eighty feet high. We did not *fall* down this, we shot over and onwards at the same angle as our previous descent, so great was the momentum. I do not remember any glorious sensation of flight, although I imagine that we must have been airborne for eighty yards at least.

That we made a landfall at that angle probably saved our necks, for we hit the mouth of the quarry where the slope resumed, and so the impact was somewhat lessened. Also, the wind swirling round the quarry had formed something of a snowdrift. Into this we crashed, and I think that for the moment I lost consciousness, for my two companions catapulted on top of me with major force on their way further. At any rate they were flung forward, clear – except of me. I remained alone, on the iron, dug in like it, into the drift.

As I recollect it, the first coherent realization was that of vast relief that we had stopped flying. Then the cries of my colleagues, who had picked themselves up and were pointing, drew my attention to the growing scarlet stains on the snow on either side of the corrugated-iron. My stuck-out legs had taken the impact of our landing, and the raw edges of the rusty metal had gouged out their own little quarries, holes on each leg, one on my right calf, one at my left ankle – not cuts, you understand, but complete cavities in the flesh, each about two inches long by almost an inch wide. Presumably these bits of me were still attached to the iron sheeting, with part of my stockings – but we forbore to search.

Browno came hurrying down the side of the quarry, in some agitation.

So there we were, in distinct disarray. What to do now? A two-mile walk back to the tram-terminus, and then the best part of an hour's ride plus a final although shorter walk thereafter?

Oddly enough, after the initial outflow, the bleeding was not heavy. By great good fortune the main blood-vessels seemed to have escaped. Little white wormlike things in the holes were probably muscles. We all produced handkerchiefs, in various stages of cleanliness, and thankfully covered up the gaping and unsightly gashes; they looked much better that way. I found that I could walk, if a trifle shakily. There was little or no pain, then, only numbness.

Somewhat silently, save for the apologetic Browno, we set out walking downhill for the road, myself pacing stiffly, wide-legged.

Today, no doubt, we would have flagged down a car. But this was 1923, cars were few and far between and thumbing lifts unheard of. So we just soldiered on. All I remember about it was that it seemed a long two miles to that terminus.

In the tram itself, of course, my legs stiffened up. The blood-stained hankies drew a certain amount of public comment, but our embarrassed non-eloquence gained us peace.

Hobbling from the second tram to my home in Edinburgh's North Side was the worst of it, supported as I was by my now somehow shame-faced friends, who seemed to feel responsible for it all and who dreaded meeting my parents. They left me at the house-door and fled.

I will draw a veil over my mother's reaction to this early return home; also the family doctor's remarks presently. Part of his trouble was that he could not stitch the sides of the wounds together, then or ever – there was this yawning gap between. So his only method of trying to join the opposing lips was to attach thick surgeon's plaster to the upper side and pull strongly downwards and then slap the lower end of the stuff on the further leg and ankle. This was not terribly efficacious, and less than comforting. And thereafter it had to be repeated every day. Not only was this in itself painful but the continual pulling off of the old plaster and reapplying new ripped out all the hairs of my already hairy legs, which in consequence grew raw, scabby and presently suppurating – indeed this treatment was more misery than the wounds themselves. Why I did not get blood-poisoning from the rusty iron or the aforementioned pocket-handkerchiefs, was a mystery.

Anyway, I had no less than six weeks off school, owing to the inability of those wounds to draw together – for which Browno could never understand my gratitude to him. He was a more willing scholar than ever I was.

Mind you, there is a moral somewhere in all this, even though I personally have never found it. They say that one lives and learns, but . . . ?

NIGEL TRANTER, NOVELIST AND HISTORIAN, IS FORMER CHAIRMAN OF THE NATIONAL BOOK LEAGUE IN SCOTLAND; FORMER (NOW HONORARY) PRESIDENT OF SCOTTISH PEN; AND FORMER CHAIRMAN OF THE SOCIETY OF AUTHORS, SCOTLAND.

Norman MacCaig

A Month that Changed Things

I don't need to think long to decide on what, in my young days, had a greater influence on me, and a more lasting one, than any other thing. In fact, I don't need to think at all, for I've been conscious of it for many years. It was a holiday in Scalpay.

My mother came from that small island in the Outer Hebrides and Gaelic was so much her first language, her 'knee language', that when she came to Edinburgh at the age of sixteen she had not a word of English in her mouth. (This was a long, long time ago.) My father was born in the Border country of Scotland, in Dumfriesshire, though his people on his father's side were also Gaels. So there were many Gaelic corpuscles wandering through my veins, unrecognized.

For my father had no Gaelic and a result of this was that I learned none at home and I thought of myself as just another Edinburgh laddie.

Then (roll of drums) I went at the age of twelve on holiday to Scalpay and a new, or, rather, an old world was revealed to me.

Scalpay has changed since then, but only materially, not fundamentally. In those days there was one rough, forked road. There was even a scatter of 'black houses' (thatched, with a fire in the middle of the floor) and most people drew their water from springs. My uncle John still went out drifting for herring in a small boat with a lugsail. My two aunts (like many others) had no English. The men's work was mainly fishing, as it still is, though they worked at the peats and grew some oats and potatoes on lazybeds (as they still do). The women wove tweed from the wool they had spun on spinning-wheels. I could go on and on pointing the differences between Scalpay and my familiar Edinburgh.

One difference was that my uncle Roderick was there – my boyhood hero, strong as a bull, full of mirth and full of songs, the like of which I'd never heard except at times when my mother sang as she was working about the house.

I fell in love with that place and the people in it – with everything about it, in fact, except the religion which they clung to with the deepest of faith and fervour. This opened my eyes, though I didn't much like what I saw. I was born an unbeliever and still am.

My eyes were opened to other things: the hard labour of both men and women to wring a living from a difficult environment; the neglect of such outlying places by the government (the beginning of politics, for me); the cheerfulness, the neighbourliness, the generosity of the people and the open, uninhibited way they showed their affection even to that skinny young townee.

But it was more than all that. The only curt way I can find to express it is that that visit gave me what I'd never had before, a feeling for the past *in which I had ancestors*. It gave me the beginnings of a sense of history in which I belonged almost as in the present. I began, slowly, to grow up, to realize that I belonged to a lot more than a family. And that was a large enrichment. Of course, I was unaware of most of this at the time. I was just a boy on holiday, playing with other boys, meeting relatives, enjoying every whole long day. But things were started that changed me forever.

Years later I wrote a poem that has something to do with all this.

Drifter

The long net, tasselled with corpses, came
Burning through the water, flowing up.
Dogfish following it to the surface
Turned away slowly to the deep.

The *Daffodil* squatted, slid ahead
Through the red Kyle with thirty crans
Of throttled silver in her belly.
Her anchor snored amid its chains.

And memory gathered tarry splinters,
Put shadowy sparkles in her bag,
Slid up her sleeve the hills of Harris
And stole Orion and the Dog.

I sat with that kind thief inside me;
I sat with years I did not know

Heaped on my knees. With these two treasures
I sailed home through the Gaelic sea.

NORMAN MACCAIG (BORN 1910) WAS READER IN POETRY, UNIVERSITY OF STIRLING 1972–79. 'DRIFTER' IS FROM HIS *COLLECTED POEMS* (CHATTO AND WINDUS, 1985).

Angus MacVicar

SALMON FOR THE TABLE

In 1924, the year we poached a salmon for the Moderator, there were only five of us: myself, aged fifteen; Archie, twelve; Willie, ten; Rona, six, and Kenneth, a baby in his cot. John, the youngest, had yet to be born.

At the time, as minister of the small country parish of Southend, Kintyre, my father drew an annual stipend which fluctuated on the edge of £350, out of which he had to maintain a Manse with eleven rooms, six dilapidated outhouses and a garden like a park, as well as a hungry family. He had never heard of such a thing as an expense account. In the circumstances, a two-day visit of the Moderator of the Church of Scotland, touring Kintyre in mid-autumn, posed for him an anxious problem. On the administrative side it posed an even more anxious problem for my mother – and for Maimie, the maid.

The Moderator, however, turned out to be a jovial man – he was the Right Rev. David Cathels, DD, of Hawick – who could discuss not only Church Law but also other more interesting subjects: fishing and golf, for example, and the Olympic achievements of Eric Liddell. He complimented my mother on her soda scones, and when Rona upset her breakfast milk on his shiny black breeches, his infectious chuckle soon chased away visions of a wrath to come.

At about five o'clock on the second evening, disaster struck. By this time the chickens and eggs supplied by kindly parishioners had all been eaten, but as a special treat for our guest at what we called 'the last supper', my mother had reserved a magnificent cold tongue. For some reason, however, the larder door was left open, and Roy, a yellow collie from the neighbouring farm of Kilblaan, saw his chance and took it. The last anybody saw of the tongue was in Roy's mouth as he disappeared over the garden wall with a flick of his white-tipped tail.

Tears were in my mother's eyes. Though guiltless, for once, Archie and I stood by her, consumed by sympathy. Willie and Rona had gone to ground beneath gooseberry-bushes in the garden: a prudent move, because Maimie was darting back and forth, scolding everybody.

'Now all we have is tinned salmon!' said my mother. 'Think of it. Tinned salmon for the most important man in Scotland, next to the King!'

My father, always inept in a domestic crisis, muttered a vague *'Dominus providebit'*, which happens to be the motto of our clan. But Archie and I exchanged looks of inspiration. We went out into the garden and joined Willie and Rona under the gooseberries.

'Listen!' I said, with an eldest brother's authority. 'There's a big salmon in the pool below the bridge: we saw him this morning. If we caught him now, he could be cooked in time for supper.'

'Your rod's broke,' said Rona.

'I've thought of something else. We'll make a landing-net out of the Dutch-hoe, a loop of fence wire and the string net from Kenneth's cot.'

Archie, the honest one, said: 'That'll be poaching.'

'Yes, but it's for the Moderator. He's a holy man, so it's okay.'

Some years later, studying Moral Philosophy at Glasgow University, we both detected a flaw in this argument. But at the time it satisfied us; and when our preparations were complete we went into action with no qualms of conscience.

A latter-day Penelope, Rona remained at the Manse to counter awkward questions with guileless words; Archie and Willie took up their positions as scouts, a hundred yards away on either side of the bridge, while I, chewing a handful of gooseberries as a rather frightened gangster might chew gum, crept cautiously to the burn's edge.

I saw him at once in the clear water, brown, red-spotted,

sensuously rubbing himself against a boulder. His nose pointed upstream; his tail moving from side to side.

Gripping a bridge support with one hand, I lowered the net with the other. In the evening quiet the only sound was a tinkle from the burn as it flowed steeply into the pool. Scent of newly cut corn mingled with a tarry odour from the bridge.

He saw the net and twitched backwards. I persisted, holding impatience in check. The white string bag moved towards him: eighteen inches, a foot, six inches. My mouth was dry and salty.

Then I decided to stake our plan on one desperate sweep. Tense with anticipation, I thrust the net forward and, as I thrust, suddenly found inside it a furious, fighting, twelve-pound fish. I tried to heave it up but lost my hold of the bridge support. I slipped and fell and splashed headlong into the water.

A shock of fair hair appeared above me. 'The keeper's coming!' said Archie.

I struggled out of the burn and killed the salmon with a stone. 'Act the decoy!' I ordered. 'Collect Willie and make your way home, round by the church.'

Then, soaked to the skin, I ran like a deer for the slope leading to the Manse. In the end, panting and almost done, but still undetected by the gamekeeper, I staggered into the kitchen and laid our catch at my mother's feet.

Archie was killed in the Second World War, on the plain of Gerbini in Sicily. Rona died in 1949, soon after winning the Gold Medal at the Gaelic Mod. But Willie, now senior skipper with the Anchor Line, he and I still remember that triumphant evening and the grace my father said as he lifted the cover off the steaming fish: '*Lord, we ask Thy blessing upon these mercies. Accept of our thanks and forgive us our sins.*'

We remember, too, that the Moderator nearly forgot to close his eyes.

From *Salt in my Porridge* (Hutchinson, 1971)

ANGUS MACVICAR (BORN 1908) HAS WRITTEN MANY NOVELS FOR BOTH ADULTS AND CHILDREN, AS WELL AS AUTOBIOGRAPHY, AND FILM, RADIO AND TELEVISION SCRIPTS. HE IS HONORARY SHERIFF SUBSTITUTE OF ARGYLL.

St Fillans

'Get on your bikes: I have the lunch in my rucksack.' Such was the sharp order from Father to sons Bobby, Ben, Frank and myself, as we set off for summer holidays. The objective was a house on the edge of the loch of St Fillans. The school year was over, and as we pedalled through some hilly country between Milngavie, Killearn and Balfron, the road began to level out. After leaving the Baillie Nicol Jarvie at Aberfoyle to our west, we headed for the only lake in Scotland – the Lake of Menteith. From there, what was then a rough track climbed the hills, from whose summit we could whisk down to Callander, the appointed lunch spot. That track was the only part of the journey where we had actually to get off our bicycles, to push them a mile or two uphill.

Arrival in Callander, however, was a great reward, for by the banks of the Leny we ate our lunch opposite a shop which kept excellent ice-cream. Furthermore, Father had a liking for stone ginger beer, and this was handed out to us in the long-gone brown clay bottles.

On again, up Loch Lubnaig, through Strathyre, to the Braes of Balquhidder. Then to Lochearnhead, with the knowledge that although the road followed the loch in gentle bends, quite flat, it was really downhill all the way as we headed 'home'.

We thought of it as home. The bonnet of a snub-nosed Morris Cowley, peering out of the back yard, announced that Mother had made it with the youngest two, Maisie and Pip, together with the baggage train required to run the holiday properly. Before us lay the prospect of climbing, walking, boating, picnics, golf or whatever we felt like doing – Ben chose more than often to be out at dawn accompanying the local shepherd when he took his flock to the hill pastures.

Why 'home'? Because Father, being a Minister, lived a peripatetic life. I, for instance, was born in Aberdeen, and at the age of one was to be found in a row of Georgian houses near the Kelvin in Glasgow: then in the manse at Milngavie, where this journey started. It was a hike of about fifty miles. We always arrived tired but triumphant, hungry but hilarious.

At Easter, we used to go by train, through a wonderful succession of now-defunct stations – Gleneagles, Tullibardine, Highlandman Muthil, Crieff, Comrie, Dalchonzie, and so to base. From St Fillans station there was a very steep hill with a ninety-degree turn at the bottom. Here, on one occasion, the wheel declined my handlebars' invitation to turn left. I hit a barbed wire fence and pitched into a field. Cuts and bruises were all part of Mother's lot. She had great faith in iodine, and, if a wound went septic, in the application of pink lint covered with some peculiar manufacture called 'gamgee'. One day on the beach, which was a short piece of cobbled stone, I stood on a bit of sharp glass, which penetrated quite deeply. Hearing my calls, Father came to the rescue. In the middle of his ministrations, a howl of anguish came from the back garden. Ben had just decided to remove the tip of Frank's index finger over the chopping block with a wood-axe. I was dropped like a hot potato. However, a charming doctor from Comrie, five miles away, sorted matters out.

The boat was a great asset. Father said we must not hoist a sail, because Loch Earn was extremely dangerous – the wind blew from the west virtually down a funnel between the hills. However, picnics in the boat were great fun. We used to set out fully-loaded, with a large Portobello earthenware teapot in the bow called 'Rebecca' – there was a picture on the outside of Rebecca at the well. It held, I later discovered by using it to draw beer from the Balgedie Tavern, about four quarts. We made a fire from flotsam, boiled the kettle, ate hunks of bread carved by Mother from a large loaf, and 'swam and swam, all over the dam'. For those who wanted, there were large beakers of milk, which was brought daily in a large can from the farm just across the loch at Ardrostan. One small visitor was reputed to have asked Mother if it was 'pasteurized' or 'boiled'. 'No,' replied the Matriarch, 'out of a dirty can.'

We ought to have been expert fishermen, but the loch was not well stocked and there was a rumour that it was as deep as the hills were high – an average of 2000 feet. If true, the result of this was that the only real fishing grounds were the mouths of the burns which fed the loch, but here the trout were small. Each year there was a one-day competition, and I used to row for the retired army officer who looked after the golf course. Competitors could fish all day. Weighing-in was at the village store at midnight, by the guttering light of a hurricane lamp. Most catches of the small trout weighed some 4½ to 5 lb. The postman, who was probably unable to get to the river before 7 p.m., almost invariably arrived, panting, at about 11.50 p.m. with a 5½ lb sea-trout which he had winkled out of some deep pool, thus winning by a few ounces.

Mr Crerar, who owned the village store, was one of those characters one finds in a small shop which has no competition. He had a small pair of rimless glasses on the end of his nose, and never seemed to know where anything was. They said that when he died, they found unsold stock, probably ten years' old, and worth a lot of money. The other 'shop' in the village was the Post Office, run by a very large woman called Mrs Scott. I remember well her taking the part of Britannia, clad in a huge Union Jack, and crowned and sceptred in the celebration of the end of World War I in 1919. We found her a little terrifying. Other supplies came from Comrie in vans. To this day I recall the delicious smell of newly-baked bread-rolls and cakes which greeted our nostrils when the baker opened the rear doors of his van. Fish and meat arrived in the same manner. There was also the coalman, Mr Menzies, called by us properly, I think, 'Mr Mingiss'. One day, sister Maisie ran after him, shouting, 'Mr Giss, Mr Giss,' and so he stayed named from that day on.

We played golf. Every Scottish child used to be given or purloined some old clubs, which would be a mixture of cleeks, jiggers, mashies, brassies or baffies, all with hickory handles somewhat bent and showing signs of use, good or bad, and redolent of the song which described some poor fellow who was 'Gowfin' a' the day, doin' na work and running aboot wi' a bag o' sticks after a wee bit ba' '. We had no bag. The other problem was golf balls. There were two bridges, one rustic for walkers, opposite the only hotel 'The Drummond Arms': one stone, and ¾-mile away towards the end of the village and which connected the northern shore-road with the southern – not much more than a track. Below the stone bridge was the third tee, and the hole ran for five hundred yards along the bank of the River Earn and was more than a trap for higher-placed golfers who would not 'wat their cork-heeled shoon'. The river was shallow, so wading in admittedly freezing water was no hazard. The rewards in partially used Dunlop 65s or Kroflites were often significant. The nine-hole course was embosomed in the lofty hills of Earn and, at one point, faced what Sir Walter Scott described as 'lone Glenartney's hazel shade'. Once a friend of my uncle gave me a niblick with a steel shaft and some *new* balls!

Sunday in Scotland, according to some, was a day of gloom and overfeeding. After church and a hefty lunch of roast beef, which was supposed to last most of the week but hardly did, we usually set off up the Birren, the hill opposite us, of about 2000 feet. There were three ways up, and it was usually a case of who, using which route, could get to the top first. Then back for high tea, which had, as well as bread and jam, scones, pancakes, and always tattie-scones.

The hills were an endless source of delight. Ben Vorlich, the highest, was a 'Munro' – in Scotland a hill of over 3000 feet. We occasionally climbed it, but it meant a five-mile bike ride to the bottom, before one started. More fun was to climb behind the house to Loch Baltichan, a small loch cradled in hillocks. Its clear water refreshed us after the climb. If we were more ambitious, then we went 'over the hump' and dropped down into Tayside near Ardeonaig and thence to Killin, where by arrangement we were usually picked up by Mother – after Father once returned from an outing with a telegraph pole figuratively wrapped round his bumper, he did not do much driving.

Evenings at St Fillans, though long in summer, were filled by games. The house was fairly big and built in good Scottish stone, faced by the relentless chipping of the stonemason. The large room on the right of the hall was divided into two by a curtain and this immediately lent itself to amateur theatricals or charades. To get to the kitchen, one went down a stone-flagged passage, with a left-hand bend in it, into a large, well-lighted room, with an enormous iron stove, which ran the whole length of the northern wall. Another short passage took one into the laundry, which was largely taken up by two huge boilers and space for ironing with the solid irons which were heated on the mammoth stove.

The house was lit by paraffin lamps, as there was no electricity: so part of one room was filled with an impressive array of lamps, which had to have their wicks trimmed and their containers filled. The larger ones gave the sitting room a mellow light, which was kind on the eyes when reading.

All-in-all, it was a marvellous base, which I missed so much that when I went to Kenya on my first appointment in 1936, I was so homesick for it that I wrote a poem about the place.

The whole question of a base for peripatetic children came starkly clear to me with my daughter and son, who were dragged with us round the world, never living in a house which belonged to them. When in 1955 we acquired a small old cottage in Hampshire, the effect on them was extraordinary. Their whole relationship with life and with us changed overnight. They could at last say, 'This is *my* home!'

SIR WALTER COUTTS (BORN 1912) WAS GOVERNOR OF UGANDA 1961–62, AND GOVERNOR GENERAL 1962–63.

Andrew Purves

A SHEPHERD'S YOUTH

I was eleven when Father decided to leave Burnfoot. He gave notice to his employer just before Christmas, the customary time for herds and stewarts, before the onset of the January hirings. We bairns knew nothing about this till we saw his situation advertised in the local press. It came as a shock especially to myself and my younger sister, who had known no other home. I gathered later that Father and his employer had not been hitting it off well for some years, but father had only tholed the unpleasantness for our sakes, because Burnfoot was so handy for the Kirk and school.

Father heard of a place in Roxburgh Newtown which required a shepherd. He went to meet the farmer, and was hired there and then. On 28 May, three carts came to flit us, and we duly landed at Roxburgh Newtown, which was to be our home for four years.

The fields were not steep and stony, as they had been at Burnfoot, but gently undulating. The stock was roughly twenty

48

score of Half Bred ewes plus hoggs. The staff consisted of shepherd, stewart, three hinds, byreman, spademan, odd boy and one or two women workers. Our house and that of the stewart were built together and stood near the steading, commanding a splendid view of the Eildon Hills. From the front window we saw some lovely sunsets, conjuring up in my youthful fancy visions of Heaven.

My eldest sister had left home two years before, and was in situation as a housemaid near Jedburgh. She used to cycle home on her day off, about ten miles each way. One Saturday, Mother, my young sister and I visited her at her place of work. We walked to Roxburgh station, took a train to Jedburgh, and walked another two miles to the house. We were quite well received in the servants' hall, where we had a couple of meals. Mother was shown over part of the house by the housekeeper. Being an ex-housemaid herself, she was very interested.

Many farmworkers' daughters preferred to go into service rather than work in the fields, these being about the only two options for them. My sister trained to be a housemaid and made that her career. She worked in various parts of the county, and as far away as London, before returning to Jedwater, where she was until she married a gamekeeper there.

As a family, we were well-fed, for Mother was a good cook. For breakfast, we had fried ham with plenty of gravy, part each of a sort of omelette fried with the ham, and made of egg, flour and milk whisked together. We carried a 'piece' to school, with a flask of tea or cocoa, or milk in summer. On our return, Mother had a hot dinner ready for us of soup, potatoes and meat or Welsh rarebit, followed by milk pudding. At about 7 p.m., we had a supper of porridge with milk, or treacle or syrup when the cow was dry. Father preferred to have his porridge for supper, and we followed suit. On Sundays, it was always tatties and mince for dinner, followed by 'Uncle Tom', a steamed pudding made with treacle. We ate large quantities of rhubarb and stewed apples in season.

One of my chosen playgrounds was the Muir Wood, a conifer

plantation at the west end of the farm. There was a lovely, green, open glade, deep in the wood, where we used to roll our eggs at Easter, have picnics and hunt for mushrooms. I used to go there alone at times to play my sheep games with fir cones. One day I had a very eerie experience. I was deeply absorbed in my game, conducting a make-believe auction sale, blethering away to myself, when I suddenly had a strange feeling that I was being watched. All at once, I felt very much alone in the silence of the wood, which was broken only by the cooing of pigeons. A sort of fear gripped me. I lost interest in my game, and ran home.

In 1926, the General Strike affected Roxburgh more than many other rural communities, since it was a railway place, and practically all the railwaymen were out. The daily papers were reduced to a double sheet only, and feelings ran high in the parish. The farmworkers were not affected, really, but tended to sympathize with the strikers. Our parents and several others took the opposite view, arguing that the strike would only make things worse in the long run. One neighbour said to my father, 'D'ye no' realize that the miners are fightin' a fight for us?' Which was a dubious argument for had a rise in farm wages resulted in higher food prices, they would have been the first to girn.

During the prolonged miners' strike which followed the collapse of the General Strike, coal became very hard to come by. The farmer got permission from the laird to have a tree felled, cut up and divided amongst the householders. All the men on the farm staff took part in the job of cutting up the tree with axes and cross-cut saws, the work being done in their own time in the evenings.

It was now that I first came across the works of Sir Walter Scott. We were right in the middle of the Scott country, and history, particularly Scottish history, was my favourite subject at school. Indeed, I dipped into it far deeper than what was touched upon in our school books. I first read *The Lay of the Last Minstrel*, which was in one of my sister's books from the High School. I got hold of a copy for myself, read and re-read it, and committed long passages to memory. Then I devoured *Marmion* and *The Lady of the Lake*.

By the time I was twelve, I had made up my mind to be a shepherd. Though I was a good enough scholar, I refused to sit the bursary examination, success in which might have taken me to Kelso High School for three or even six years. My parents and headmaster were dismayed and angry. Although Father had always encouraged me to take an interest in the sheep, he had cherished the hope that I would make a career in some other direction.

Apart from my deep interest in shepherding, there were other factors, which made me scared of going to the High School. My sister's books and the subjects she studied overawed me, plus the piles of homework she was saddled with. Then there was my ingrained hatred of woodwork and of the PT teacher, who had been a visiting teacher at my school – both of which would have confronted me at Kelso. It all seemed an appalling prospect.

Though I am certain today that I might have done well for myself academically, I never really regretted my choice of career, nor did I neglect the intellectual pursuits. I remained an avid reader, quite a bookworm, in fact. There is no reason why a person should not work happily with his hands and still retain an interest in things of the mind.

Extracts from an autobiographical manuscript

ANDREW PURVES (BORN 1912) WAS A SHEPHERD UNTIL HIS RETIREMENT. HIS THREE SONS, THE ELDEST OF WHOM IS AN ACCOUNTANT, ALL WENT TO UNIVERSITY.

David Daiches

MAIDS AND MAIDLESS

—

While my mother was well, my father had little contact with the maid. When he was not out at one of his innumerable meetings or at the Synagogue he stayed in his study, reading or writing, and his study was a sacrosanct room which no maid entered, except when he was out, to dust it. But the maid had the duty of answering the door, and ushering into the study people who called on my father, who would range from heavily bearded emissaries from rabbinical colleges in Eastern Europe to the Professor of Hebrew or of Logic and Metaphysics at Edinburgh University. Some of the callers knew no English, and curious mutually unintelligible dialogues between maid and visitor would go on at the front door until my father came out to see what was going on or my mother came to the rescue. Sometimes an extremely impressive looking visitor would turn out to be a crook: I remember a venerable looking couple of gentlemen who claimed to be collecting for some European *Yeshivah* (rabbinical college) but whom we later discovered, with the help of the police, to have been collecting only for themselves. My father was continually being visited by collectors, beggars, émigrés, scholars, talmudists, clergymen, distressed persons, eccentrics, fakers, and he was generally able at a glance to distinguish the genuine from the counterfeit – something which I was never able to do, for I found myself nearly always most impressed by the least worthy. I remember once two young men arrived at the house, speaking only Yiddish, and alleged that they had just arrived by cargo-boat at Leith from some Baltic port, and were penniless and starving. My mother made them a huge meal, while my father cannily telephoned the appropriate offices at Leith to find out whether in fact a boat from that Baltic port had arrived that day. He found that none had. It turned out eventually that the men had arrived by train from Newcastle, and that they were making a systematic tour of the Jewish communities of Britain, telling a different hard-luck story at each one and collecting free meals and substantial sums in cash. Such gross abuses were, of course, infrequent; most of the distressed persons who arrived at our house in search of help were in genuine need; but the well-known charitableness of Jewish communities towards needy brethren from any part of the world did encourage the occasional confidence trick.

My mother had to be ready at a moment's notice to give any one of this miscellaneous collection of visitors a meal. She was not often caught unprepared, but I recall one Wednesday afternoon (early closing day, when the shops shut at one) when she was suddenly called upon to provide a substantial repast for a hungry *meshullach* (emissary from a *Yeshivah*) at the awkward hour of 3.30 p.m. The only food in the house was for the family's dinner that night. I was sent to borrow some eggs from a neighbour and the *meshullach* had to be content with boiled eggs and vast quantities of bread-and-butter, which he ate, it seemed to me, with an almost contemptuous air. On another occasion my mother had just prepared supper for my father and herself and, by some chapter of accidents, had nothing in the way of food left in the house apart from what she had prepared, when a venerable looking gentleman made his way unannounced into the dining room. My mother, in some embarrassment, explained the circumstances, and apologized for not being able to give him a meal, at which he smiled and sat down at her place and fell to. My mother went into the kitchen and shared the maid's supper.

To the maid, my father was always 'the Master' or 'the Doctor', and was referred to with a certain amount of awe. 'We must have lunch prompt today', my mother would say, 'because the doctor has a meeting at two o'clock.' The maid must have thought of my father as moving in a mysterious multi-lingual world, full of oddly-dressed characters and strange and impressive rituals. After the main meal of the day we would say the long Hebrew grace, singing out the beginning and the end of certain paragraphs, and the maid would move around the table collecting the dirty dishes and listening. If my father introduced a new tune, as he would occasionally do, the maid might comment to one of us later in the kitchen: 'Yon was a nice tune the doctor had today.' When we were very young we had no self-consciousness at all in discussing these matters with the maid; but as we grew older we became more reticent.

When my mother was ill, and she had a number of spells of illness, sometimes fairly long, in the 1920s, my father would come into closer contact with the maid. He would have to go into the kitchen sometimes and give orders himself, speaking always in a tone of extreme politeness, and referring to my mother as 'the Mistress'. 'Oh, Mary, the mistress would like you to bring up a cup of tea. Would you please do that?' 'I think we might have dinner now, Mary.' He was not exactly shy of the maid, but he clearly felt that this was a kind of human being of which he had no real knowledge and he spoke to her with a certain caution, as one might speak to an animal of whose disposition one was ignorant. There were sometimes quite long periods when there was no maid, and mother was ill, and my father would wrestle with domestic affairs himself. There was one period when he used to get up early and make porridge while we children helped in various ways (I used to light the fires and clean the shoes), and I have a clear picture of him standing by the stove in his dressing-gown, stirring the porridge while admonishing us to hurry or we should be late for school.

The most serious problem that arose when we had no maid was the lighting of fires and the turning on of the gas on the Sabbath, when such activity was forbidden. There was a little grocery shop, Cameron's, round the corner, where we used to get some of our groceries, and they had a messenger boy ('message boy' was the term we used) whom we were sometimes able to get to come in and put a match to the fire or the gas stove. The boy regarded us as quite mad. 'See,' he said to my mother the first time he was asked to come in and light the gas, 'it's quite easy. Ye just turn this wee handle and then pit the light tae the wee holes.' 'I know how to do it,' replied my mother calmly, 'but this is the Jewish sabbath and I may not strike a light.' The boy's jaw dropped, and he looked at her sideways, half scared. But later he came to take it all for granted. Sometimes, when Cameron's boy was not available, my mother would go into the street and ask anyone she could find to come in and light the gas. I remember an occasional bewildered stranger being led into the kitchen to put a match under the soup. When I was a little older I would ask my father what one was supposed to do in a community where everybody was Jewish and there were no '*goyim*' to light the gas, but I cannot remember ever receiving a satisfactory answer. The logical answer, I suppose, would have been that everybody would have to stay cold, and we had some experience of that state on winter Saturday afternoons when there was no maid and no temporary substitute.

We always had dinner about one o'clock on Saturdays, soon after we came home from *shul*. After dinner my parents would take a nap and we children would be left to read in the dining room (which was also the living room). On a winter's day when we had a maid, we would sit round a roaring fire and read, helping ourselves at regular intervals from a large bag of boiled sweets which Mother provided every weekend; they came from Cooper's, the large Edinburgh grocers with branches all over the city, and were technically known as 'Cooper's finest boilings', a description we considered expressive and appropriate. When there was no maid, we would huddle round a small electric radiator which would warm only those parts of the body immediately in front of it. I don't think I have ever been so cold as I have been sitting reading in our unheated house in Edinburgh on a winter Saturday afternoon. On one such afternoon I was reading an account of Scott's final and fatal expedition to the Antarctic, and the coldness of the scene described in the book mingled with the coldness of the room to produce in me the impression that I was slowly freezing to death, and it was a long time before I felt really warm again. The South Pole, Cooper's finest boilings and the coldness of our dining room are still connected in my imagination.

The electric radiator – which did, I suppose, make some difference, though memory links it only with extreme cold – could be switched on and off on the Sabbath, as the electric light also could, in accordance with a decision of my father's which differentiated his position sharply from that of my grandfather, patriarchal rabbi of an orthodox Jewish congregation in Leeds, who would have been shocked if he had known how cavalierly we treated electricity. Gas light or heat, which required the striking of a match, was another matter: that was clearly prohibited. But electricity was a phenomenon unrecognized by the Talmud, and my father felt free to make his own interpretation of the nature of the act of switching on the electric light or heat. He decided that it was not technically 'kindling a fire', which a biblical injunction prohibits in the home on the Sabbath.

From *Two Worlds* (new edn. Sussex University Press, 1971)

PROFESSOR DAVID DAICHES (BORN 1912) IS A LITERARY HISTORIAN AND CRITIC.

Peter Brodie

'McBride'

The years of my early schooling in a Lanarkshire town covered the miners' strike, the National Strike, a period of depression and postwar reaction. Of course, such matters did not concern us, none the less we were the innocent victims of society's bungling and confusion and war-shock.

Our school was built in 1876, so said the carving on the masonry – at the height of British Imperialism. None of the then very up-to-date facilities like drinking water and wash-hand basins were functional by my time. They had long been stuffed with stones and earth. One of these – only one – was carefully protected by the teachers and I remember still the smell of strong carbolic soap beside it. We used slates and 'slate-com', and frugally-issued jotters in the higher classes. Once I remember a slate go hurtling towards a teacher. I waited for the world to stop. Now I wonder, did the teacher not just tantalize too much a breakfastless lad with no place on a littered table to do his home-work.

Could I say our school was classless? On the one hand there were miners' children from the 'miners' raw', poorly dressed and ill-fed. On the other, a few of the pupils lived in the big villas east of the school and their parents made their money as local drapers, grocers or chemists, and a few were works' managers or professional people. In between were the children of parents who were skilled tradesmen and clerks from offices and factories.

The class lines were there, I suppose, but I didn't think of them operating in school; certainly not in the playground, where rank and authority were very differently distributed. There we tolerated no snobbery and brain power was doled out in different proportions from wealth. However, there were marked differences in dress. Duncan, from a house that stood in its own grounds, always had a new grey flannel suit every term and wore a cap. The School had no motto for his cap, however. McBride from the miners' raw had a ragbag variety of clothes and as often as not an exposed shirt-tail. A safety-pin held his shirt closed at the neck. His stockings were never darned: just holes and more holes. He, and, I suspect, a third of the boys at school, never knew the joy – at least I felt a thrill when I had anything new to wear – of being taken into a shop and having shoes, jersey or trousers specially bought for them, wrapped up in brown paper and handed over by the shop assistant. They wore 'hand-me-downs' and the residue from some Kirk jumble sale. Nothing ever just fitted. Colours never matched.

Monday morning was not the happiest time in the school week because it meant that the freedom of the weekend and the Saturday matinee were over and a whole long week of school lay ahead with the nagging question 'would the hero stop the train in time?'

Frankly, I never liked school and the only thing I hated more was going back after being absent through illness. But it had one bright spot. Before going up the short brae to the imprisoning gates, the lucky ones, flushed with weekend money, made for Robertson's sweetie shop with the false assurance that wealth gives. They were going to buy a new slate pencil with its half-wrapper of a blatantly imperialistic design wound around it, a Scot's Gray pencil and some chocolate 'bricks'.

The less lucky approached furtively and surrounded us sycophantically, hypocritically greeting us as their best friends when we emerged with our treasures. They hoped for some crumbs to fall from the rich man's table. Before long, as nothing fell, their tactics changed to threats and intimidation. Here we could see McBride hovering around the fringe, generally pursuing quieter and sneakier tactics. The bigger boys left us but McBride trailed behind right to the school gates and sometimes was lucky, a 'poke' with some sorbet left in the corner or a new slate pencil that had got broken.

McBride played quite a part in our school life. We, that is my little gang, liked him, were sorry for him but irritated by his treasonable hit-and-run tactics. His ill-nurtured, seldom-washed body, his more seldom-washed clothes combined to give off an animal-like odour that repelled.

My friend and I took what I now think of as a mean kind of pleasure in being sent to bring in truant McBride. We saw ourselves, no doubt, as policemen taking in a baddie, not an uncommon sight in those pre-Black Maria days. He didn't come quietly, often he didn't come at all. He was eel-like and evasive. When we did get Tam dragged into the classroom door, there the teacher waited – and the belt! Miss Allan felt it was her duty and responsibility – vocation was not then a dirty word – to teach for present needs the multiplication table and for future the Shorter Catechism. Both to be found in the same little booklet. What, after all, is the chief end of man but to glorify God and to enjoy Him for ever?

Miss Allan, not really a fearsome creature and, I suspected even then, sorry for McBride rather than sore at him, gave our prisoner three of the strap and marched him to his desk. The same ritual would be repeated another day.

Tam McBride could not philosophize but, as I now think about it all, he instinctively felt his dignity insulted that he had to mingle with the fat and the clean with their new school bags, nicely covered books, a big Mansion Polish tin for their sponge, new slate pencils; and he, his book covered, if covered at all, in cheap wallpaper and his slate-com two inches long and no sponge, just his jacket sleeve to clean the slate.

Time passed and we, my chums and I, went on to the high school. Society was changing and armaments were beginning to create new wealth and ease the dole queues. McBride, kept back, was now of little concern to us and yet I always exchanged a few words when I met him hanging around the Old Toll.

Then he ceased to be around. He had joined the army. 'They'll sort him out', we all said, and though we laughed, I think we were a little sad. The Army in these days did not have a good image, and were there not distant noises of war?

I didn't pass the Old Toll so frequently now that I had gone to 'varsity, but I saw McBride once in his army kilt. There wasn't much swagger. He had stout shining boots, heavy stockings and a tunic. They were all new, presumably tailored for Tam, and still they did not fit. He was a new and brawnier man, but, even so, the early years of malnutrition undermined the Army's chances.

Tam was taciturn and had nothing of the braggadocio I had seen in some new recruits on home leave. I felt there was more of a gulf between us than years ago, though now he had money in his pocket and was warmly dressed all according to a pattern. I was a student short of cash and wearing older clothes than he, but Tam saw me as 'them' and himself as 'us'.

Once, a year or two years later, one of the miners at the Old Toll gave me a shout. 'Did you know McBride won the MM?' 'No,' I replied, astonished but pleased – Where? How? In the desert some place, said my not very well-informed former classmate. 'Good old Tam, good old Tam,' we both said, one after the other and made a gesture with our breasts.

I did see Tam again, demobbed and in the most unbefitting 'demob' suit I ever saw. He looked pale and listless. I was on the other side of the road and just waved. He waved lethargically back.

When next I passed the Toll I heard a loud hail, 'Hey, big yin.' I stopped, for I hadn't been called that for a long time – since low school. 'McBride's deid – his chest.' No more was said. We just parted. Our silence was mourning for Tam.

The Very Reverend Dr Peter Brodie (born 1916) is Minister of St Mungo's Parish Church, Alloa, and former Moderator of the Church of Scotland.

Maurice Lindsay

PETER PAN

Do you believe in fairies?, the eternal boy asks
as a waving spotlight fingers the darkened stage.
If so, applaud. Self-consciously, we applaud.
A joke, of course. Mere children's make-believe;
for who would hold back time to disengage
the failures knowing secretly forbode?

Good, good! Then Tinkerbell is saved,
a wish that no experience corrodes.
The children laugh as public adult masks
relax for them, and eagerly clutch the sleeve
of one, at least, secure; their household god;
not knowing who it was he thought had waved.

MAURICE LINDSAY CBE (BORN 1918), POET AND CRITIC, WAS CONTROLLER OF BORDER TELEVISION AND, LATTERLY, DIRECTOR OF THE SCOTTISH CIVIC TRUST.

Iain Moncreiffe

KIDNAPPED

At the age of four I was kidnapped from my mother and stepfather by 'Nursie'. My father was dead, and Nurse Archibald, the local district nurse who had been called in when I had a recurrence of malaria, thought my life in danger if I remained in East Africa. So, on my recovery, she simply uplifted me and brought me by ship to this country.

I was taken over by my father's brother, Uncle Guy, afterwards the ninth Baronet and 22nd Laird of Moncreiffe, and his wife, Aunt May; my mother's protests were silenced by my worried grandmother, who controlled the family purse-strings; and 'Nursie' returned to Africa for ever. I never saw her or my mother again, although we always corresponded happily.

Uncle Guy's two children were Elisabeth, then aged three, and David, aged one. We lived in the country with a succession of nannies, and later French or English governesses. One of our earlier nannies was a girl of character called Nurse Kate. David in his pram was still too young to be affected, but she made a lasting impression on Elisabeth and me.

The last of Nurse Kate's exploits proved her undoing. She would enter the nursery of a morning and say: 'You're naughty.' Elisabeth and I suspected that she might be right, but weren't sure how much she knew. So we would ask, 'Why?' She had the standard grown-up riposte to this: 'Don't answer back.' Then she used to fill our mouths with mustard, put sticking plaster across them, and lock us up alone in the dark in our separate bedrooms.

Being lazy, this didn't bother me much; except that I couldn't breathe well through my nose which was usually blocked by scabs, and so had to ease one end of the plaster loose so that I could breathe through the corner of my mouth. While we lay in the dark, in my case having placid day-dreams about treasure islands and the like, Nurse Kate was off on her usual joy ride and picnic with the chauffeur. On her return, as she unlocked our bedroom doors, I used to smooth the end of the sticking plaster back into place; just in time for her to be able to rip it off savagely in the often vain hope that it hurt.

Nurse Kate's fun life came to light when Uncle Guy, who had been a submarine commander and loved mechanical contraptions, took in that his prized motor car was clocking up too many miles. Poor Nurse Kate was sacked with words of contumely. Uncle Guy and Aunt May sent for me and Elisabeth, and asked why on earth we hadn't reported all this long since. We had no adequate reply, as most things grown-ups did seemed so mad to us, we had thought it was everyday life.

Sir Iain Moncreiffe of that Ilk (born 1919) was an author and genealogist. He died on 27 February 1985, shortly after writing this piece.

LAUGHING TATTIES

It was dark November, and that particular November evening seemed very dark and cold to me as I trudged my way home from school. We were living in little huts at a farm called Arn Bog, halfway between Meigle and Eassie. The huts are still there, down an old road at the corner of a field.

It was about four miles' walk to Meigle school. 'All the other bairns are home long ago,' I thought. 'I wish that teacher wouldn't keep me in every night.'

Children from cotter houses and farms along the way also had to walk home from school. Though they often chanted, 'tinkie, tinkie, torn rags' to me, and didn't walk with me, I could always follow a bit behind them, and I was not so frightened.

I transferred my little school case from my frozen left hand to my right, then put my free hand into my bosom to try to get feeling back into it. Out of the murky darkness a big crow came marching, nearly up to my feet. It was searching for food. 'Are you hungry, too?' I said aloud. I was very hungry myself. They did have a soup kitchen at the school, but it cost a penny a day, and many mornings there was no penny for me to take – nor anything else. So apart from a drink of tea in the morning, I had not yet broken my fast.

Just then, a human figure walked towards me, and my heart was in my mouth for a moment before I recognized it as my mother. Mother was tall for a woman, and in spite of having been pulling turnips all day, walked very straight. She was wearing heavy muddy boots, and I could hear the water squelching in them with every step she took. The front of her dress, too, was all wet and muddy.

'Did that silly teacher keep you in again,' she greeted me.

'Aye Ma,' I answered.

'Instead of trying to fill your head with book learning, better she would go and learn some sense from someone herself. That is if she can find anyone with sense. God pity her, would any woman with sense keep a wean till this time of night, in the dark, dead months of winter. She kens the road you have to come.'

Mother ranted on about the stupidity of the country hantle (non-travellers) for about fifteen minutes, then suddenly the tone of her voice changed. 'Never mind, wean. You've two whole days before you have to go back again. In the morning when I get my coppers from the farmer, I will buy you a pair of warm stockings, and maybe a sweetie.'

I had just reached the age of seven, and had started going to Meigle school in mid-October. Before that, I had been potato-picking. Traveller people's children only needed two hundred attendances; then they were free to roam at will. The parents were given a card which stated that a child had attended school for a hundred days, and which could be shown to any policemen or to the 'cruelty' – usually a member of RSSPCC. Sometimes they would be accompanied by a nurse, who would examine the children's heads for vermin, look inside the tents, and check the children's physical appearance, asking numerous questions as they did so. Very often there were few children to examine. At the first wind of these people's presence, the children scattered like rabbits into hiding – up trees, inside harvest stooks, in the middle of whin bushes, or to whatever place they could find. This was not because they were verminous, but because the examination was an insult to their dignity.

Of course, the people sometimes did find children whom they considered to be neglected. These children were forcibly re-moved from their parents and put into 'homes'. The 'homes' were often founded by people who imagined that they were doing a great service to humanity, and who honestly believed that travell-ing people were so low in mentality that the loss of their children would put them neither up nor down. Actually, children were loved beyond telling. One seldom sees travelling people without a host of bairns around them. So the suffering of those whose children had been taken was pitiful to see. Especially as they were not allowed to visit them, under threat of prison – a fact which quite a few old travellers will verify.

That night near Meigle, Mother and I arrived at the wee hut very cold and hungry, but we were cheered to find the stove well alight, and a big pot of 'laughing tatties' on top of it – laughing

63

tatties was the name Mother gave to unpeeled potatoes which had burst their skins in the cooking.

Katie, my older sister, who was fourteen, had put the pot on when she came in from work. She was working with the Irish potato workers, who lived in the adjoining hut. They worked very hard indeed, and lived as cheaply as possible, sending most of their wages home to alleviate the poverty of their families in Ireland.

Lexy, the other member of our family, was only three. She had to play about in the field where Mother worked all day. As she worked, Mother would tell Lexy wonder tales of enchantment, to keep her from getting too weary and falling asleep in the cold. Almost every evening, she would tell us those tales, too, but in a voice specially lowered to lull us to sleep.

As we ate our laughing tatties, a pleasant Irish voice shouted through the window: 'And what are you doing burning a candle, and us with a big can of paraffin next door?' It was Dunyen, one of the young Irish lads.

'We can't expect you to keep us going with things when we run out,' Mother answered, as she opened the door.

'Sure and didn't you share your last shilling with us when we arrived here penniless, until we got our pay.' He picked up our lamp as he spoke. 'Give me your water-pails too. We're going for water anyway.' A wee burn, a field breadth away, was our source of water.

Our Irish neighbours were a real blessing, and the best of company that rather dreary winter. Daddy was in hospital, and we children too had been in hospital earlier that year with diptheria. That was why we were living there, away from all our traveller relatives and friends – lest any of their children might catch that dreaded disease from any lingering germs that we might be carrying. We had caught the infection from a drain.

There were seven of the Irish – four lads and three girls, and in spite of the hard work they were doing, they sang beautifully, danced, played music, laughed and joked almost every night. They always asked us to join them. Little Lexy had us all in stitches with her version of the Charlston. Katie was adept at the Irish clog dance before winter was over.

My teacher persevered with me every evening, until I caught up with the rest of the class. Then she stopped keeping me in at nights. The other children gradually thawed towards me, asking me to join them on the way home.

By March, I had put in two hundred attendences. Daddy was home and was strong and healthy again. Soon, we were on the road, wandering from camp to camp, enjoying the company of other travelling folk, happy as the day is long. Ere the yellow was on the broom, Daddy and his brothers were pearl-fishing the river Tay. Mother was selling hardware from door to door. Katie was looking after Lexy and me. Waiting for nature to ripen the fruit, the grain and the potato crops.

Then I would be back at some little country school, where some other poor teacher would have the task of helping me catch up on the other bairns.

BETSY WHYTE (BORN 1919) IS A TRADITIONAL STORY-TELLER AND SINGER. THE STORY OF HER EARLY DAYS, *THE YELLOW ON THE BROOM*, WAS PUBLISHED IN 1979.

George Mackay Brown

HAMNAVOE

My father passed with his penny letters
Through closes opening and shutting like legends
      When barbarous with gulls
      Hamnavoe's morning broke

On the salt and tar steps. Herring boats,
Puffing red sails, the tillers
      Of cold horizons, leaned
      Down the gull-gaunt tide

And threw dark nets on sudden silver harvests.
A stallion at the sweet fountain
      Dredged water, and touched
      Fire from steel-kissed cobbles.

Hard on noon four bearded merchants
Past the pipe-spitting pier-head strolled,
      Holy with greed, chanting
      Their slow grave jargon.

A tinker keened like a tartan gull
At cuithe-hung doors. A crofter lass
      Trudged through the lavish dung
      In a dream of cornstalks and milk.

In 'The Arctic Whaler' three blue elbows fell,
Regular as waves, from beards spumy with porter,
      Till the amber day ebbed out
      To its black dregs.

The boats drove furrows homeward, like ploughmen
In blizzards of gulls. Gaelic fisher girls
      Flashed knife and dirge
      Over drifts of herring,

And boys with penny wands lured gleams
From the tangled veins of the flood. Houses went blind
      Up one steep close, for a
      Grief by the shrouded nets.

The kirk, in a gale of psalms, went heaving through
A tumult of roofs, freighted for heaven. And lovers
      Unblessed by steeples, lay under
      The buttered bannock of the moon.

He quenched his lantern, leaving the last door.
Because of his gay poverty that kept
      My seapink innocence
      From the worm and black wind;

And because, under equality's sun,
All things wear now to a common soiling,
      In the fire of images
      Gladly I put my hand
      To save that day for him.

From *Selected Poems* (Hogarth Press, 1977)

GEORGE MACKAY BROWN OBE (BORN 1921) IS A POET, NOVELIST AND WRITER OF SHORT STORIES.

THE POWER OF GRACE

———

Once, in the all but dear dead days beyond recall, there lived in a tenemented street in Clydebank, a woman called Mrs Gilhooley. As the name would suggest, she was Irish, with a soft, southern accent. She was straight of carriage and, to my child's eyes, tall. Her eyes were glinting blue. She was pale-complexioned, with features that were firm, almost gaunt, but kind – though harrowed maybe just a bit at the eyes and mouth by little lines of time and disappointment. On all days she wore a black, satin-trimmed, velour toque hat, and a faded but genteel brown costume with black brocading on the pockets and lapels, of a length that must, in the mid-twenties, have been ten years out of fashion. She was a milder, more patient, less imperious, less intimidating Betsy Trotwood to whom I played a very young, very Scottish David Copperfield. I was, at the time, maybe four-and-a-half. Many a day she, returning home with food for her day's needs (meagre enough, I'm sure, those must have been for a single soul, as most of the time she was), would pause in the street where I was making pies with what passed for mud in the Clydebank gutters and engage me in conversation. It varied from day to day, but might run as this, particularly remembered, did.

'You're in a terrible hurry today. Would you ever – would you wait a minute?'

'I can't.'

'Can't? I see, you've turned all high and mighty on us all of a sudden. What's all the rush?'

'I've got to get up for my dinner.'

'Oh! Is that it?'

'Yeah.'

'But sure wouldn't your dinner wait a minute or two – are you starvin' or what?'

'No, it's not that.'

'I'm glad to hear it. What then?'

'I've got to get back to my work.'

At this, light descended on her countenance with a breathed sigh of understanding.

'A-a-ah! Is that it?'

'Aye.'

'Well, that's different.' A short pause. 'I – eh – I – eh – I never knew you were workin'.'

'Oh. Aye.'

'Would you mind – could I ask you then – where is it – where is this you're workin'?'

'Singer's.'

'The sewing machine factory?'

'Aye.'

'I didn't know. Your Aunt Lizzie never breathed a word of this to me.'

A shrug of masculine indifference, at this, from me.

'And, when was it now you got a start?'

'A what?'

'A start. When did you begin your work?'

'Last week.'

'Is that right?'

More than a little intolerant of this feminine ignorance and incredulous that she knew so little of matters so great in import to my masculine world, I moved to foot it up the two steps at our close-mouth and be gone.

'Here, before you go – I won't keep you. I know you're in a hurry.'

'I've got to get back.'

'Sure aren't you goin' to get your dinner?'

'But after. I've got to get back before the horn.'

'Oh! I see – I can see that, but tell me this. A job like that – what is it you're doin', by the by?'

'Ingineer.'

'Engineer?'

'Aye. I make ingines.'

'Make engines, is it? Well, I never. You an engineer!'

'Aye.'

'You'll be making a queer lot o' money at that.'

Here, she paused, moved her weight from one foot to the other, drew her raffia message-bag closer, and stooped just a little towards me, before asking, with that wonderful, all but whispered air of Irish confidentiality, 'How much – if you wouldn't mind me askin' – how much wages do you make in that kind of a job?'

'Twenty-five shillin's.'

The answer was immediate, and not without the pride of a well-to-do artisan of the time.

'A week?'

There was a pause while I worked that one out. 'Yeah.'

'God! You'd be queer and rich in no time with that kind of a wage every week.'

'Yeah.' Another pause, and then: 'Well, I have to go. I'll be late.'

'Indeed. And that would never do. A man in your position. But, just before you go – would you tell me? What d'you do with all that money you're earnin' – the twenty-five shillin's?'

'Gie it to m'auntie.'

'Ah.' Here the Irish sentimentality crept into her voice. 'Aren't you the good one right enough. Oh, well, she's a lucky woman, is all I can say, havin' a fellow like you bringin' in money the likes of that every week.'

'Aye.'

'Well, now, I'll not keep you. I can see you're rushed right enough, so I'll get on and let you do the same.'

I was off up the close with never a word nor a backward glance, with only her final-called farewell reaching me in that gentle soprano of hers against the echo of my steel-tipped little boots on the granolithic floor.

I cannot guess what her age might have been at that time – maybe forty, maybe fifty. To the child, age above his own is eternity. She was a friend of the aunt who brought me up and was often in our house. Her husband, whom I never set eyes on – I think he was a seaman – she referred to in conversation as what I thought was 'my own'; a phrase I found even at that early age over-affectionate, even fanciful. But on reflection, years later, I suppose his name was Owen – Owen Gilhooley. Her Christian name, I never knew.

We left that street a few years after that, bound for a council house with dahlias, red and yellow, and pink London Pride in its garden. I neither heard of nor saw Mrs Gilhooley ever again. And yet, even now, I hear that gentle voice inflecting a question, expressing wonder, murmuring deference at my impatience, but never, never giving a glint of matronizing laughter, nor the sentimentality of any word of fondness or foolishness. I hear only her respect for another human being, child as he was, for his individuality and his imagination; and I hear, too, perhaps a trace of her own loneliness and the courage with which she dignified it. I weep, now, older myself than she was then, that such a good, early friend should have passed from my careless ken with never a backward glance from me to see, was she standing there still where I left her each day? But looking back, vanished though she be, like a figure in a dream, like a character, minor but essential, in a good book, I find, too, a quiet joy in her memory, treasured within me for its impact on my life, gentle and wise and quite out of proportion to the time I knew her.

Tom Moore, could I but find the right quotation, would say in conclusion more accurately and, being her countryman, more fittingly, what I feel. I say only that I thank the vanished grace of Mrs Gilhooley and will carry a trace of her spirit in my own, as I have done since childhood, till my ending. Come to think, that would have been the right Christian name for her; maybe indeed it was; maybe she was Grace – Grace Gilhooley.

FULTON MACKAY (BORN 1922) IS A STAGE, FILM AND TELEVISION ACTOR. HE WAS FOR MANY YEARS WITH JAMES BRIDIE'S CITIZEN'S THEATRE IN GLASGOW.

THE SINGERS AND THE SONGS

One of my earliest memories is of sitting at the window of my parents' home in Airdrie watching the gaily bedecked Clydesdales as they plodded their way over the common to the horse show. The carnage and slaughter of the First World War was over and my father, like some fathers, though not all fathers, had returned to his 'little grey home in the west'. The jingling bells and the bright ribbons on the harnesses of the horses heralded the return to the simple pleasures that had almost been forgotten in the mud of Flanders.

I was lucky to be born into a happy home. My mother and father always seemed to be singing – which is perhaps not surprising since they first met in the choir of the Airdrie Baptist Church and my father was an active member of the Male Voice Choir. And so I and my brother and two sisters – all older than me and so good to me – grew up absorbing the words and tunes of the late Victorian and Edwardian era of our parents' youth. 'Come into the Garden, Maud', 'The Last Rose of Summer', 'Somewhere a Voice is Calling', 'Love's Old Sweet Song' and, later, 'All in the April Evening' were part of our environment. We learned Burns' songs without ever seeing them written down. My father and his six brothers each had his 'own' song, which he was expected to sing at family gatherings – especially weddings. My fathers, rather surprisingly, was 'Trumpeter' (though he later changed it to 'Afton Water' with the advent of the Second World War, when I was in the forces).

We were not a rich family; my father was an insurance agent and so our pleasures were simple ones. Nearby, the Woodbine Park was Hampden in winter and Lord's in summer, where my pals and I became Hughie Gallacher, Jackie McDougall or Bob McPhail (yes, they all played in Airdrieonians' cup-winning team of 1924 and I was there to see them parade it through the town). There were other Airdrie men, Alan Morton for example, but he played for Rangers and so we didn't impersonate him. Our cricket wicket was a primitive one, but since I was Larwood, who cared?

My cousin Donnie (Bradman, of course!) would come down from Lossiemouth on holiday and play with us. Ironic that he, a minister's son, should perish during the Second World War in the icy cold waters of the Arctic in a convoy carrying munitions to Godless Russia.

The annual Sunday School trip, on foot to a neighbouring park with 'tinnies' jangling, was a great event. It was only years later that it ventured to Helensburgh. Holidays, too, were generally nearby events – Ardrossan, Saltcoats and Dunoon come rapidly to mind – but they were none the worse for that, for the sun was always shining! Some summers we would go to my father's brother, the Baptist minister at Lossiemouth. It was he, by the way, who gave me my first book on Natural History and thus helped to set me on my biological career. I loved the countryside and was at my happiest even when a wee boy, walking and camping with my pals. My sister Mary added a further dimension by reading to me the works of the 'Nature' poets – Wordsworth, Shelley and Keats. I still go back to them with pleasure. Holidays at Lossie were a mixture – there were glorious days on the beach presided over by Aunt Nelly and her picnic basket, but there were no visits to the 'Tallie's' for ice cream and no activities other than church-going on Sundays.

Back in Airdrie too, Sundays were rather curious days – church in the morning, a walk (about three miles) to the cemetery in the afternoon (we took the 'special' bus if it was wet) to buy flowers and pay our respects (in our best clothes) to those family and friends who had gone before us; pausing at each gravestone to ponder his or her good points. I did hear it said, too, that cemetery visits performed a useful social function. Many a grieving widow and sad widower rebuilt their lives together in the shadow of New Monkland Churchyard. Church again in the evenings or sometimes a walk to the Monkland Glen to hear the brass band. But whether church or glen, tea at Aunt Mirren's (high tea, but we never called it that), where my father would play the organ and the triumphs of Moodie and Sankie were relived and resung by both young and old generations.

Of course, not all days were Sundays. On Wednesday nights my mother would take me to the pictures, where contentedly we would view the silent world of Norma Talmage, Harold

Lloyd, Charlie Chaplin, Ramon Navarro and Adolph Menjou.

There was one very exciting evening in 1929 when the whole family went to the Theatre Royal in neighbouring Coatbridge to see and hear our first 'talkie' – Al Jolson in *The Singing Fool*. I remember yet how disappointed I was when Jolson said he would 'sing a million songs' and then sang only three – but one of them was 'Sonny Boy'. But the talkies took a long time to catch on in our family. Even when there was only one cinema (out of four) showing silent films, we would go there, for my mother preferred a good 'society' picture to the talkies, which were dominated by musicals. And father was too busy for the talkies.

While mother and I were enveloped in the dream world of the upper classes, he was fighting hard to change that world through the ILP (Independent Labour Party). One of my jobs was to go down to Airdrie Cross to meet visiting speakers coming by tram from Glasgow and bring them home to tea before the meeting. Thus I met Jimmy Maxton, John Wheatley, Davie Kirkwood, Pat Dolland and many more. I even learned to read the *Forward* and we took the *Daily Herald* because it was a Labour paper. But I revelled in *Puck*, *Tiger Tim* and later the *Rover* (have any of the young generation heard of Cast-Iron Bill?), the *Wizard* and the *Magnet* (how I loved the adventures of Harry Wharton, the 'bounder' Vernon Smith and the 'fat owl' Billy Bunter).

In the street, games had their seasons – we went runs with our 'girs' and 'cleeks' in the spring; we played football and went sledging in winter; cricket in summer; and 'glessies' in the autumn, long after the leerie had lit the street lamps. Heiders with a sixpenny rubber ball were also popular, as was cat-and-bat and hunch cuddy hunch; and when the wind blew, we flew our 'draigons'. Peever and jumping ropes were generally left to the lassies, though sometimes we could be persuaded to join in.

I went to school, too, of course, and fought with others to get front seats in winter because they were nearest to the fire. I can still see the 'jannie' coming into the classroom two or three times a day to put on more coal and to note the attendances on the slate which hung behind the door. Thinking back, some of the boys and girls in the class with no shoes or stockings even in winter had more need of the fire than I had. There were no jotters in those days – instead we used slates, and many a teacher's nerves were shattered by the screech of the 'slate combs' on the slates. Although our teachers exhorted us to bring wet sponges to erase our masterpieces, more often we used spittle and the cuffs of our jerseys. How the public health buffs of today would shudder at that! Particularly as infectious diseases were rife. The 'fever van' was a constant visitor to our street and it struck terror into our young hearts. As indeed did the 'school board' whose tap at the door made you bury yourself more deeply in the bedclothes, particularly if you had no legitimate excuse for plunking the school.

But the happy times far outweighed these little worries. It has been fun to live them again.

W. W. FLETCHER (born 1918) IS EMERITUS PROFESSOR OF BIOLOGY, UNIVERSITY OF STRATHCLYDE, AND A BROADCASTER AND WRITER.

Ian Wallace

OVER THE BORDER

On to the stage of the Golders Green Hippodrome walked the well-known entertainer Stanley Holloway. 'Ladies and gentlemen, I've had a request, which I can hardly refuse. It's for wee McGregor down there on his birthday.' He pointed to a small boy in a kilt sitting in the front row. He then launched into his famous monologue about Sam and his 'moosket' at the Battle of Waterloo. I'd wondered where my father had gone in the interval.

That incident took place in the late 1920s when I was eight and had been given my first kilt, a sartorial extravagance that I kept very quiet about at school in Highgate. Yes, my firmly-expressed claim to be a Scot has to overcome the objection that I was born and brought up in a north London suburb.

My father had married in his mid-forties a girl from Glasgow. He hailed from Kirkcaldy and had started as an office boy in a linoleum works there over thirty years earlier. When he was promoted in 1915 to head the London office he brought his young

74

bride south. I was born four years later. If I am cautious by nature it is hardly surprising.

My parents were not the sort of exiled Scots who go to Burns suppers or join Caledonian societies, nor did they indoctrinate me with Scottish culture or folklore beyond the pile of records that sat beside the small wind-up gramophone in its mahogany case. Every single one of them had the name – Harry Lauder – on the label. I loved them all from 'I Love a Lassie' to 'The End of the Road'. Indeed they were played so frequently that they developed frying noises, particularly at the beginning and the end.

Many of our neighbours were Scots who had been attracted by Highgate, perhaps because it was near King's Cross and Euston, more likely because it stands high above the city and is what estate agents call 'leafy'. We went to the Presbyterian church, where I experienced the exquisite agony to a small boy of extempore prayers, punctuated by long pauses for meditation, or maybe inspiration. It never occurred to my parents to remove me after the children's address.

There were no other Scots boys at the schools I attended in Highgate or Hampstead, and there were few at the C of E public school to which I was sent at the age of thirteen – Charterhouse. The only moment there when the subject of Scotland arose was my very first afternoon. The musical director, a Dr Thomas Fielden, rounded up all the 'new bugs' and auditioned them for the choir. My piping treble was embarrassingly loud and clear and for a moment the crowd of little black-suited wretches forgot their homesick apprehensions and giggled. 'What's your name?' 'Wallace, sir.' 'Ah, a Scotch boy. Well, Wallace, pay no attention and remember that old Scottish saying, "They say. What say they? Let them say!"'

Invariably we went to Scotland for our summer holidays and the pattern seldom varied. Our first port of call was Kilmacolm in Renfrewshire where my grandfather and his daughter, my auntie Peggie, lived as residents in the Hydropathic (since demolished). Auntie was my mother's sister who never married, and more of her in a moment. The Hydro in its own grounds had a swing and a putting course to say nothing of a cold plunge where I learned to swim, dangled in the water by Tom Kyle, the masseur. My webbing belt was attached to a stick by a length of cord. Tom, a tall thin man with an authoritative moustache, also presided over the cold buffet at lunch time. The residents all seemed to me to be very old, though some of them went to work in Glasgow each day, descending the Hydro Hill to the station in a horse-bus driven by a sharp faced Irishman in a top hat called Jimmy, who would run up the steps into the front hall and blow a whistle to announce his arrival.

From there we proceeded to St Andrews – The Grand Hotel, that impressive red pile that stands behind the eighteenth green of the Old Course. It is now a university hall of residence, I believe. My parents played golf by day and bridge by night, while I made do in the early years with a girl engaged to look after me. One day I gave her the slip and a frantic search-party found me strumming my ukelele and singing a Gracie Fields' song at a talent contest put on by the seaside pierrot troupe. I won a box of chocolates and what my father described as 'a scud on the lug'.

It would be quite wrong to assume that I had unfeeling parents. Quite the reverse. But it was hard for my father to communicate with a boy 51 years his junior and, at holiday times, my mother, who spoilt me for the rest of the year, felt that my father should have most of her attention. He was, until I was much older, a benevolent but remote figure.

We also went to Kilmacolm for Hogmanay, when the Hydro became truly magical for the sort of boy who enjoyed parties and dressing up. The elderly residents were augmented by large family parties from Glasgow, Bearsden and Helensburgh. Matt Feggan and his orchestra played at teatime as well as in the evening and I was initiated into such mysteries as military whist and the steps of the eightsome reel. The great night was the Hogmanay Fancy Dress Ball. After the judging, everyone had to pose in groups before a huge camera. The blinding flash was spectacularly provided by a white chemical ignited on a small metal tray held high above the photographer's head. No wonder so many of us had our eyes shut in the pictures.

In London, the only real whiff of Scotland was when grandad and auntie Peggy came on a visit. Auntie had a lovely soprano voice and could accompany herself on the piano. Grandad was a born comedian (though journalism was his profession) and he also possessed a charming light baritone voice. Their visits to a household where neither of my parents really liked music were as welcome to me as food parcels to a beleaguered garrison. I got auntie to the piano as often as I dared and it was she and my grandfather who have to bear the heavy responsibility of enchanting me with the idea of being a musical entertainer.

On reflection, if I had to pick out one day of my childhood as truly memorable it was one of our visits to Kilmacolm. Grandad, sensing that I was bored by the elderly company and endless rounds on the putting course, took me on the train to Gourock where we boarded *The Duchess of Rothesay* for a sail round the Kyles of Bute. The thump of the paddles and the strains of the fiddler and piano accordionist on the deck playing O'er the Hills to Ardentinny as we forged away from the grime of Port Glasgow towards unknown delights, munching our fresh ham rolls – now that was an adventure!

IAN WALLACE OBE (BORN 1919) IS A CONCERT AND OPERA SINGER, ACTOR AND TELEVISION PERSONALITY.

Molly Weir

THE SUMMER WE ALL WENT TO THE SEASIDE

When we used to cluster in the back courts and begin to talk about summer holidays, I was fascinated by the terrific number of places there seemed to be in Scotland where there was sand and sea, and you could paddle in salt water, and play with a spade and pail and make pies and sand castles.

I had absolutely no idea of distances, and to me Irvine and Stevenston had the same magic and were as far off as Aberdeen and Montrose, and from the bottom of my soul I envied those chums who talked enthusiastically of the bathing boxes (not that they ever aspired actually to go inside them – they undressed on the beach – but the fact was that the boxes were THERE). In my imagination, I could see the rich holiday-makers emerging from those bathing boxes, like Mack Sennett bathing beauties, wearing striped costumes and fancy caps, and racing towards beautiful breakers, plunging in, splashing and swimming effortlessly in the waves, and later gazing roguishly at one another over the tops of mountainous ice-cream cones!

Apparently the seaside also had something known as pierrots, who sang and danced and told great jokes in those marvellous holiday places, and the fish and chips were streets ahead of those we could buy in Springburn, for of course the fish came straight out of the sea. I'd never given a thought to where the fish lived before they arrived at our fish-and-chip shops, and I certainly never thought they swam about among the legs of people who were on their summer holidays. In fact, on the whole I think I would have preferred not to know this. But I drank in all the rest of the boastful stories of marathon swims, sand-castle building competitions, races along the shore, and competitions on an actual stage at the pierrots to find the best singer or dancer among the holiday-makers.

Oh WHY did my grannie not like the seaside? WHY did she have to be different from everybody else in the tenements, and prefer the country? Grannie came from Crieff, and her idea of bliss was to return to her roots after twelve months in the treeless tenement life of Glasgow, there to rejoice in green grass, long gardens bright with flowers and rich with fruit bushes laden with gooseberries, currants and raspberries, and to eat eggs straight from the hens and drink milk straight from the byre.

It wasn't always Crieff. Sometimes it was Balfron, and sometimes it was Auchterarder. But wherever it was, it wasn't the seaside. After we got to 'the country' of course, there were so many differences from tenement life that we forgot spades and pails, and settled for fishing for baggies in the burns, filling our mouths with stolen fruits from the gardens, terrified at the same time that God would poison us and strike us dead for our wickedness. Fish and chips soon faded from our minds. The fresh eggs, the farm milk, the peas we'd picked ourselves and fine locally grown tatties had us rushing in for meals, starving and enthusiastic for all that was laid before us. When we returned to

Glasgow, we were rosy-cheeked and more than ready to swop our 'country' tales for stories of the sea from the other back-court chums.

We were delighted to find that the exotic delights of Irvine seemed to pale a little in the light of our exaggerated accounts of all the fruit we'd stolen and eaten, unpunished! Not a word of our feelings of guilt at the time, of course. Just rolling eyes, as we described the 'haun-fu's' of currants and raspberries and goose-gogs, and 'dizzens' of pea-pods we'd devoured. Aye, they could-nae get thae things at Irvine or Stevenston, so they couldnae, and we ran home realizing, not for the first time, that oor grannie was different from everybody else, and the country wisnae sae bad after a'.

But when grannie died, and I drooped and grew pale and thin and seemed to lose interest in everything, even sweeties, and my mother was at her wits' end wondering what to do to rouse me, she found the answer when we started looking in the *Times* for holiday addresses.

At the first mention of 'lookin' fur a wee hoose for the holidays', I hadn't shown any interest. But when my mother added, apparently quite idly, 'I think we'll maybe try the seaside this year, hen. Seein' ye've been gettin' thae swimmin' lessons at the school, ye'd be able tae get yer feet off the bottom if ye went intae the sea.'

I rushed over to the table, and so did the boys. 'Oh mother', I gasped, 'Can we go to the seaside? Is there a wee hoose there? Can ye afford it?'

'Ah'm gettin' a spade an' pail,' shouted Willie and Tommy, 'an' a fitba' maybe. Well, a painted ba' onywey.'

'Wheest,' my mother cried. 'Ah canny see whit ah'm lookin' for, for a' that noise.'

We were silenced immediately. Holding our breaths, we leaned over her as she ran her finger down the columns. 'Oh here's a nice yin,' she said, as if she could actually see it. 'To let. Girvan. Small holiday house, kitchen, two double beds, outside toilet, low door, own key.'

GIRVAN! Nobody in the tenements had ever been there. We would be the very first to come back and describe it to envious ears. The price was right, and my mother assured us it was the seaside. 'Hurry up and write mother,' we urged. 'Hurry up in case somebody else has seen the wee hoose is to let and they'll get it first.'

When the letter was written, on the pad kept for writing to auntie in Australia, we rushed to the post office for a stamp and never drew an easy breath until the postie brought us the glad tidings that Mrs Gray would be pleased to reserve the wee hoose for the desired fortnight, and if we would let her know which train we would be coming on, she would be there to show us where everything was.

There was no time to be lost. We would start saving our modest pocket money right away to buy a spade and pail. If we ran extra messages for the neighbours, we might even have enough for a painted ball. We expected no luxuries. We'd live as we did at home, for we knew no other life style. It was the SEASIDE we wanted, that was all that mattered. Oh it would be great! We couldn't wait.

It seemed an eternity of waiting before my mother got out the hamper to pack it with all our things. We had to take our own sheets and pillowcases, tablecloths and towels – dull necessities that half-filled the hamper – before we could add the bathing costumes and the sand shoes, the socks, pyjamas, and a change of clothes for each of us in case we got wet. WET! At the SEASIDE! 'My Goad,' said my mother, 'it's no' Australia ye're gaun tae. It's juist Girvan, and it can rain there juist the same as it can in Springburn. It's no' that faur away.'

We stared at her. 'Oh but it IS far away,' we cried. It's the other side of dreamland, I thought, it's magic, and the rain COULDN'T be the same as it was in Springburn.

The hamper was fastened down, a long metal rod like a poker slotting through two loops to secure it, and as we had no man in the house we indulged in the breathtaking luxury of having it collected, conveyed and delivered by the Railway. If you took it down to the station yourself, it cost two shillings to have it conveyed and delivered. But collection, conveyance and delivery cost three whole shillings! For us the excitement started with that knock on the door, when a uniformed railwayman consulted a piece of paper, and checked that we had a hamper to be delivered to such-and-such an address in Girvan, to arrive on Saturday July the 18th. 'It's to be conveyed too,' we cried. The man laughed and said, 'Oh aye, that tae.'

The station was seething with Glasgow Fair holiday-makers when we got there on the Saturday forenoon, and my mother was in a ferment of anxiety in case any of us would fall out of the train door. 'Keep away fae the door,' she cried, if we as much as stirred. 'Don't hing oot the windae,' if we rose to see which station we had reached. As all the other parents shared this belief in the murderous possibilities of trains, nobody really enjoyed the journey very much, and we tumbled out at our various stations, radiant with relief at having safely surmounted all dangers.

We walked from the station to the address clutched in my mother's hand. My heart gave a great bound when we found the street we sought – it ran straight down to the sea. And, joy of joys, the holiday house had a red pipe-clay doorstep and the door opened right on to the pavement. After living two storeys up in a Glasgow tenement, this was the very stuff of story-book holidays.

The door opened to reveal a nice couthy-looking woman who swept us inside with a welcoming, 'I've put the kettle on so it'll no' be long in coming to the boil.' As soon as she'd gone, we rushed around our new home. 'A lovely clean sink,' my mother beamed. 'Nice cutlery too, and the dishes are a' hale, so mind you're no' to be breakin' ony, for we'll hiv tae pey for them.' This was a fate worse than death, for anything spent on breakages meant less left over for 'fancies' like cakes or pokey hats. We only had my mother's holiday pay, and nothing for extravagant tragedies, like breaking dishes.

'We've got a lavy. To oorsels,' I announced, after exploring the small compartment outside the back door. Fancy, a back door! This exclusive use of a toilet was a luxury beyond our imaginings until that moment. Each tenement stair lavy was shared by three families, which in our case meant sharing with a dozen people. Now we had one entirely for own use. What bliss!

Everything about that holiday was unforgettable. It was all far, far better than the back-court stories had promised. The shops were excitingly different from the familiar Glasgow stores. Ice-cream parlours were filled with brightly dressed holidaymakers, eating sugar wafers at 11 o'clock in the forenoon. Not one of them apparently bothering their heads that it would put them off their dinners!

Even with the wee-est, totiest pokey hat, they gave a generous squirt of raspberry vinegar, a mouth-watering delicacy not possible at home unless you spent the impossible sum of tuppence.

The morning rolls were crisper and bigger and the farm milk was sweeter and creamier. And the holiday breakfasts were great. We didn't have porridge once. Grannie was the one who had always insisted on starting the day with this good warming meal, but the Girvan weather lived up to my confident hopes, and gave us days of blue skies and hot sunshine. So my mother decided we'd have rolls and butter, or rolls and jam, or maybe rolls with an egg between two of us, just for a wee change. It made a glorious start to the day, and we never missed the oatmeal from our diet.

When we craiked for chips, and were refused because the holiday money was vanishing fast, we asked the farmer if we could go in and pick up the wee tatties left by the tattie-howkers because they were too small to be worth wasting their time collecting. The farmer made no objection, and we got down on our hunkers and soon gathered a basketful, which we presented to my mother for chips. 'Ah'm nut peelin' thae wee bools,' said my mother. 'If youse want chips fae such wee totties, youse can scrape them yersels.' What would have been unthinkable at home became a game on holiday. We perched up on the sink and the draining-board, and scraped those tatties which were no bigger than Willie's 'jawries', and in the end they were transformed into what I christened 'Lilliputian' chips (I'd just read *Gulliver's Travels*). They were delicious, and all the sweeter for having been gathered and prepared by ourselves, and in the knowledge that they had cost nothing. We had the dripping in the house anyway, and that didn't count.

When we saw the sea on the first night, before we went to bed, I made excited plans to paddle to the big rock standing out on the horizon. My mother laughed. 'I think maybe Paddy's Milestone is faurder than ye'd think, hen – that's Ailsa Craig.' 'Well,' I said, 'I'm going to explore it in the morning.' It looked so near, I couldn't believe it was all of thirteen miles away. Tactfully my mother never mentioned it again, nor did I.

The sea itself, to my surprise, was far colder than the baths.

'My Goad,' said my mother when I came out after the first attempt at swimming with my feet off the bottom, 'look at her. She's blue wi' cauld. Ye steyed in faur too long.' 'It was great,' I said, my teeth chattering. 'It was as warm as onything.'

The boys preferred the rowing boats to sea-bathing, and only an acute shortage of cash prevented their spending every minute pretending to be sailors escaping from a stricken ship, and heading for a desert island. My mother was terrified they would be 'cerried oot to sea' if they left the safety of the harbour area, and they had strict instructions 'No' tae staun' up in the boat or they'd cowp it, and naebody would jump in an' rescue them.'

We all adored the pierrots, and lined the railing outside the paying area (we hadn't a spare curdy for seats), and joined in lustily with all the choruses and fell in love with the comic and the lovely wee soubrette, and couldn't stand the big serious baritone or the soprano. 'Waste o' time,' we complained, 'when everybody knows the comic is faur the best.' Who wanted to hear 'I must go down to the sea again', or 'A brown bird singing' when we could have been roaring out 'Where does a little liver pill, when you're ill, know where your liver is, eh?'?

The excitement when they came round with a dainty bag for 'offerings' was palpitating. We longed to see them at such close range, and smell the 'poother' as my mother called it, but we had no money to give them and so had shamefully to take to our heels before they reached us.

I swaggered up and down the kitchen of our wee holiday house imitating those pierrots, acting out their songs to my heart's content, but nothing could persuade me to get up on that stage and enter the competitions. Not even the unexpected flattery of the boys telling me, 'But you're faur better than the wee lassie that goat the prize. You're daft no' goin' up.' Maybe some sixth sense told me I must wait until I knew beyond doubt that I was good enough to please myself.

Oh yes, it was a very special holiday. An unforgettable time of family joys, of innocent pleasures, of healing, of happiness which was utterly independent of material possessions, and of having our mother to ourselves for a whole perfect fortnight, with no thought of real work.

The seaside was everything I had longed for, and as a Pisces I was entirely in my element. And I discovered something else. A holiday sink is nothing like the one at home.

The Greeks sum up the best stories for children with the words, 'And they all went to the seaside', to indicate a happy ending. Well, we all went to the seaside, and we returned with tanned cheeks and limbs, healthy bodies, and a serene confidence that whatever the winter offered, we could take it.

The final flourish was enjoyed when our hamper was collected, conveyed and delivered to our tenement for another well-spent three shillings. We were well content.

MOLLY WEIR IS AN ACTRESS, BROADCASTER, JOURNALIST, AND WRITER OF BOOKS ON COOKERY AND ABOUT HER OWN LIFE. THIS ARTICLE FIRST APPEARED, IN A DIFFERENT FORM, IN *PEOPLE'S FRIEND*.

Veronica Maclean

THE WATERFALL

I was brought up in a large, pink, sandstone castle in the heart of the Highlands and Clan Fraser country. Beaufort, the 'new' Castle of the Lovats, took so long to build that three Victorian architects died in the making of it. This is fairly evident from the front elevation, but more so from inside, where the immense impracticability of the castle's internal plans could never have been achieved by the ingenuity of a single brain. But, from the back, where the land falls sharply to the River Beauly below, the castle stands up pink and proud above the soft greens of its escarpment, a perfect monument to the Highland romanticism of the day.

Of this we children were unaware, for the river itself was a far stronger influence than any man-made building. It was a living thing, and it ran through our lives and moulded our characters, and taught us many things that only river children know, and for part of my childhood I felt I belonged to it, and loved it almost as much as a third parent. It was on the river that we learnt to swim, to row, to fish, to skate, to rock-climb, to poach, to risk our necks and to get away with it. And it was the river that determined each year where we would spend our summers – for, if it was let with the Castle to rich fishing tenants, the family would have to up-roost and retreat to whichever shooting lodge or house on my father's estates that was un-let.

Sometimes we would follow a family tradition and join our favourite cousins on the West Coast where the white beaches of Morar and Arisaig look over the sea to magic outlines of Hebridean islands – Rhum, Skye, Canna and Eigg. Here we would pack into a small over-crowded farmhouse at night, but live all day on the sheltered dunes and beaches, digging little pink cowrie shells out of the tide-line with our bare brown toes while the older cousins dug revolting rainbow-coloured lug worms for bait.

The favourite shooting lodge, without doubt, was Stronelairg, at the top of Stratherrick, where ten miles of single-track glen road stopped and the hills began. It wasn't only the lodge, or the wildness, or the sport or the peaty bath water which looked like Guinness with a head on it when the burn was in spate (and made your skin feel like silk), but the MacFarlane family who lived there, who were, of course, the chief magnet. Archie MacFarlane had been a sergeant in the Lovat Scouts during the 1914–18 War, had won the Military Medal for supreme courage, and had been decorated on the field, a rare thing to happen, even to a Highland soldier. My father had made him head stalker and gamekeeper at Stronelairg after the War. He revelled in his work, and if there was a happy man whose job was his hobby, it was Archie. And one could almost say the same was true for Mrs MacFarlane. She would open the wind-battered door of their sturdy, granite house, and just one look at that beaming, rosy, bonny face – so like the other little faces crowded round her or peeping out shyly from behind her skirts – was welcome enough. But she would immediately ask us in. 'You must be just starving with the cold, you poor *moichens*! And how about a bite? There's a batch of scones on the girdle and a pot of tea on the hob . . . it'll be no trouble, mind, no trouble at all. . . .' Mrs MacFarlane's work was the ten fine, rosy, curly-haired children she had born Archie over the years. Strong, beautiful children with fine resounding names – William, Mary, Archibald, Clarissa, Georgina, Robina. . . . For many years a new baby had turned up 'regular as clockwork', Archie would say with a wink, and was immediately christened with the name of the previous season's shooting tenant, if it was a boy – if it was a girl it would be named after the tenant's wife. Mrs Mac was always on her feet again by the Glorious Twelfth, ready to provide the perfect packed lunch or those tremendous stalking teas for which she was famous.

In those days our County Educational Authorities favoured a 'pupil teacher' system for bringing enlightenment to the remote glens and islands where there were too few children to justify the building of a school. The 'pupil teachers' or students in their last year of training would lodge in one of the parents' houses and teach in an extra 'school' room that could be built on to it. Though they may have lacked experience in teaching, they certainly made up for it in keenness and freshness.

A Miss McArthur had recently come to lodge with the Mac-Farlanes and one happy summer term I had the good fortune to be taught by her in their schoolroom. There were nine of us, four MacFarlanes, me and two pairs of shepherds' children from further down the glen who walked four miles to and from the schoolroom every day except when they 'managed' a lift with the mail van. Our ages ranged from six to twelve and I think sometimes a MacFarlane baby would be allowed in, as long as it was quiet, to scribble contentedly with crayons in a corner.

Any illusions of superiority I may have had when I first entered that bare little room were soon dispelled. The MacFarlane children knew a good deal more than I did, in almost every subject except French, which they had just begun, and the older ones had even started Latin, which to me seemed the height of intellectual achievement. We had a bell in our schoolroom which Miss McArthur rang at 9 o'clock when morning lessons began and *we* rang at 12.30 when we were dismissed. As soon as that bell was put back on her table we tore out of the classroom as if someone had shouted 'Fire!'. It was then a race, a wild stampede across the green and down to the bridge, into the almost dried-up bed of the burn, hopping from stone to stone, with incredible speed and agility, till at last we reached our destination – the one deep pool by the waterfall that was all that an unusually sunny June had left of its swift brown waters. Here, all was dark and silent except for the noise of the water. The high cliffs of rock and bracken shut out the sunlight on two sides, and lower down through the bared peat of the crumbling bank you could see the black bones of ancient tree roots. Here there were huge granite boulders and shelves of rock over which we hung for hours at a time – gently feeling for the fat, brown, speckled trout that slept below, nose in, tail outwards, dreaming perhaps of dragon flies and spate waters – gently, gently we felt, our arms plunged deep into the icy water, gently, slowly, till you knew that your delicate searching fingers were touching something more solid than water and your pulse quickened and your heart began pounding so loud that the trout must surely hear it, and your fingers began stroking, gently, gently, till your arm ached like a tooth with the coldness of it, and you slowly began changing the position of your hand, but slowly, gently, stroking and turning until *WOOMF!* You suddenly clutched with all your might, throwing your arm and your whole body back in one fleet movement, and sometimes, not very often, but *sometimes*, there would be a greeny-brown, opaque yet shining little fish with a dark cream belly and red spots on his dappled side, gasping there in the heather beside you – and a distinct strange fishy smell in the air.

A trout caught this way made me inordinately proud, and however small it was, I would take it back to the lodge kitchen, to Geggy, and tell her I'd got something to 'help out' the breakfast: and sure enough it would turn up next morning to my intense pleasure, sitting all alone in a silver entree dish, with a lid, and I would generously halve it with whoever I loved best at the moment and then sit back and watch them with beady eyes while they ate it, making quite sure they appreciated every single morsel.

The Stronelairg School experiment had gone off so well that my mother seriously thought of continuing it, but there were the practical difficulties of distance and the long, hard and sometimes snow-bound winters – and perhaps she had not altogether liked the calluses that were beginning to show in my sensibilities as well as on my small, bare, brown feet. We had not been long back at Beaufort before a letter arrived for my mother from MacFarlane, a much tear-stained, pathetic letter, telling us briefly that Georgina, the merriest and sweetest of all his children, had fallen while playing in our waterfall pool and, striking her head against a rock, had stunned herself. The smaller children had not been strong enough to pull her clear, and by the time they had raised help, the pretty, vivid, dancing little Georgina had drowned.

LADY MACLEAN (BORN 1920), SISTER OF LORD LOVAT AND WIFE OF SIR FITZROY MACLEAN, HAS COMPILED SEVERAL COOKERY BOOKS.

Cliff Hanley

RELUCTANT PUGILIST

It's all very well talking about fights, but it's a different thing fighting them except when you know you'll win and you won't get hurt. I never liked getting hurt. There was one afternoon I deliberately picked a fight with a boy in the class who wore an expensive blazer and had curly hair and a transparent complexion and talked like a jessie, and maybe he was a jessie, but his arms were about two feet longer than mine, and every time I made a run at him I ran my face straight into one of his fists, and when I started running back from him his arm could still stretch faster than my feet could move and all I wanted to do was be somebody else, in another country for preference. It wasn't the humiliation that worried me so much as the discomfort of being punched on the face, and once he had discovered the thing could be done, he was all for doing it all night. But I knew later how he felt because I had it the other way round and this time I didn't want the fight in the first place.

To be frank, I had given up the fight game for life. But there was a crowd of older boys with a pack-sheet tent pitched on the coup one evening, and they sponsored the match after this other boy of my own height and weight had landed an unprovoked stone on the back of my head. They wanted sport, and I felt that I was armed with justice, so we squared up. I'm not even sure of the other boy's name, but I think it was Hannah.

We sparred for a few minutes, and the big boys got impatient and shouted for action, and at last I forced myself to aim straight at his face, and hit him hard in one eye. I was ashamed at once and sorry for him because I knew what it was like to be punched. But although he was half-hearted about it and didn't fly into a killing rage, he went on fighting, and I hit him in the face again. The big boys cheered me and patted me on the shoulder, and I felt flushed with victory, but I hated them too and they disgusted me, for they were risking nothing themselves and nobody was punching their faces, and I hated myself a bit for playing up to them. I was hoping Hannah would run away, and I wouldn't chase him very fast, but he suddenly kicked me.

Dirty foul! One of the spectators was so hot on fair play that he was making to kick Hannah from behind to prove it, but missed him, and I was smarting slightly from the kick on the shin and justifying myself while I hit him again. And then it got hellish. He was either blinded or posing as blind, and it doesn't matter which, because he just stood with his hands in front of his face and I punched through his hands and hit him again and again until a man working in a garden across the street came over and stopped the fight and gave the big boys a telling off and said I was a bully.

'He hut me furst!' I said.

'Get away home out of here,' the man said, and I went.

It was always bad to see older boys urging young boys on to a fight, because they were always liable to throw in a clout or two themselves, if they didn't like one of the fighters, and they were just as liable to turn nasty with their favourite if he didn't produce enough action. Even among ourselves I didn't often see a fight that was deliberately sought and willingly fought. There was a standard practice at this time for satisfying honour. Fights usually started in the playground, and the contestants couldn't fight there. They would promise or threaten to meet up the Muck at four o'clock, and by four o'clock the thing would be forgotten.

The Muck is a piece of made ground with a cinder track on it used for training by Shettleston Harriers. It may have another name, but nobody knows it.

In the playground one afternoon I was tripped on my face by Willie Cairns. He was one of a big family of Cairnses who lived in a little low old row of cottages in Shettleston Road, since de-molished and gone, and the Cairnses, about five of them all at

89

school, were known for two things. They were all sneaky wee pukes and their mother was a terror.

After I was tripped, Willie was laughing in his Cairns way. I said:

'Ah'll get you.'

'Ah'll ge-e-et ye!' he mimicked. It was a catchphrase. 'An' if ah don't get ye, the coos'll get ye!'

The bell rang. 'You wait,' I warned him. 'I'll see you up the Muck at four.'

'Gi'e him a towsin', Willie,' one of his supporters said. 'Don't worry,' Willie said. We glared at each other as the lines went in and made a threatening gesture with our right fists. For this gesture, the left shoulder is pushed up and forward and the right forearm is tucked well into the body pointing towards the chin, and the fist is clenched, but with the thumb poked through between the first and second fingers. We regarded this form of fist as correct for a killer punch. In practice, if you landed a punch with the thumb like this, a stab of pain shot up your arm to the shoulder and paralysed the thumb.

I knew my Willie. There would be no fight up the Muck at four. In the crowd leaving school at four o'clock, it was easy to get quietly lost before anybody could find you. But I had friends, and Willie had friends, and friends love somebody else's fight. Willie would have got clean away at four o'clock, and good luck to him, but for his friends who wanted his honour defended, and my friends had me trapped before I was out of the classroom. We took our positions before an audience of fifty or sixty, or rather, inside an audience of fifty or sixty, for everybody wanted to crowd round for a ringside view.

I had no fear of Willie. On the other hand, even a Cairns fist can be sore against the nose and was undesirable. We set to in the first position, arms tucked into the body and right shoulders forward, and then we did the usual thing. I said:

'Well?'

And Willie Cairns said:

'Aye – Well!'

'Well, whit'll ye dae?'

'You'll see!'

'Well, whit?'

'Ah'll dae a loat.'

Somebody in the crowd shouted:

'Aye – in yer troosers!' Shouts from every direction. 'Hit 'im wan!' 'Gi'e it tae 'im!' 'Whit kinna fight is this?' 'Baste 'im!' 'Gi'e 'im the auld wan-two!' Some of the spectators would demonstrate the kind of uppercut they fancied, and accidentally nudge another watcher, and arguments spurted up here and there. Willie Cairns and I were breathing heavily at each other, then I made the first attack, by leaning forward and bumping him on the shoulder with my shoulder and upper arm. He missed balance and staggered back a step, then stepped up and gave me a dunt with his shoulder.

'Well?' I said. 'You want a fight – let us see ye fight.'

'Ah never wanted a fight – you asked for it!'

'Ah don't want a fight.' These were the only honest remarks made all day.

'Well, yur gonny get wan!' a spectator shouted. Everybody was blood-mad to fight; except me and Willie Cairns. Somebody shoved Willie from behind to get him started, but he kept his balance and swung round angrily to curse the shover. It was a diversion that might end the main fight, but the crowd stayed in a solid ring and he finally had to give up arguing and turn back to face me. It never occurred to me to punch him while he was off guard. I don't say I was too honourable. He might have punched me back.

Somebody shoved me, and I was off balance. I cannoned into Willie and he fell back shocked. 'Hit 'im!' 'Uppercut!' 'Solar plexus!' I didn't know where the solar plexus was. Willie straightened up and aimed a swinging punch at a point two feet in front of my chin. 'Get in therr!' I aimed an uppercut about eighteen inches from Willie.

As I swung it, somebody shoved him again from behind, and his face crashed on to my fist. 'Uppercut!' the crowd shouted. 'Oh boy, did ye see that?' Spectators demonstrated the uppercut that I had landed. I danced about now, red and heavy-breathing and looking as if I meant business. I had put an uppercut right on the button. I was a real fighter. Willie swung like a woodsman again, but this time he was peevish and didn't care even if he hit me. He hit my shoulder and I lashed out, terrified of myself, at his face, and struck bone. I never liked Willie, but I was grateful to him

91

then. He didn't get angry, he surrendered the fight. He put his hands to his face as if he expected the jaw to be smashed, and reeled about drunkenly and decided not, after all, to fall down. It was a poor fight, as usual up the Muck. But my friends loyally made the best of it, and there were even some sycophants from Willie's camp who wanted to shake my hand and pat me on the shoulder. Soon I let them persuade me that I was a real killer. I lapped it up. I went home with fans on both sides of me and behind me shouting:

'You basted 'im! It was a massacree! Wan, two, bang!'

They stopped shouting. One or two of them left the procession and hurried ahead, or turned aside. We had reached Shettleston Road, and a big red woman was ten yards away facing us. She had Willie Cairns by the hand, and he was weeping floods and moaning. His eyes, which I had never laid a finger on, were raw red where he had rubbed them himself, and he had apparently sprained a knee and broken both arms on his way home, from the way he was walking. The big woman was Mrs Cairns.

'Aye, it's me! You come 'ere tae ah get ye, yah wee devil! Proud ae yersel', eh? Ah'll soart ye!'

'He started it!' I retorted. I was just as angry as she was, and I wasn't afraid either.

'Aye, an' ah'll feenish it!'

I ran like hell. She shouted after me:

'Ah know where ye live, ya bullyin' wee nyaff! Ah'll get ye!'

That was something I could worry about later, as long as I got out of reach of Mrs Cairns in the meantime. She wasn't like Willie. Mrs Cairns *could* fight.

From *Dancing in the Streets* (new edn. Mainstream, 1983)

CLIFF HANLEY (BORN 1922) IS A NOVELIST, JOURNALIST AND BROADCASTER.

W. S. Graham

ALICE WHERE ART THOU

Alice where art thou sings the girl across
The language slipped into a time in Greenock
In was it thirty-three? Hark how through at
The edges of the language in its time
Comes Christine's voice. She was my very first
Girl as a girl grown up walking beside me
After the kirk on the Whin Hill in the summer.

These are real names. She is alive or dead
Humming whichever way we look at it
Maybe Alice where art thou. She set her mark
On me for ever, a young apprentice to Love.

If you would like to see us through the slow
Camera of the time, there we are
Not speaking hardly touching walking under
The West End sycamores of Greenock dying
Of sheer love. That was me as a boy
Not yet come into the language which was
To pretend to discover me. I can hear
Her now singing ALICE WHERE ART THOU at
Fifteen and us standing there in the dusk
Inside weeping for love looking between
The railings of the bowling green.

W. S. GRAHAM (BORN 1918) LIVED LATTERLY IN CORNWALL. HIS *COLLECTED POEMS*
WERE PUBLISHED IN 1980. HE DIED EARLY IN 1986.

My Aunt Grace

I don't suppose you knew my Aunt Grace. Even so, you would certainly have given her a second look as she walked purposefully down Albert Street. Not that she was bonnie. In fact she was downright plain. But with her black, flowerpot hat well anchored, her black leather handbag stowed under her arm, her jaw jutting out a fraction more than nature intended, and her determined marching stride, here was a woman who knew her own mind, and was capable of giving a bit of it to any Nethergate shopkeeper who thought he could reduce the filling in a Forfar bridie or who showed incompetence in calculating change to a farthing.

Yet she wasn't the businesswoman in the family. Business was left to Jessie and Kate who had the milliners' shop at the top of the Hilltown, just opposite the big clock and the public toilets. As the discerning matrons of Dundee were well aware, Jessie and Kate were the artistes of their profession in the area. Hadn't most of them followed Jessie when she left Draffen's department store to set up for herself in the nether Himalayas of the Hilltown? And couldn't Kate do more with a satin ribbon than a Roumanian gymnast?

But Grace was the family's solid centre. Mainly for Jessie and Kate, for she was custodian of the flat in Clepington Road, but also for Mary, the one sister who had married and believed that life was made up of crossword puzzles, and for Lizzie, who lived in opulence in Beverley Hills but graciously summered in Dundee. Then there were the brothers. Hadn't she nursed George through one imaginary illness after another till he died, and made William's unsteady life as comfortable as possible? William d . . . k.

Alec, who had flown the Dundee coop, was her favourite. He even looked like the young man she may or may not have lost in the Great War and her affection for Alec was readily, effusively even, extended to Alec's children of whom I happened to be one.

These were the days when part of the holidays was spent with

Aunts, and it was to Grace's daunting old arms that we were generally sent.

For she was very old. Perhaps fifty. But at least she knew everything of importance: at which shop in Victoria Street to buy a knife, how to jump on and off the shaky Downfield tram without too great injury, where Broughty Ferry was, and how to get the boat across the Tay to Newport.

For no obvious reason, she added, accurately, columns of figures in her head, she read the *People's Friend* avidly but sceptically, and she loved the Royal Family.

She knew with certainty that Dundee had the most beautiful situation in the whole of Europe, probably in the world. Where else was there a city overlooked by a hill as distinguished as the Law, with a broad river sweeping round its base into a silvery firth? Maybe the bit between the Law and the river might have been better laid out and put to better use, but that was an error that could be remedied.

And she always asked her nephews the right question: what did we want to do next? We wanted to go to a football match.

Clepington Road was too close to Dens Road for Grace not to know that there were two senior football teams in Dundee. But at that point her knowledge of football ended. She had work to do.

She began a study of the sports page of the *Courier and Advertiser* with intensity and care. Dundee Football Club was going through a difficult period; it was not going through one of its infrequent periods of success. But there were things in the team's favour. Hadn't it recently won the Scottish Cup? Well, twenty years ago, but two decades is as a moment in football lore. Wasn't Bill Marsh, the present goalkeeper, an Englishman? What other team in Scotland could possibly boast of having an Englishman as goalkeeper?

Grace decided that Mr Morrow, her next door neighbour, would have the answers. Although his knowledge was only slightly greater than Grace's she prised from him that the game was played with a round leather ball, that there were eleven players in a team, and that the idea was to score goals against an opposing team. He believed that Dundee was not good at scoring goals, but had a sound reputation for dirty play. He also thought it inadvisable to watch Dundee playing football if it was against the Rangers

95

or Celtic from Glasgow. Quite apart from the fact that Dundee would be defeated, the supporters of these clubs were not noted for their charm of speech or manner.

From Clepington Road to Dens Road is not much more than a long throw-in. Her bonnet, now with just a touch of blue satin ribbon in it – the team's colours came in the market research – was even more squarely placed on her head as Grace marched, with two small boys in tow, into the home of Dundee Football Club. For ninety minutes she sat through a game she didn't understand and would never grow to like. Still she had done her duty to the best of her not inconsiderable ability, with results that only time would·tell.

One result is that I have supported Dundee Football Club for fifty-five years, and there is no way that I shall change my allegiance now. On reflection, as Grace surely knew, loyalty to the team as to the family is one of life's enduring joys.

SIR CAMPBELL FRASER (BORN 1923) IS CHAIRMAN OF SCOTTISH TELEVISION, AND WAS PRESIDENT OF THE CONFEDERATION OF BRITISH INDUSTRY 1982–84.

James Thin

A SENSE OF WONDER

Can we go back? No of course we can't. How can I possibly feel the immense surge of excitement at finding dozens of squiggly black tadpoles in a puddle? Or the great adventure of the first day at school? Or the pain when I slammed the garage door on my fingers?

Can I again experience the horrified fascination of watching a battle royal between a spider and a wasp caught in the web? Or the terror when I accepted a dare to walk through a small wood alone in the gathering gloom? Or the sheer misery and sense of loss when my ice cream fell off the cone and plopped into the sand?

I may remember these things vividly, I may recall them with nostalgia, but never again can I think as I did then, or feel as I did then, or react as I did then. Naturally, for I am a different person. That is why, sadly, a father's advice to his children can often be so futile. He is trying to transpose himself as he is now into a different age, a different outlook, a different person, and different circumstances. The child is not the father, nor is the father himself as a child. The years have moulded and changed him, sometimes almost beyond recognition.

All the same, I think it is worth making the attempt to throw ourselves back, for this can sometimes give us a refreshing simplicity of outlook. I do not believe that we can achieve this on our ordinary working days, when life can seem pretty hectic and complicated; but I suspect that the mood can creep up on us unawares when we are on holiday. Then we can occasionally be surprised at how different things look, how simple our complicated problems become.

What we so desperately need is a sense of wonder. We used to have this, and we have lost it. Possibly it was the most valuable thing we ever had. Is it too much to hope that it might come to us again, even if only in rare unguarded moments?

JAMES THIN (BORN 1923) IS IN THE BOOKSELLING BUSINESS.

Ian Hendry

CRICKET AND THE COVENANT
OR
SATURDAY AFTERNOONS AND SUNDAY MORNINGS
—

Friends who live south of a line drawn from Montrose to Oban hear with ill-concealed scepticism and condescension my claim that cricket was played to a high standard in the northern county of Moray, indeed along the shores of the Moray Firth from Dingwall as far south as Aberdeen.

97

What about the weather? they ask, thus revealing their ignorance of the fact that nowhere in Scotland does the rain fall more lightly or the sun shine fairer than on that blessed strip of fertile land between the Grampians and the sea. No less a character than Banquo invests my native town with immortality when he asks in *Macbeth*, Act 1, 'How far is't called to Forres?' and King Duncan himself finds exactly the words to describe the climate that cricketers more recently have sought:

> '. . . the air
> Nimbly and sweetly recommends itself
> Unto our gentle senses.'

My senses were captivated early by the game of cricket. My memories of school are much less sharply etched. With regret, tinged with shame, I have to confess that my first contacts with Shakespeare, Racine and Goethe have left no indelible impression; even the bitterness of my first, joyless excursions into mathematics has lost its edge, but a sniff of linseed oil brings back for me into sharp focus the cricket pavilion, the fragrance of mown grass and old cricket boots, tea intervals with cream buns and, of course, memories of the giants who bestrode the turf of the Grant Park in those days.

Even my doubting friends do evince some evidence of interest when I tell them that the Australians played at Forres in September, 1934. For lack of permission to be absent from school, due to the Headmaster's failure to recognize the importance of the occasion and grant at least a half-day's holiday, I felt compelled to absent myself for most of one day; for lack of funds I did not present myself at the normal point of entry but wriggled into the ground under the canvas. The first crime was detected and punished in the traditional Scottish style; the second I believe I have now expiated in what my family find a disproportionate expenditure of my time and money on cricket and its literature!

I sat rapt at the boundary's edge on that day, gazing in wonder at the great men in action; I still see clearly the bristles in Fleetwood-Smith's moustache as he patrolled the boundary line beside me; I remember the mixture of disbelief, horror and pride that was my reaction to the sight of the great Donald G. Bradman being bowled by our local fast bowler for seven and two. It is true that Bradman was immediately thereafter whisked away to hospital for an appendicectomy. But the scorebook has nothing of this. Records do, however, show that the town had fifty-five hours of sunshine during that week.

The same fast bowler was a sculptor in the town and I often joined him on sunny Saturday mornings in the very elegantly laid-out cemetery on a wooded hill overlooking the cricket ground, where, as he chiselled away at inscriptions on gravestones, we talked of the famous names of the game, of stirring events at Lord's or the Oval, and, inevitably, of our prospects for the afternoon, when fate and the umpires would take over.

We had, it seemed to me, a highly idiosyncratic body of umpires, who reached their decisions by processes of thought that had not been significantly affected by MCC's rulings on the laws of the game. But we learned to accept the vagaries of fate with a good grace, believing that any bias at one end would be compensated for by a similar lack of impartiality at the other and that on balance an approximate form of justice would result.

Promoted early to the 2nd XI, I became, for some reason, the apple of our team umpire's eye. He always carried a ¼lb bar of Cadbury's chocolate for the top scorer and was, of course, best placed to determine week by week the destination of the award. On one occasion I snicked my second ball into the Elgin wicket-keeper's gloves. I started to walk towards the pavilion but was stopped by the umpire's call: 'You're not out, Ian!' I returned somewhat diffidently to the wicket. The opposition shrugged their shoulders. As I prepared to face the next ball our umpire wagged his finger at me and called down the wicket: 'If ye dae that again, Ian, yer oot!' I hope I had the grace to blush as I pocketed the bar of chocolate that week!

This element of predestination in the award of the chocolate could perhaps be seen as foreshadowing the Calvinistic flavour of the Scottish Sunday that followed the Saturday of cricket. The contrast was stark. We were up early, carefully scrubbed and dressed in our best, ready to accost a day that was significantly different from the other six days. No school work was allowed. Sunday papers were unthinkable. We spent the morning before church grappling with the Shorter Catechism from a small cinnamon-coloured booklet with the burning bush on the front cover and the multiplication tables on the back – a juxtaposition of the basic tenets of the faith with the elements of sound arithmetic that John Knox would have whole-heartedly approved. We had to learn the question and the answer, beginning with the fairly straightforward 'Q. What is man's chief end?' 'A. Man's chief end is to glorify God and enjoy Him for ever'; and from there on to the much more complicated definitions of such matters as sanctification and justification, taxing work at any time, but especially so on sunny, summer Sundays!

Looking back, I sometimes ask myself why we were not more rebellious about having to be so different, or why, at the very least, not more envious of our schoolfellows, making headlong for perdition by swimming on Sundays, reading the *News of the World* or doing their homework. I suppose the answer must be that Sunday was a day when we were insulated from the rest of the world, a family day with its own well established routines and observances and we played this game, too, according to the rules which were arbitrary but, curiously enough, not harsh.

After church, books were allowed, but only such as were likely to improve our moral and spiritual condition, missionary stories, chief among them those of Mary Slessor, David Livingstone and McKay of Uganda, but the hard core of our reading was expected to be that book which should be on the book list of every young Scot, Alexander Smellie's *Men of the Covenant*. When, in the depths of winter, I would sit with *Men of the Covenant* on my knee, gazing into the fire, my heroes of the cricket world would intermingle with the gaunt, hard Scotsmen whose fire and passion kept them suffering for their faith on bleak, inhospitable Scottish moors, just as Jardine and Larwood were doing battle on hard and hostile Australian wickets for an England that was not entirely sympathetic to their efforts.

And so, although my two worlds touched in imagination from time to time, the chasm between them was real enough, real enough for me in later life to wonder at and even envy the English, who, in their village life, managed to fuse cricket, the pub and the church into an aesthetic, harmonious whole.

On further reflection I am now grateful for the two very disparate disciplines that dominated my youth. When now, from the safety of my armchair, I watch the England XI in action, I wince to see professional batsmen take their eye off the ball and I groan when they fish speculatively outside their off-stump. Then I feel sure that what is needed is an injection of the iron that was in Douglas Jardine and in his covenanting forebears, but then, come to think of it, a similar injection of the iron of the Shorter Catechism might do something to stiffen our national, spiritual backbone!

IAN M. HENDRY (BORN 1922) WAS RECTOR OF DUNOON GRAMMAR SCHOOL 1969-75, AND RECTOR OF DOLLAR ACADEMY 1975-84. HE DIED IN DECEMBER 1985.

Evelyn Cowan

STREET GAMES

About eight of us were jammed into the musty narrow back close. There was Jacky, Wally and myself the only girl, not quite converted to full-time femininity. The crowd included Harold, a blankfaced pale boy of about ten. Big Doddy Hertsfield, a dod of a boy in a man's body, Ginger-Snotty Hornstein, Julie the Jewel, a flashy boy, and Peeshy-Paishey, a boy of thirteen with a heavy growth of hair on his face.

'Now, listen carefully.' Jacky addressed himself to Harold. 'This is part of your test to join our gang.'

'Aa right. I'm listening.' Harold became paler.

'Well,' Jacky went on, while the rest of us stood around in silence. 'You go up to the top of this building. Count up to fifty by fives. Then come jumping slowly down the stairs singing out loud, "It was me! It was me!"'

'You mean,' interrupted Harold, 'that's all I need to do?'

'Yes,' nodded Jacky, 'for the moment, anyway. Just do what you're told. And whatever happens, don't stop singing.'

Jacky gave the new boy a violent shove. 'Right, now! Away you go up.' Harold climbed the three flights of strange stairs. When he had gone, we all tiptoed up to the second storey. We tied a long string across the landing from the door handle of one flat to the bell-pull of the other. Working quickly, we did the same on the first floor.

Then I ran up and rapped at the door with the tied handle. I did the same on the landing below. I then disappeared down into the dark back close where the boys were waiting.

Meanwhile, the first lady opened her door, and in doing so, pulled her neighbour's door bell. By this time, Harold was on his innocent descent, singing at the top of his voice, 'It was me! It was me!'

The two irate women caught hold of him. 'Oh, it was, was it? Can't you find anything better to do than ringing folk's bells?'

Harold received a few good slaps on his face. Then he continued down on to the first floor, where the two neighbours there grabbed him and boxed his ears. He was crying, but still bravely singing, 'It was me! It was me!' – and was a fully-fledged member of our gang as he joined us in jumping over the dyke to escape.

We raced along the lane beside Motherwell's flour mills and turned across the tramlines towards Oatlands. This was a district forbidden to us, notorious as it was for gangs. We mooched alongside the dim shop windows. There were no kosher butcher shops here. But mainly, cut-price bacon, ham, and egg shops, and dusty windows displaying pails and ropes and sticky notebooks with erasers to match. Then we turned off into a side-street. Jacky called us to halt, we were far away from the noisy tram-clanging street. There was dead silence. Suddenly in the distance we heard the cry, 'Here come the Billy Boys!'

'It's the gangs,' shrilled Harold. 'We better get out of here quick.' In a flurry of excitement, we started to run for our own district. My heart thumped like a war drum. This was not the first time we had been chased by gangs. We spoke of them in whispered awe. Yet we were never caught.

And, strangely but truthfully, in all the years that I lived my childhood in the Gorbals of Glasgow, I never saw a gangfight or a razor wielded in an attack.

We raced back across the tracks, turned into Apsley Place, ran through the first close and huddled together in the darkness. The noises of running feet could be heard passing by and voices shouting, 'A Billy or a Dan, or an old tin can!'

A Billy was a Protestant and a Dan was a Catholic. And an old tin can was a Jew. So if you admitted you were an old tin can, you got kicked around the street just like that piece of metal. Vaguely, we always knew of someone who got beaten up by the gangs. But it was never one of our immediate circle. Still, we shivered thrills of anticipation and the real dangers never quite penetrated our minds.

When the 'all clear' signal came from Julie, our temporary lookout, we formed a circle round the lamp-post on the pavement to decide what to do for the rest of the evening. A motley assortment of shapes and sizes we were. From Big Doddy round to Jumbo-Jacky, pale Harold, wee Wally, Skinny Julie, Snotty Hornstein, and ending with my small female self enveloped in a ragged cast-off football jersey.

Big Doddy said, 'Let's go down to the river under the bridge and see the wind blowing up the lassies' skirts?'

'Na,' said Julie. 'That wouldn't take up much time,' I interrupted. 'Anyway, that's no interest to me.'

'Aye. I forgot about you being a girl.' Doddy shuffled his feet.

'You've only forgot since my brother Jumbo punched you up OK.' Doddy fidgeted. 'Well, how about a smoke?'

'Haven't the price of it.' Wee Wally looked up at six-footer Doddy. 'Anyway, it'll stunt your growth.'

'Och, never mind all that,' Ginger Hornstein sniffed. 'How about a game of football?'

'It's too dark. You'd never be able to see the ball.' Jacky recovered his authority. 'That reminds me. What about Miss Duncan? We're about due a visit there.'

By a majority, we voted to have our revenge on Miss Duncan. Now, she was a lady who lived down our street in a main door flat. She had a beautiful patch of garden on each side of her front door, which faced the street. The gardens were guarded by medium-high spiked railings. Inevitably, when we played a game in the street, our ball went into Miss Duncan's well kept garden. She must have been waiting at the ready. For the minute the ball touched her ground, she dashed out through her little side gate, into her garden, snatched the ball and in front of our very eyes cut up the ball with big scissors.

Our pleas and cries fell on deaf ears. She just kept on cutting. Tales were told in the street that Miss Duncan was more than one person, and that, supposedly, there were two Miss Duncans. But this was never proved. They were both tall, wore long black tunic coats, and kept their grey hair drawn back in a tight bun.

One of them appeared to be slightly fatter than the other. But this may have been the one and only Miss Duncan after a big dinner. We were never sure. Her appearances in public were rare and swift. The other story about Miss Duncan was that she had been jilted on her wedding day by Paleface the Polisman. And that's why they always exchanged angry glances and both hated children.

It was usually afternoon, after school, when all our games were played. But now it was evening. In pairs we drifted through the close into the yard at the back of Miss Duncan's flat. We threaded a safety-pin on a reel of black thread, fastened one end of the thread to a knob outside the spinster's window, reeled out the thread and span it along until we were far away. Then let the pin slide down the thread until it tapped on the window.

'Tap . . . tap . . .' went the metal pin on the windowpane. Miss Duncan opened her window and put her head out. Quickly we tilted the thread downwards, leading the pin back to us. Seeing nothing, she withdrew and closed the window. We were round the corner in the darkness of the backyard.

As soon as she closed the window, we let the pin slide back on to the pane. 'Tap . . . tap . . .' Miss Duncan's head emerged again. There appeared to be nobody there. We repeated this for about an hour until Miss Duncan was nearly demented.

'Hey, you kids! Hooligans! I know you're out there.' she shouted into the darkness.

We giggled. She went on shouting. 'You just try it once more. And I'll call the police.' Wally yelled back at her, 'Pay us back for the balls?'

'Throw us out the money,' shouted Jacky.

Far away we could hear Ma's stentorian voice resounding along the street. She was leaning dangerously out of our high window – 'Jacky, Wally, Ebby! . . . Nine o'clock!' It was time to go home. We trailed up our three flights of stairs. In the kitchen my sisters had steaming cups of hot cocoa and bread and jam prepared. We washed our hands. And while we sipped our nightly beverage, we enjoyed watching Annie and Rina play their kind of games. My sister Kate sat in a corner by the fire engrossed in her library book.

Annie and Rina were dressed up like ladies in Ma's old gowns with high-heeled shoes and big floppy picture hats. They had attached a rope to an old flatiron. This was their imaginary poodle. So now they were two smart society ladies out shopping and meeting for a chat. Annie tugged at her rusty iron poodle. 'Good morning. Miss Florence Nightingale, is it?' This greeting pleased Rina, for her ambition was to be a nurse. She had been diverted by Ma from choosing this occupation because Ma thought it was not a suitable job for a nice Jewish girl. However, Rina eventually made it into the nursing profession, although she was a grandma before she passed her final exam.

Back in the kitchen, Rina replied to Annie, 'Oh, yes. That's me. Pleased to meet you.' The two girl-ladies shook hands. 'And what's *your* name, my dear?' Rina waved her broken umbrella cum parasol. 'Oh, don't you remember me?' Annie simpered. 'We met at the Royal garden party in London. My name is Mrs Marjorie Seldon.'

The girls played out their gossipy act. But Annie's choice of Seldon as a name was not purely imaginary. For my father's real name had been Simon Zeldon. According to his traditional story, when his ship docked about the year 1900, Papa disembarked at Greenock. With hundreds of other refugees he queued up in the landing shed. Eventually he reached the desk of the immigration official. The busy officer looked over my father's papers. 'Your papers are in order.' He fingered the document. 'But I can't make out your name. What is it?'

My father, with only a few words of English at his command, could not comprehend the man. 'I said,' the officer was getting impatient, 'what is this name? How do you spell it?'

Papa Zeldon shook his head, pointing to his lips and then to the identity book, indicating his lack of language. 'Och, what's the odds?' The man was already wielding his rubber stamp, 'Let's call you Cohen like the rest of them.'

He wrote 'Cohen' across the illegible foreign words, rubber-stamped the document, and let my father through. The official could not know that such a name could never be bestowed, but only inherited. We were never real Kohanim, who are priests of the first tribe of Israel and very highly respected in all prayer assemblies.

My mother used the name 'Cohen' for a few years, then changed to 'Cowan' long before I was born. First of all, it was more Anglified, or should I say Scotified? And, secondly, there were so many people in the Gorbals called Cohen that it became extremely confusing. My sisters liked the anglicized version of Zeldon and often called themselves Seldon in making dates with new admirers.

From *Spring Remembered* (Canongate, 1974)

EVELYN COWAN (BORN 1926) IS A NOVELIST AND JOURNALIST.

David Donaldson

'COATBRIDGE TO GLORY'

I was fifteen and some months, when my childhood was interrupted. This was on my arrival at the Glasgow School of Art in Renfrew Street in January 1932, long before being a Charles Rennie Mackintosh enthusiast was a recognized way to the top.

I had no formal qualifications, thus presenting an embarrassment to the administration. It was, after all, their concern to keep the affairs of the institution tidy. Any deviation from the accepted norm created problems. I was that kind of problem.

My childhood and schooling had shaped me to be an outsider. Not that I wished to be so, for I was anxious to be accepted. Regretfully, I seemed unable to interpret rules correctly, a difficulty that experience has not overcome. School was a trial. Counting beyond ten made my life a misery, and that of my teachers, 'patient beyond all understanding', a battle against the odds.

Happily, being a child at Coatdyke Primary School was not just a dreary round of ill-understood arithmetic. How could it be, when Corky Lovell was Headmaster – so called because he had an artificial leg. Totally Victorian, complete with velvet jacket and velvet smoking-cap, peering through steel-framed glasses. He was kind to wee boys with diarrhoea or any other ailment, treatment for which was dispensed in his room – senna tea, poured out into a saucer, and, the ultimate consideration, blown to an acceptable temperature. Corky understood, too, the need for surprise half-holidays. Perhaps his leg ached, or maybe he had run out of senna tea.

Tumult and shouts at playtime. Peeing over the wall. 'An airyplane in the sky!' Hysteria! 'Sixty miles an hour,' it was rumoured. Impossible speed! Hunch, cuddy, hunch – two opposing teams, the lowers making a long line of bent backs, heads between legs, twelve backs in all. Hurling oneself along the line, holding on until the count of ten – collapse, acrimony, accusations.

'Lucy Gray' and 'Sir Patrick Spens' in the afternoon, while later in the gathering darkness the janitor lit the gas. Then singing songs from Shakespeare – 'Come away, come away, death', 'In a cowslip's bell, I lie' – as a correction to joy.

Most of us had boots, but there *were* those who would arrive at school with bare feet. In such cases, boots were supplied every so often (belated thanks to the Education Authority of Scotland, which walled us in with concern).

My family earned a living in the rolling mills of Coatbridge. Being artisans, they lived in larger houses than the single-ends allocated to the 'roughers'. Here lived those who kept 'pouters' (pigeons) or made the Houses of Parliament in fretwork from thick six-foot egg-boxes, still stained by the occasional broken egg. These same egg-boxes doubled up as beds, hauled up by pulley to the ceiling during the day. One 1914 soldier named his daughter Mons, after the battle in which he fought. Another went mad and was taken away and shut up, after bringing a herd of cows to graze on the drying-green within the building.

There was wonder, too, when the great black horses and hearse came into the building to act out the Victorian drama of death. It was all clatter in those days – horses drawing milk carts or 'mickey carts' (the cleansing), all traffic loud on iron wheels on cobblestones, and manure being gathered with a shovel. 'Katie with the

Iron Teeth' and 'Jock with the Hairy Waistcoat' were minor demons introduced into our culture, bringing spice and exhilaration. The fear was enjoyable.

We climbed the social ladder to a council house up-town. So, too, I advanced to secondary education, and to the Scouts. I went off to camp a few miles outside the town, staggering under the burden of a huge kit-bag, supporting the popular conviction that solidity and weight meant worth. The experience of that first night! Wide-awake till dawn, lost in the beauty of the green light flooding through the tent. There was porridge in the morning, immovable in the billy-can; later that day, custard, turgid and congealed, with grey ash dropping like impetigo on the sulphurous yellow skin. I preferred to have it with stewed rhubarb, similarly sprinkled with ash. Commands from Reggie Begenstein, our Patrol Leader. How did Reggie ever get there, I wondered? He was a German boy, lean and scraggy, with a furious stutter, who wore the kilt like all his men – Camerons, Seaforths, Black Watch and Hunting Stewarts – represented in that force.

Secondary school opened up a vast academic minefield, wherein any hope of a polite and profitable career was instantly destroyed. But there *were* survivors, and their achievements throughout the world bear testimony to the excellent teaching that was available to us all. Nor was the art class a haven for me. Shading and assessing the contours of a jam jar found me woefully inept, and jealous of those better able to understand the rules of the game. I realize now that on my part there was a resistance to organized teaching, and that my dreams had other values and disciplines.

In such a steel town, the sub-culture was lurid – much of it, as no doubt it still is, concentrated below the navel. Squeals in the dark, trigonometry forgotten! The swimmings baths offered other hazards and delights. On a Friday, the entry was one penny, and we splashed in a broth of water, on the surface of which floated, forlorn and sodden, corn plasters and car tickets. Threepence on the Saturday bought clean water, but at a price! Whichever day it was, the entry money assured one of a towel, reeking of bleach – for health reasons, I suppose. Broken biscuits, from a nearby bakery, satisfied our hunger after our exertions. A few coppers bought a day bright with incident and substance.

To my knowledge no one suffered who patronized that spa.

Religion meant Sunday School – another infringement on one's liberty. Scrubbed and dressed overall as a midget refugee from a pipe band, you arrived at the Baptist Church with a penny for the plate. Tedium and disbelief! The rest of the Sabbath was calamitous with boredom, for everything was forbidden. No running, no bike, and stewed rabbit for tea. I refrained from reading *The Pilgrim's Progress*, and sought diversion and information in the family medical book, wherein 'pop-up' lungs and intestines sprang to life with a most edifying display. It was probably this required reading that influenced me to consider medicine as an alternative to boredom.

Release on Monday blew away such heady fantasies and supplanted them with others, equally unobtainable, like being a drummer in a jazz band.

The Baptist Church offered other routes to salvation. I sat among the congregation of black-clothed ladies on soirée nights, their men safely exposed to the dangers of white-hot iron on the night-shift. Listening to the minister, listening to the rustle of sweetie pokes, awaiting the arrival of tea in the polished brass kettles, new-burnished for the occasion, resplendent with blue bows. Waving to friends across the holy sea, as we waited for the main event, a convert from Glasgow, playing a selection of sacred melodies with milk bells. There was hushed admiration as four bells were rung to strike a chord. 'Rock of ages'. Admiration, too, how the bells were silenced on a baize table.

There was no formal response to this kind of litany such as may exist in other churches. But on the occasions that I witnessed, it was to rise and sing with stout conviction:

> Nothing to pay,
> No, nothing to pay:
> Straight is the Gate
> And narrow the Way.
> Look ever upright,
> Start right away,
> Coatbridge to Glory,
> And nothing to pay.

Another cup of tea from the kettle, and straight into:

> We are travelling to the Mansions
> On the Happy Day Express,
> And the letters on the engine are
> J.E.S.U.S.
> And the guard shouts, Off for Heaven?
> And we gladly answer, Yes,
> We are travelling to the Mansions
> On that Happy Day Express.

Then a sincere good blessing, and out into the night to hear mothers and grannies discussing operations past and to come, and legends of pain endured, devoted championship of various local doctors, and proud boasts of visits to the Glasgow Royal for whispered diseases. With this kind of medical background so easily available, I invalided myself out of the educational process at one point. The surgeons at that great hospital in Glasgow, the Royal, took out my appendix and showed it to me next day – as a treat. Maybe it wasn't mine. Who knows?

The party was over. I had to forget carbide bicycle lamps, and so much else. Then, full of dreams again, I presented myself at the Glasgow School of Art.

DAVID DONALDSON (BORN 1916) IS HER MAJESTY'S PAINTER AND LIMNER IN SCOTLAND AND WAS, UNTIL HIS RETIREMENT, HEAD OF THE DEPARTMENT OF PAINTING AT GLASGOW SCHOOL OF ART.

Rikki Fulton

HAPPY BIRTHDAY?

My family, as I remember them in my pre-teenage days were as follows. One father, somewhat small (maybe five-five, no more), and rather shilpit. One Mother, even smaller (an unbelievable four-feet-eleven-and-a-half-inches), and two assorted brothers, also rather on the short side, and my elders by fourteen and eight years respectively.

The system under which we lived was matriarchal and *my* Mother ruled her four slaves with a rod of iron. (I've always wondered if it was significant that when talking to me, my brothers referred to Her as '*your* Mother'.)

She was, it must be said, a remarkable little thing. She had the stamina, energy and drive of ten of us, and so in awe of her were we that, if one of us crossed her, even unwittingly, and found ourselves the object of her displeasure, the other three would immediately form a frantically supportive chorus to her argument, while in our heart of hearts grateful indeed that we were not the poor wretch in the dock.

Imagine, then, the panic one Saturday morning in September when we all realized that the anniversary of Her Birth had come and almost gone without its being marked. And here we stood in a trembling assembly – sans card, sans prezzy, sans hope of reprieve, allowing the full horror of the situation to possess us completely.

What to do?

My father, with a rare show of decisiveness, positively shot into town to return laden with goodies which he quickly thrust into our nervous hands at a hastily reconvened meeting.

We stood wide-eyed and shivering in the living-room, listening to the great bumps and bangs and thumps which emanated from the sitting-room upstairs whither She had repaired to vent Her wrath on wardrobes, bed-settees, arm chairs and any other object large or small which dared defy Her avenging washing-clout.

My father approached the foot of the stairs like a sergeant about to lead his men over the top at the Battle of the Somme.

'Aaaaaaaaaaaaaaay,' he quavered tentatively.

The bumping and thumping suddenly stopped, leaving an eerie, nail-biting silence.

My father cleared a dry throat and bravely ventured on.

'Would ye – er – come doon a wee minute?'

His use of the diminutive should be noted. It made his call an invitation, a supplication even – not a command.

He withdrew and rejoined his men. We squared our shoulders and braced ourselves for what was to come.

What was to come certainly took its time coming. The silence persisted for a good two or three minutes while the four of us stood and sweated in anticipation. As, indeed, we were meant to.

And then we heard it. The first soft fall of a size three on the top step of the stairs, followed by a measured series of others as She descended like some pinnied Cleopatra from Her carbolic throne.

Suddenly She was there. Straight-backed and defiant, proudly reaching for her full height of four-feet-eleven-and-a-half-inches in her shoes, her hair slightly awry, her face ruddy and glistening from her exertions, with a large piece of soapy-wet flannel dangling from one hand, She glared at us with a glare that Medusa would have envied.

My father seized the initiative once again. (He was surpassing himself.)

'Er . . .' he stammered ingratiatingly. 'We just wanted tae say – er – that – er – it's yer burthday. And . . .'

But he got no further. Her eyes black and remorseless and unforgiving swept the tide of her offspring and flooded us with such scorn that we could only hang our heads and cover our faces.

We heard the size-three's re-mount the stairs, and clip across the room above. Within seconds the banging and the thumping and the bumping had resumed with renewed energy and violence.

We silently commiserated with one another, knowing without saying that we were dug in for a long period of unrelenting winter.

But, surprisingly, the thaw came much sooner than anyone could hope. When the family foregathered for what we expected would be a pretty gloomy tea-time, *my* mother was in fine fettle and chattered away happily as if nothing had ever ruffled her pretty feathers. Gratefully and unquestioningly we accepted the restoration of the status quo.

Of course I was much too young to understand the ways of grown-ups, particularly Mothers and fathers, and their moods and hurts and fancies . . . but I *do* just remember that when we got home at tea-time, all the birthday presents – that pathetic little bundle of gaily wrapped and beribboned parcels – had been put away.

Methinks my father chose well . . .

RIKKI FULTON (BORN 1924) IS A FILM, STAGE AND TELEVISION ACTOR.

INDIAN SUMMER
—

I was brought up to be interested in history, particularly that of the British Empire, and also enjoyed as a child short travels abroad not just to the places visited but also for what I considered to be the glamour and excitement of just even getting on a boat or a foreign train to get to and from the chosen destination; even if it was only across the Channel to France and more so as far as Malta, which seemed at the age of twelve to be a real adventure.

When my father was appointed in 1934 to the Governorship of the Madras Presidency in South India for five years, I was thrilled at the prospect of possibly visiting the 'Exotic East' during his term of office. Having spent one term at Eton College, I was disappointed (to say the least) when I learnt that the Headmaster had refused my father's request to release me for three months or so on the grounds that it would 'interfere with my education'. Correspondence ensued which ended with the Headmaster's capitulation after my father's pithy question to him, 'Who's son is John? Yours or mine?'!

So my two younger brothers and I travelled by sea in 1935, passing by the Rock of Gibraltar and through the Suez Canal, docked at Aden and after landing at Bombay, proceeded by train to Madras, stopping at the even then legendary military establishment of Poona. On arrival in Madras, we learnt, with some dismay, that we had been booked in as day boys for one term at the Jesuit Loyola College, not far outside the City, to ensure the continuation of our schooling. This proved to be a real experience, even though we were segregated. Our Latin was improved by Father Bassenach (an Alsatian) and our French and Mathematics by other teachers, none of whom were Britons.

During that time in 1935 I must have begun to realize that denominations of the Christian faith and also other religions (I was baptized and confirmed into the Church of England and am now an Elder of long-standing in the Church of Scotland) are not all that different, hence my valued friendship now with many people whose religion or sect of it is different from mine. It was, for instance, food for thought that some high-caste Hindus were so devout that although having accepted the invitation to a lengthy banquet at Government House, they sat throughout the feast with an orange on their plate and never even touched it or anything else.

I was lucky to go back to Madras again in 1938 at the more receptive age of seventeen. Having specialized in history at school, this afforded me the opportunity to see what was to be part of the last few years of the British Raj. There had been a considerable move towards self-government and this was gradually and carefully being introduced into the political scene by my father, according to British Government policy. In fact the peaceful transmission of authority in the Southern part of India to the Indians was, I believe now, due to the confidence which existed between government and governed during the ensuing years and prevented in Madras the holocaust which occurred in the north after the War.

To sum up, my eyes were opened to the educational benefits of travel, to an understanding and respect for people of other religions (and I met many during my service in the Army during the 1939–45 War and have since), to the benefits which usually accrued to the indigenous populations through British rule in the Empire and finally a complete distaste of any headmaster who dares to say that the sort of thing which I experienced would be or was an 'interference with my education'!

THE EARL OF MAR AND KELLIE (BORN 1921) IS THE PREMIER VISCOUNT OF SCOTLAND AND HEREDITARY KEEPER OF STIRLING CASTLE.

George MacDonald Fraser
(Dand MacNeill)

A MERRY VERY CHRISTMAS

There was a silk blouse, with some sort of ornamental collar, and a kilt in dress tartan, and white socks, and black buttoned shoes, and that was me ready for the Dunlops' Christmas party. I can still feel adult hands tugging the collar into place, and brushing my hair with a briskness that set my head nodding, and a voice exclaiming proudly:

'There, now, that's a fine little man. Isn't he smart? Now, you'll remember to give Desmond his present' – a brown paper parcel was thrust into my hands: it contained, I knew, a splendid canoe with an Indian paddler with a real feather in his head and was, in my opinion, a lot too good for Desmond Dunlop – 'and to be very polite and not to make a noise and not to eat too much and when you're coming away to say: "Thank you very much indeed, Mrs Dunlop, for such a lovely party." Will you do that?'

'All right,' I said. 'I'll remember.' I was holding the parcel wondering what present I would get off the Dunlops' Christmas tree; one thing was certain, it wasn't going to be as nice as the canoe with the Indian.

'That's nice. I'm sure you'll have a lovely time; such nice children. You'll have lovely games. And you'll remember to say "Thank you" nicely . . .'

I didn't want to go to the Dunlops'. A few days earlier my sister and I had been to a huge party for the railwaymen's children – our father was the railway doctor. It had been in a great smoky hall, and there had been hundreds of kids and we had all run about shouting and having a tremendous time. There had been orange juice and jelly and scones and sweets, and the chief of the railway police had come in as Santa Claus, red and roaring, and I had got a Dick Turpin shooting game from his sack, and my sister a little sewing set. There had been streamers and singing and disorder; it had been great fun. The Dunlops', I knew from experience, would not be like that.

Mrs Dunlop was large and stout and blue, and once she had gushed at me in welcome and commented on my kilt (everybody always did), I stood nervously in her large, dim hall, listening for the sounds of children's voices from far away upstairs – shrill, hostile voices they seemed – while adults conversed in the air above my head.

'So nice . . . lovely . . . do hope he behaves . . . lovely . . . awfully cold . . . quite sure he will . . . good little boy . . . dreadful weather . . . such a busy time . . . lovely . . .'

I stood with Mrs Dunlop's large, soft hand on my head. It must be so serene and pleasant up there where she was; I was down in the half-way-up world where small children live, watching a thin boy in Eton jacket and spectacles coming down the hall.

'Oh, Desmond,' said Mrs Dunlop, 'here's Dand. Come and shake hands, darling.'

We shook flabbily, he smirking uneasily.

'Now be a good little host and take Dand upstairs to take his coat off, and then go into the playroom.'

We clumped upstairs, and the sounds of the other, grown-up world drifted up behind us.

'. . . so much rain . . . frightful . . . lovely . . . so nice for the children . . . goodbye.'

There was the subdued, final sound of the front door closing, and the shrill noises of children came closer; a nervous lump came into my throat.

'Is that parcel for me?' said Desmond. I handed it to him, and he tore the paper off, halting on the turn of the stairs.

'I say, that's not bad. Will it float? How much did it cost?'

'A merry very Christmas,' I said.

He shrieked with laughter. 'A what? I say, did you hear what you said? You said "a merry very Christmas" instead of "a very merry Christmas." I say, Jacquie, do you know what Dand said? It was so funny. He said . . .'

He was addressing a small girl in red with sandy hair in pigtails and freckles, who was patting a balloon about at the top of the stairs. She glanced at me and said: 'Merry very, merry very. Maybe that's how he talks all the time. Merry very.'

'A very merry . . .' I began, but they had gone off, Desmond calling, 'In there,' and pointing to a cloakroom where a little girl in white was taking off a velvet cape and putting on dancing pumps. I hung up my coat, and she looked gravely at my kilt. She had black hair cut in a fringe, and wore a small bangle on one wrist.

She said something incomprehensible, and I said something back which she didn't understand either, and we talked in mutual misunderstanding, as children will, until Desmond reappeared and led us into the brightly-lit playroom, where there were paper chains and a Christmas tree, and about a dozen children all thoroughly at home. I didn't know any of them well; one or two I remembered from last year.

'Here's yours, Alice,' said Desmond, lifting presents from the tree. 'And yours, Dand.' I opened it, hoping against my better judgment, but sure enough, it was *The Deerslayer* and it looked pretty dull.

'A merry very Christmas,' said Desmond, and everyone laughed; apprently they had all heard about it already.

'Thank you very much indeed.'

'You ought to say "Much very thanks",' said a ferret-faced boy with yellow hair, and they laughed even louder. 'Is that a kilt?' he went on.

I said it was.

'Are you Scotch?'

I said I was.

He thought for a moment. 'Scotchmen must all be girls,' he said, 'or they wouldn't wear skirts.'

'It's not a skirt. It's a kilt.' Suddenly I was very angry. He must have realized this, for he began to chant: 'Dand, Dand, funny old man, washed his face in a frying-pan,' and everyone seemed to be laughing. I knew I would either have to cry or hit him, but he suddenly said: 'Here, I say, shake hands.'

Relieved, I put out my hand, and he seized it and twisted it behind my back. He was larger than I, and stronger, but when I struggled we both went down in a heap. I hit out at him, and at that moment Mrs Dunlop came in.

Amid all the babble of childish voices she made motherly rebuking noises, and set me and the other boy, who was called Berkley, on our feet. I mustn't fight, she said, and now we would all play Looby Loo.

So we played Looby Loo, but I unfortunately didn't know the

steps. Berkley did, of course, and in putting his right leg out he made sure it landed on me; then we played Blind Man's Buff, and it seemed that when I was blind man there was more squealing and shoving than usual, and when we played balloon race, in which everyone got a prize, I thought – or was it just imagination? – that there was less applause when I won mine.

After a while there was supper, and I sat next to Alice, whose language was still incomprehensible, but who seemed quite friendly. Berkley sat opposite, and looking at me, he said: 'My brother's going to a public school next year. I shall be going later. Where do you go to school?'

'The Grammar School,' I said.

'I knew you weren't at Upperby House,' he said down his nose. 'The Grammar School must be pretty oickish.'

'It's one of the oldest schools in the world,' I blurted out. I knew that, if I knew nothing else.

'Old and mouldy,' said he. 'I say, Desmond, isn't the Grammar old and mouldy? Do they let you wear a skirt there?'

We were at the trifle stage, and I simply scooped up a handful and let him have it. It caught him nicely, and he never looked better, and Mrs Dunlop chose that moment to look down the table. Much Dand-ing and my-goodness-ing followed, and I was sent up to the playroom in disgrace. There I wept, softly and intensely, among the decorations, until presently I heard them coming up from the dining room and they all burst in, Berkley in the lead.

'There he is!' he shouted. 'Now, savage Scotchman, you're going to fight me.'

'I don't want to fight,' I said. Even at that age, I knew my limits. He was too big for me.

'Cowardy, cowardy custard! He's been crying! He is a girl, after all!'

At that I just put down my head and went for him, and after a few minutes' tussle he punched me in the eye. I got up, and he knocked me down again, and everyone yelled: 'Good old Berkley!' He moved in and pummelled me, and in pain and rage I quite lost my head and kicked him square and solid.

He went down, howling, and I was assailed with cries of 'Pig!' 'Beast!' and 'Not fair!' The row brought in Mrs Dunlop, and there was a dreadful scolding, with me standing like a small, resentful Highland bull, and Berkley martyring it bravely, and I was banished again, this time to the cloakroom. After a bit they brought me back, and showed me the lump on Berkley's leg, and said wasn't I ashamed. I wasn't but said I was, so I was allowed to join in the games again, and above the sound of the gramophone I could hear Mrs Dunlop: '. . . dreadful child . . . absolute ruffian . . . that school . . . disgraceful . . .'

But Berkley left me alone, and by the time it was all over and I was being collected in the hall I suppose the signs of tears and conflict had all disappeared. In the presence of my parents I thanked Mrs Dunlop and Desmond according to ritual, and she beamed at us down the steps.

'Yes, frightfully cold . . . not at all . . . delighted to have him . . . awfully good . . . good-bye . . . good-bye.'

Berkley, leaving with his parents, who were also ferret-faced, called cheerfully: 'Good-bye, Dand.'

'What a nice boy. It seems to have been a lovely party. Did you enjoy it?'

'Oh, yes. It was nice.' We were out in the dark, the sound of car doors slamming and voices behind us, and I was going home, home, home, at peace again.

'You must have had lovely games.'

'Oh, yes. They were good fun.'

'I'm so pleased you thanked Mrs Dunlop so nicely. They seemed very nice children.'

'Yes, they were all right.'

'Good. I'm so glad you enjoyed it.'

I see my own children coming home from parties, and hear them saying what fun it was, and how they enjoyed the games, and liked the other children, and looking at their shining faces I feel a slight relief. Obviously they mean it. Maybe I was an odd child. But sometimes, now and then, I wonder.

GEORGE MACDONALD FRASER (BORN 1925) WAS DEPUTY EDITOR OF *THE GLASGOW HERALD* 1964–69. AS A WRITER, HE IS BEST KNOWN FOR HIS NOVELS ABOUT FLASHMAN. THIS ARTICLE ORIGINALLY APPEARED IN *SCOTLAND'S MAGAZINE*.

Ewen Bain

An introduction to cinnamon stick

Fatherly advice

EWEN BAIN WAS BORN IN GLASGOW IN 1925 OF HIGHLAND PARENTS. A FORMER ART TEACHER, HE HAS BEEN A FREELANCE CARTOONIST SINCE 1969.

Sid Robertson

SALT OF THE EARTH

Many horticulturalists can boast of starting their career in vast acres in the grounds of a mansion house, or in a large municipal park, or even in the surrounds of a palace. My interest in gardening started on a plot for the unemployed.

My Dad, like so many others, was thrown out of work in the thirties. He tried and tried to get work, but no matter how industrious he felt, there was no place for his energy and his powers of innovation. Then, one day, he was offered the tenancy of a one-acre plot of land, provided by a local Dundee benefactor. This not only steered his life on to a different course, but it changed mine completely, too. Although I had won a bursary to Morgan Academy, once smitten with the joy of growing things, and with the feel of the soil under my feet, I decided to leave school at fourteen, to be a gardener. It was the right move, and my enthusiasm remains as strong today. I have met some grand people . . . and some fantastic plants, in my time.

My father's plot was a gigantic chunk of ground – an acre is 70 × 70 yards – and he had just a spade with which to turn it over. He was a remarkable man, for he only had one arm. His other had been blown to smithereens on the Somme in 1916. Nothing ever stopped him, no matter how difficult the situation. I never knew him with two arms. And just as another lad might have a father who wore a different coloured tie, or had a longer raincoat than my father, so my father had only one arm. That is how I viewed him through my childish eyes.

My Dad dug that whole acre with a lady's spade and one hand. Folk at the roadside would watch him perform, but when a crowd gathered, he would steal away for a bit. When he was digging, he would stand on the tread, sink the blade to the hilt, and slide his hand down the shaft to the neck of the spade. Then, with the shaft behind his forearm, he would lift and toss over a measured cube of soil, catching it deftly with the point of the spade, so that it would lie where he wanted it. He had a failing, though, for as he dug, his furrow always veered to one side. I'm sure it was a result of his lopsided anatomy, but we used to joke that his work looked like the east coast of Scotland!

Our home was a Dundee tenement, and the plot was some four miles away. We often walked both ways, and my legs ached, but I could hardly wait for Saturdays to come. Then, we would set off early to open the greenhouse ventilators, and to work among the plants. I learned that brussels sprouts grew up the stems of the plant, and carrots grew underground. There were rasps and strawberries in abundance, and my Mum really started something when she invited a couple of adjacent plot-holders over for a plate of strawberries and milk, with sugar over the top. Our green-house-cum-potting-shed had fruit that is still to me unmatched, and our place became a meeting point for everybody, as they arrived on their bikes. The bike was the standard beast of burden, then. A hundredweight bag of fertilizer could be squeezed into the frame and wheeled along with comparative ease. Bags of tatties and poultry food were treated in the same way. Garden rakes were often tied along the bar; cardboard boxes, bundles of bamboo canes, and other nondescript loads were carried, too. And if the string on the bundle of canes broke . . . Whoops, went the lot!

All the plotholders were inexperienced townfolk, and there were lots of gardening failures. One chap mistook my Dad's Dutch iris bulbs in growth for onions! Carrots collapsed – nobody had ever heard of carrot fly. Nobody knew that potatoes had to be earthed up, or that the tubers would turn green. One character thought he would make his fortune by growing mushrooms, but his entire crop was a few buttons which he donated to the communal frying-pan, and we all tucked into them together. This was my first experience of gardening folk, the salt of the earth.

An old Irishman who kept poultry was advised by a Government inspector to cull half his stock, as they were disease-ridden. Little wonder, for the poor birds paddled around in a small muddy run in all weathers. Nothing that lives can prosper in a poor environment, and as time went on I discovered that that applies to plants . . . and to people, too.

Growing crops had hazards of its own. Selling the crops was another, and anything the plotholders grew had laboriously to be carted back to town. Nobody had, or could afford, a car. The élite had two-wheeled barrows. The bike remained the standard form of transport. However, others carried sacks of vegetables on their backs, or occasionally caught the bus. One wee man stopped the service bus to town. When his foot was on the step, he announced that he had two bags of tatties, a bunch of onions, and half-a-bag of neeps! The conductor protested, but the passengers cried, 'Let him on!' Then it all happened in reverse when the bus reached town. There was laughter all round, and the man bowed graciously to the passengers, who waved as the bus drove away.

My Dad sold vegetables and flowers to neighbours. During the week, it was usually vegetables. A typical order might be 7 lb potatoes, a cabbage, peas and maybe a cauliflower. The orders were made up in the cellar of the tenement. There were no lights, apart from a simple paraffin lamp. Next day, early in the morning, he would be up and down those tenement stairs, delivering the orders.

Saturday was 'flower day'. Each week saw a different make-up of bunches. The bunches were mixed, so that all the flowers we grew could be used. Even a couple of stalks of the most common flower were used to make up a bunch. I learned a bit about economics in those early days, too.

I still grow many of those simple flowers – asters, sweet william, cornflowers, wallflowers, candytuft – as well as more exotic types, but those early days taught me never to worship the label more than the flower. Have you ever looked down inside a simple nasturtium? It's beautiful.

It's true that there is a horticultural ladder, and many garden lads achieve well paid, and worthwhile, jobs, and gain great acclaim. And every one of them has his own story about how it all started. But any real horticulturalist has a garden of his own, and the dirt which gathers under his fingernails reminds him of all sorts of elementary things, and where it all began for him. Like myself.

SID ROBERTSON (BORN 1924) IS A HORTICULTURALIST, BROADCASTER AND JOURNALIST, AND A REGULAR CONTRIBUTOR TO *THE DAILY RECORD* AND TO BBC SCOTLAND'S *LEISURE TRAIL*.

LONDON OR SCOTLAND?

Which was home? London, where we lived ten months of the year, where my father worked, and where we went to school, or Brucefield, our home in Scotland where we spent the summer holiday and a few weeks at Easter?

If we ever asked ourselves this question, Brucefield would have been the answer, despite our having an English mother born in Chester and preferring London. I believe that anyone who has lived in a place with a mountainous horizon will if possible choose that place as their home, and most certainly if the horizon is the Ochils seen from the south. That outline, from Dumyat in the west to Seamab in the east must surely be imprinted on the mind of every child born or brought up within ten miles to the south. It must have been carried all over the world for the last two hundred years in the minds of those labouring in the farthest outposts of the Empire, as it was carried by us as children, accurately we believed, until asked at school to draw a range of hills, when we would find its exact delineation more difficult than we expected.

No excitement could equal that of seeing the furniture van loaded in Bedford Gardens W8 on the day of our departure for Scotland. Why so much luggage had to be taken on holiday, I cannot imagine, but I am sure I can remember the heavy cast-iron lawn roller being loaded into the van together with innumerable leather trunks.

Having arrived at King's Cross, we would go and inspect the LNER locomotive before settling into our four-berth third-class sleeper. Most of us would of course want to be in the top bunk, but the disappointment of being in the bottom bunk overcome, we gave ourselves up to the delights of the journey. Peeping illegally round the blinds in the middle of the night to read the signs of 'York', 'Doncaster', 'Darlington', and 'Virol, Anaemic girls need it', by early morning we were dashing along the coast of North-umberland watching the rolling grass fields and red Midlothian soil, and feeling the thrill of the immense North Sea.

We would prove to ourselves we had arrived at Brucefield by

feasting our eyes on familiar sights. The first thing to do was to find our bicycles, and we would soon be whizzing down the hills, noting with satisfaction the sites of previous years' spectacular crashes.

Buried in the country, a family of six children and two parents did not bother much with the outside world, so that everyone who came was an object of great interest. Mr McAinsh, the postman, gave us a particularly delicious variety of boiled sweet from a tin concealed in a waistcoat pocket, having walked all the way up from Clackmannan to deliver and collect the post at all the intervening houses and farms.

The giant elder Fotheringham brother with his axe of unbelievable size, who came with his brother to fell some large oaks, requisitioned during the War. The sight of the chips flying as they prepared the base of the tree, the ringing sound of the big cross-cut saw, and looking up, seeing the leaves of the crown shiver to the clink of the wedge being driven in, till, very gradually, a widening gap emerged between this crown and its neighbours, as it slowly accelerated – till crump! These sights and sounds are clearer than the details of yesterday's journeys.

Very occasionally cousins and aunts had to be collected in our open 1930 Morris Oxford from Bogside, our local station. Once we saw, under some trees near the station, the flickering light of a bonfire illuminating the faces of some tinkers, in particular a big man with a big smile singing and accompanying himself on an accordian. Bewitching sight and sound! We returned many times to look for them, to find no one interested in telling us where they could be found.

It was during the War that we first came to understand the delights of winter. Tramping down to the millpond every day to test the ice during a week of hard frost, Dad finally allowed us to venture onto it. He would calmly put on his old English-style skates, advise us about tying our laces, and stepping out onto the ice set off in a series of long comfortable swooping strides. Loud sounds of 'Crrrock' came from the ice as cracks raced from the middle to the edges of the pond. We skipped nervously off the ice shouting warnings to Dad. Unconcerned, he skated on to the sound of further bangs and cracks, explaining as he circled round that it always cracked like that at first.

The greatest excitement was family ice hockey, when no one was allowed just to watch. Everyone would have to come on the ice, on skates if possible, or in wellingtons if not, with hockey sticks or walking sticks. The most thrilling battles took place, when we found in the desperate necessity of getting to the puck, we progressed in our skating ability more in half-an-hour of ice hockey than in a day of practising by ourselves.

Another excitement that particularly comes to mind was making gunpowder. Having produced it from a recipe learned at school, we took it to our gamekeeper to ask him if he could help us make a cannon. He rapidly obliged by making one from a bit of heavy pipe, and he clearly enjoyed firing it just as much as we did. However he thought our gunpowder was rather feeble, and found at the back of a drawer some gunpowder made by Eley Kynoch. There was much speculation about how much better it would be, and we applied the lighted match to the train of powder with some trepidation. Unfortunately, it turned out to be about a hundred times more effective than our own manufacture, and the shattering explosion it produced stunned us all, and somewhat impaired my brother's hearing.

When invited to write this piece I asked, 'How long is childhood?', wondering how far up teenage I could look for ideas. I was told there was no age limit, and have found this to be true. Discussing these things with my brother we remembered the delights of a rope we suspended from the branch of a tree over a road running through a cutting which we crossed Tarzan-like to the other side.

Excited by this memory we went out and erected for the children a bigger and better one over a deeper cutting and found it as exhilarating as ever. Fortunately childhood is not yet over, with only a few years to go to the OAP ticket.

LORD BALFOUR OF BURLEIGH (BORN 1927) IS DEPUTY GOVERNOR OF THE BANK OF SCOTLAND AND CHAIRMAN OF THE EDINBURGH BOOK FESTIVAL.

Iain Crichton Smith

CHILDHOOD INCIDENT

When I was young they took my Western magazine.
Wild Bill Hickok with a posse was riding west
towards, I think, the blue hills of Wyoming.
I never read the end of the story. Dispossessed,

I shall always see him, never quite catching the villain.
The hills are blue, so blue, and the cactus burns
in a furious sunset like a skeleton,

and the world's a music of expectant guns.

IAIN CRICHTON SMITH OBE (BORN 1928) IS A POET AND NOVELIST IN BOTH ENGLISH AND GAELIC.

Robert Crampsey

WILLINGLY TO SCHOOL

It was at Holy Cross School that I first saw poverty at close quarters. I had about a mile to travel to my parish school which was in Govanhill, nearer the centre of the city. At first I was taken down by tram, but it was a short run, only two stops, and as soon as I could I preferred to walk, especially as I was allowed to keep the halfpenny so saved, a formidable inducement.

I was a marked man from the day I entered the L-shaped, ridged, red sandstone building in Daisy Street. My Aunt Julia, younger sister of my mother, taught there, so that even before my arrival I was known to the rest of the staff. Most of the teachers were young, female and pretty; a couple were old, female and daunting, not least a Miss McKenna who affected a lorgnette and a chiffon handkerchief trailing from the sleeve of her blouse as she wafted her eau-de-cologned way between the narrow passages. The headmaster was formidable but curiously remote, and we had more to do with the other male teacher, his second-in-command, Mr Kelly, an amiable man whom the more daring amongst us referred to as Mr Kettlebelly.

There were not more than half-a-dozen Catholic families living in Mount Florida at the time who had children of school age, and the great bulk of the children came from Crosshill and Govanhill. Although there were a few pupils from far out in King's Park, I was still something of a frontiersman, in that few of my classmates lived anywhere very near me. Socially, I suppose I was just in the upper half of the class, which was more truly comprehensive than anything that has been devised at the present time. At one pole, there were the doctors' and lawyers' children of Queen's Drive, Queen Mary Avenue, and Myrtle Park. Most exotic was the fluffy blonde girl whose father had fought for the middleweight championship of the world and lost narrowly. She arrived every morning in a chauffeur-driven limousine, and as she passed my house on the way, I was often given a lift to the school gate. At the other extreme were the children from Robson Street and old Polmadie. In that time of crippling unemployment, there were several in the class who received their clothing from 'the parish', always distinguishable by its uniformity and the heaviness of the boots.

It did not differ in style from the garb of the more affluent. The woollen jersey and matching tie were the order of the day, although the parents of one boy, fortunately tall, well set-up and a useful fighter, dispatched him to school in a sailor suit. There were about forty in the class, and of that number, fully one-third were not required to find the halfpenny which was the nominal charge for our interval milk.

We were well taught, although much of the instruction was by rote and would now be condemned as stultifying and unimaginative. I am persuaded that for most of us it was the means of thoroughly grounding us in the traditional three Rs.

In the earliest class we worked with red and blue counters to teach us to add. We read with great anxiety 'Will the dog go to Nell?' and this first sentence of the reader was the occasion of the first joke. One of the Robson street boys who was actually important enough to have a brother in Borstal yelled out during one interval: 'Will the dog go to Nell? Will it hell?' We looked on, astonished that he was not struck dead on the spot.

There was great emphasis laid on handicrafts, in the baby class. I was not long in discovering that for anything involving manual dexterity, I had an ineptitude of the first order. I liked the pungent smell of plasticine, but while my neighbours could make dogs and giraffes, I could do no more than roll it up into hot grubby balls. The cards through which one pulled tagged, coloured laces soon became an irreducible tangle, and all that I could achieve with the rather messy crayons was to draw ships of an impossible rectangularity.

We chanted from morning until night:

> Nine and ONE are ten,
> Eight and TWO are ten,
> Seven and THREE are ten,

and so on.

We extended the same liturgical chant, appositely enough, to our catechism answers for, since it was a Catholic school, great stress was laid on the teaching of formal religion. We were very firm about it all. 'These three persons are NOT THREE GODS, we recited in Unison, 'the Father, the Son and the Holy Ghost are all one and the same God.' In the same satisfied vein we recited what Christ would say to the wicked: 'Depart from me ye cursed, into everlasting fire, which was prepared for the devil and his angels.' The force of this anathema was only slightly weakened for me by the fact that for some time I was under the impression that the fifth word in the answer was 'custard', and was rather troubled by the fact that the Deity had such a seemingly irrational dislike of pudding.

Occasionally, one of the curates from the parish would pop in to hear us, and no matter how abysmally we sang our hymns, or said our prayers, there was a kind word said to us. Much more imposing were the periodic visits of the Bishop, whose conversion from the ministry of the Church of Scotland had caused a considerable stir some three decades previously. He had perhaps adopted the tenets of the Church of Rome, but he retained an austerity which would have pleased Knox and Melville, and he certainly overawed us. He put his questions to the accompaniment of a gentle prod in the stomach from the board pointer. He was much given to inspect the teacher's register, which he would gloom down at from a height perceptibly in excess of six feet. On cold days he had a 'dreep at his nose', as the local phrase had it, and we would watch mesmerized as the drop of moisture would hover ever nearer the page, until, at the last possible second, he would flick a coloured handkerchief from his pocket with the speed of a Western gunman and, passing it across the end of his nose, avert the sullying of the register.

The windows of the classrooms were set high, and through the wooden partitions one could hear the sing-song of the class next door. There was the very odd diversion, perhaps a visit to the Drill Hall, where we marched like giants, tiptoed like fairies and threw beanbags to or at each other as the mood took us. Occasionally too there would be visits from a peripatetic music teacher, who wore her grey-streaked hair in a severe Eton crop. She had a squally soprano voice which no one could hear and be unmoved – to mirth. Her choice of song now seems almost malevolently in-appropriate; there were few converts to be made to music amongst young hardy Glaswegians when the chorus ran:

> With my chip-chop cherry-chop,
> Fol-de-rol de-riddle rop.

For a certainty, she killed music for many.

There were few decorations or pictures on the walls; in general we got on with the business of learning and were always more than relieved when the janitor, Simon Carr, rang the big handbell that signalled the end of morning or afternoon. There were two playgrounds, one for either sex; we were forbidden the girls' yard but were constantly in there. Neither was big enough to play football in with comfort, so at intervals we tended simply to run around aimlessly, or to play Scotch-horses; this was done by linking arms across one's back with another boy, while a third acted as driver. When young blood stirred, a variation was to run straight at another couple of Scotch-horses and endeavour to knock them to the concreted playground.

When this seemed too physical, we played a game with cigarette-cards called 'Face-or-a-blank.' For this, your opponent held his cards concealed in his doubled fist. You said: 'Two a face, or Seven a blank', as you thought best. If he held the cards face upwards in the first instance, he gave you two, if he had them with the writing on top, you paid up. The cards covered a very wide range of boyish interests, Famous Footballers of 1938, Squadron Badges of the RAF, Aircraft of the World, Ships of the Navy, Flags of Europe. There was a series on fish, one on motor cars, one on film and radio stars, and, almost last of all, and very sinisterly, one on Air Raid Precautions. These often beautiful cards disappeared with the outbreak of war and proved to be permanent casualties.

Geography, however, dictated that most of my friends would be pupils of Mount Florida School, and the great bulk of my playing was done with them. It would be generally accepted, I think, that with the exception of Belfast, religious animosity is more virulent in Glasgow than anywhere else in the United Kingdom. I cannot remember that in ten years of living in the Mount I ever had any altercation with my almost exclusively non-Catholic friends over our religious affiliations. This was partly due to the district, partly to our own good sense, partly I suppose to my scarcity value; there is after all no Eskimo problem in New Hampshire, and Eskimos are somewhat thicker on the ground there than Catholics were in the Mount Florida of the Thirties.

Not that I was religious, by any stretch of the term. One of my more spectacularly disgraceful episodes took place in the early autumn of 1938 on the night of my Confirmation. I had been resigned to being confirmed; I made no formal opposition and evinced no enthusiasm, especially after my mother vetoed my choice of Edward as a Confirmation name, and insisted that I should be Joseph, a name for which I have always had a violent and illogical dislike. On the morning of the Confirmation, I was horror-struck to find that less than half-a-mile away from the church, Third Lanark were to play Partick Thistle in the Glasgow Cup, and the famous Anna Neagle, the film star, was to kick off. All my suggestions that the Bishop, he of the fast-flicking hand-kerchief, would not miss my face among scores of others, were ruthlessly disregarded. In vain I offered to be confirmed the following year. I was dispatched to church, but as the tram passed Cathkin Park, the venue of the match, I jumped up, momentarily evaded my aunt, and legged it for the turnstiles. Unfortunately, she, being young and lissome, soon close-hauled me, and the ceremony proceeded without hitch, although I cannot remember that I underwent any marked access of spirituality.

ROBERT CRAMPSEY (BORN 1930), NOVELIST, SHORT-STORY WRITER, RADIO AND TELEVISION BROADCASTER, CHURCHILL FELLOW AND FORMER 'BRAIN OF BRITAIN', IS RECTOR OF ST AMBROSE HIGH SCHOOL, COATBRIDGE.

Duncan Glen

THE GULLION
—

I can mind the gullion
ayont the midden and the auld Alvis.

I can mind the ducks waddlin out the gate to dook.
And Peter goose takin out his wives
through the slap – hissin and streekin his neck.
The gullion for cuttin nettles wi a scythe and whettin-stane
– or bill or heuk nou I mind the words.
And cuttin new gress for pownies owre in the field.
And boontree canes – for bows and arrows.
The gullion for takin out the pownie on a halter
for special grazin when it's dried out. The gullion
for cuttin fails.

I can mind the gullion wi the swings
and muckle puddles for jumpin. And the stane dyke
for setting up tin cans for shootin at
wi a point two five – I think. And the speugies
and stookies and craws – and blackies e'en.
And waas to sclim to fields for shootin
foxes – ae fox – and maukins and rats. And huntin
out peeweeps' eggs or stanein wasps' bike
– and rinnin for the gullion.

I can mind the gullion and aa the lans ayont.
I went back   and fund
a wee bit boggy grund.

From *In Appearances* (Akros, 1971)

NOTE: THE POET EXPLAINS GULLION IN THIS CONTEXT AS 'A SORT OF DOMESTICATED QUAGMIRE'.

SIX-THIRTY A.M.

It's day shift and six thirty
and my faither still in bed
as if on the dole. But that's no his
escape. He's a lucky ane in safe staff job
wearin collar and tie
and polisht buits. Lucky at his hie-heid ane's
desk. But each Spring he taks to bed
and tremblin haunds and dizzy turns
and risin nausea and turnin tummy
as he tellt me lang efter. But then aa talk o heat
and cauld frae office to furnace
and back again. But still in bed
his books and papers are out and he's countin
countin, countin . . . I'm impressed
but ken nocht but toom words
stocktakin, orders, spare capacity . . .
And freendly visitors sayin
'Still I hear you're slack the nou.'
My mither says, 'His bluid has turnt to watter
wi the heat and the cauld.' And men
at the door:
'Ony chance o a job afore owre lang?'

From 'A Sort of Renewal' in *Realities Poems* (Akros, 1980)

PROFESSOR DUNCAN GLEN (BORN 1933) TEACHES AT TRENT POLYTECHNIC, AND IS A POET, PUBLISHER AND TYPOGRAPHICAL DESIGNER.

BAR-MITZVAH BOY

I was the first person in synagogue. Father has a last-minute panic about his top hat. He had worn it only once before, seven years ago, and it was now too small. Mother advised him to wear a homburg, but he wouldn't have it. 'A homburg on a Bar-Mitzvah? Never!' They were still arguing about it when I left, but father for once had his way and he arrived breathless and triumphant, with the topper balanced on his head like a jug. It fell off about twenty times in the course of the morning. Once while he was standing by the ark with the scrolls of the law in his hand, it toppled over, rolled down the short flight of stairs and settled in the aisle. But the real calamity had nothing to do with father or his hat. It came during the service when I was being addressed by the Rabbi. I stood in the front pew between the synagogue wardens like a prisoner in the dock, directly facing the pulpit, while the Rabbi's words flowed over me. He had a long face, made longer by a pointed beard, and long arms which, in his turbulent, black canonicals, looked like vultures' wings.

'My dear Bar-Mitzvah boy,' he began, but I was not listening. I gazed at him for a while, then my hands wandered round the congregation. My father, with one hand to his hat and the other to his ear; Uncle Motie, with his thin moustache coming down the sides of his mouth as if it was melting; Uncle Boruch, with his face raised to heaven, fast asleep; Uncle Yehudah looking into his prayer book with a pained look on his face; Uncle Peter picking his nose; Uncle Freddy, eyeing the women; Uncle Reuben, facing the Rabbi, with his shoulders drooping in sleep. I looked up to the gallery: a few old ladies scattered loosely about the place, and a glossy cluster grouped round my mother, all silver foxes and straw hats. When the sermon was over I would have to go upstairs and kiss them; I steeled myself for the task. An occasional sentence from the pulpit reached me: '. . . remember therefore that you are standing in the congregation of Abraham, Isaac and Jacob. . . . Children can err, but only man can do wrong, and henceforth you are a man. . . .'

I sank into a reverie and began to tally up my Bar-Mitzvah presents: thirty-two pounds in notes; forty-seven pounds in cheques; the Five Books of Moses, five times over; a child's version of the Talmud; the life of Lord Nelson; two histories of Mary Queen of Scots; *The Decline and Fall of the Roman Empire*; seven books on Jewish ethics; five sets of prayer books; three wallets; a trouser press; eleven ties; four watches; a pair of gold cuff links; five pairs of non-gold cuff links; a bottle of Palestinian wine made in Manchester; a manicure set; and eleven fountain pens. And I continued to comfort myself with my riches, when the raised voice of the Rabbi burst in upon me:

'. . . and therefore I say to you, there are two roads in life, the road of iniquity and the road of virtue. Which road shall be yours?'

'The road of iniquity,' I shouted before I could recover my bearings. And at once the whole synagogue rose in commotion.

Father did not think this a happy omen, and when I went upstairs to kiss mother and my aunts, mother boxed my ears before the full congregation.

The reception which was to have taken place the next day was cancelled because mother became violently ill and for the next fortnight the house was busy with the passage of comforting aunts. That same Saturday, Kadisch won some piffling prize scholarship. I can't remember what it was, but his picture appeared in the *Evening Times* and it didn't help mother's recovery a bit. By then I was beginning to give up the race with him, but mother did not. 'I wouldn't bother if I thought you were an idiot,' she said, 'but you're not. There's nothing wrong with you which good tuition can't cure.' Uncle Boruch was the only one who took my side on this issue: 'Are you sure,' he asked, 'that there's nothing right with him which bad tuition might spoil?' But Uncle's philosophy was never highly rated in our household and for several years there was hardly an evening to the week which was not darkened by some bleak-faced tutor. I was a form of outdoor relief for superannuated schoolmasters. Happily, there was always the Sabbath.

From *Jericho Sleep Alone* (Chapman and Hall, 1964)

CHAIM BERMANT, BORN IN POLAND IN 1929 AND BROUGHT UP AND EDUCATED IN GLASGOW, IS A NOVELIST AND JOURNALIST.

THE WAR BEGINS

My memories are of Easter Ross in the days before the War. My great aunt had a cumbersome wireless, whose batteries needed constant, almost incessant, renewal. We heard, through a long autumnal night, Tommy Farr going 15 rounds against Joe Louis for the heavyweight championship. I was not supposed to hear it, but I did. The rest of the time the wireless was used to listen respectfully to the morning service, so beloved of Sir John Reith (and of my great aunt); the choir's singing is still in my head.

It was also turned on to hear the Prime Minister, Mr Chamberlain, tell us if we were at war with Hitler's Germany or not. My family had waited for three days with disbelief as Poland was knocked about, praying for him to make good his promises. His voice was, as I remember, reedy. He said what had to be said, and we were glad of it: at least we had kept our word. We did not think about how many countless millions were to die. Out in the Cromarty Firth the grey ships disappeared, and people gossiped about where the *Hood*, the indestructible *Hood*, was going. We had seen the oil tanks spreading inland from Invergordon; stray planes went overhead from Evanton and Novar. One morning, cycling down to Delny station for the *Glasgow Herald*, I saw the territorials, in the kilt, marching towards whatever destiny the War Office had thought up.

The war brought money back. It got the fields back from the sheep, though it cut down the woods again, only just after they had recovered from the Canadians in the First War. I dug a slit trench for my great aunt to sit in against Goering's bombers; she said the horse had looked at it and didn't like it either. She died, sensibly, before Hitler could ever do anything against her. Her dog, Rex, not letting anyone near her, had to die too. Between them they had understood a world in which the croft, its well, its animals, its jobs, its habits, its calf in the spring, its snares for the rabbits, its potato drills, the byre and the midden, had been the normality of generations, and now was removed for good. I was sent away to school.

Sir Alastair Burnet (born 1928) is Associate Editor of ITN's *News at Ten*.

Jimmy Logan

SHOW BUSINESS

I had a very happy, but an unusual childhood. I was one of five children. I had two older brothers and two younger sisters; and my mother and my father were in show business. In fact, not only my mother and my father, but my brothers, sisters, uncles and aunts were in show business too – my brother Buddy sang with all the leading dance bands of the day. And those relatives who were not actually earning a living on the stage still had the talent to entertain. One favourite uncle played on the saw. My brother Bert grew up to be the world's worst xylophone player, which pleased him greatly, as he always liked to do anything better than anyone else! Come to think of it, life was rather like a talent competition.

I had a wonderful mother and father. My mother was a comedienne, expert at raising laughter, and she was the backbone of any comedy sketch. She also had a beautiful voice, and could sing her way out of trouble, as we would say in show business. My father was the producer and presenter of the show. He used to get together a company of Scottish artistes and sail them over to Ireland, where he put on the summer show at the seaside resort of Bangor. In order to do this, he would borrow a hundred pounds from my grandmother – Scottish grannies are wonderful. If, at the end of the season, he could pay her back and still be left with some money over, life was considered to be pretty good.

We used to take over an old hall with a bare platform. We worked very hard to build a stage, mount the lights, and arrange seats for the audience. One brother worked the lights, the other brother sang on the stage; I, at the age of seven, sold the programmes, chocolates and cigarettes.

The show was called *The Jack Short Entertainers* and my father was very conscious of publicity. We were all given large piles of leaflets advertising the show, and were sent all round the town to put them through each door. I found this the most boring and tiring job in the world. Many a poor housewife would find a pile of thirty or forty bills that I had pushed through the letter box in an effort to get rid of them as quickly as possible. On another occasion, my father dressed me up as a cowboy – wearing a Scottish cap and with a red nose – and sat me on a donkey to go through the town with a sign on my back and front, saying, 'I am no ass. I am going tonight to *The Jack Short Entertainers*'. I don't know which of us was the more embarrassed – I or the donkey!

The great day came when I was allowed to appear on the stage. I was dressed up in jodhpurs, black coat and top hat. The jodhpurs, though small, were meant to come to somebody's knees; they came down to my ankles. I came on in the finale of the show, to sing a song – 'Will You Drive with Me to the Lakes of Killarney'. I was meant to be an Irish jarvey, the man who drives the jaunting-car. I sat at the side of the stage, patiently waiting until the curtain rose. The first house lasted for an hour and a half. I appeared in the finale. Then I sat patiently, waiting for the second house to begin. Nine times out of ten, when it came to my song at the end of the second house, I was asleep.

On special occasions, my father would put on a Scottish Night. This was an added attraction. He would get a lot of haggis, prepared by the local Irish butcher. Cardboard saucers and wooden spoons were provided, with a small piece of haggis in each saucer. My job was to go round the audience and make sure that everyone got a taste of haggis. I don't know why, for I certainly never starved, but I used to nip behind the seats and finish off what was left of the haggis, before distributing it to the rest of the audience.

I remember sitting in a garden, with the sun shining, and listening to the Prime Minister telling us that we were at war. I did not understand, but my father, who had been badly wounded and had lost a limb in the 1914–18 War, was white-faced and quiet, and my mother sat crying.

To me, it seemed rather an adventure. Shortly after that, we sailed back to Scotland and arrived at the River Clyde. We crowded on to the upper deck of the ship to look at our first British naval vessel. It was a trawler, with a gun in the bow. With this defence, it did not seem possible that the Germans would be stupid enough to attack us.

I was settled down with my aunt and uncle in Gourock. He worked in the Royal Naval Torpedo Factory. My aunt was a second mother to us all. She regarded her sister's children as her own – and still does. We lacked for nothing while my mother and father were touring in various theatres. Every morning when we left, Aunt Jean would be waiting for us at the door with a large tablespoon of emulsion. It tasted like fish oil, and seemed to stay with us for the rest of the day. A pity, really, because we had always had such a wonderful breakfast.

I helped on the ferries at Gourock which took the seamen out to the merchant ships and brought back those who were going on leave. Although I was only a boy, I felt very grown-up then.

With my younger sister, Heather, I used to take part in charity concerts. We were asked once to appear on the same bill as Scotland's greatest entertainer, Sir Harry Lauder. It was a Sunday concert, in aid of Royal Navy funds. To be on the same bill as Sir Harry was an honour indeed. At the rehearsal there seemed to be a crowd of people milling around on the stage, many of them not connected with the concert, but just there to help if needed and to see what was going on. Suddenly, like a bush telegraph, a message came through that Sir Harry was at the front entrance. Instantly, all the extra people melted away from the stage, and stood hidden in the wings. Voices were heard approaching. Then there was silence as Sir Harry came back stage. A chair was set at the front of the stage, and he sat down to rehearse with the orchestra. Everyone watched each move he made. I did, desperately anxious to learn the slightest thing about the secret of his success. He was, of course, meticulous. He knew how his music should be played, and he was not content with any second-rate performance. He demanded the best of the orchestra, and they gave it to him. That was a wonderful night in the theatre. When Sir Harry stepped on to the stage, you could feel there was a magic in the air. He soon had the audience eating out of the palm of his hand.

My parents later settled down in Glasgow, and I left Gourock to join them there. I have appeared in many shows since then, all over the world, and I have learned to marvel at what my mother did. Although the show was changed every week, and there were new songs and a new production to rehearse, and although as star of the show she had to do more than anyone else, we children never suffered. Nor did we ever lack for love or kindness. Once, when I was appearing in Vancouver, a Scot who had emigrated there many years before said to me, 'Well, Jimmy, we're both the same. We used to run around the streets with no shoes on and the tails of our shirts sticking out the backs of our trousers.'

I said to him: 'Never! That's an insult to my mother's memory. If she had seen me in that condition she'd have murdered me.'

JIMMY LOGAN (BORN 1928) IS AN ACTOR, THEATRICAL MANAGER AND PRODUCER.

Alasdair Gray

DUNCAN THAW DRAWS A LINE
——

Duncan Thaw drew a blue line along the top of a sheet of paper and a brown line along the bottom. He drew a giant with a captured princess running along the brown line, and since he couldn't draw the princess lovely enough he showed the giant holding a sack. The princess was in the sack. His father looked over his shoulder and said, 'What's that you're drawing?'
Thaw said uneasily, 'A miller running to the mill with a bag of corn.'
'What's the blue line supposed to be?'
'The sky.'
'Do you mean the horizon?'
Thaw stared dumbly at his picture.

'The horizon is the line where the sky and land seem to touch. Is it the horizon?'

'It's the sky.'

'But the sky isnae a straight line, Duncan!'

'It would be if you saw it sideways.'

Mr Thaw got a golf ball and a table lamp and explained that the earth was like the ball and the sun like the lamp. Thaw was bored and puzzled. He said, 'Do people fall off the sides?'

'No. They're kept on by gravity.'

'What's ga . . . gavty?'

'*Grrrrr*ravity is what keeps us on the earth. Without it we would fly up into the air.'

'And then we would reach the sky?'

'No. No. The sky is just the space above our heads. Without gravity we would fly up into it forever.'

'But wouldn't we come to a . . . a thing on the other side?'

'There *is* no other side, Duncan. None at all.'

Thaw leaned over his drawing and drew a blue crayon along the line of the sky, pressing hard. He dreamed that night of flying up through empty air till he reached a flat blue cardboard sky. He rested against it like a balloon against a ceiling until worried by the thought of what was on the other side; then he broke a hole and rose through more empty air till he grew afraid of floating forever. Then he came to another cardboard sky and rested there till worried by the thought of the other side. And so on.

Thaw lived in the middle storey of a corporation tenement that was red sandstone in front and brick behind. The tenement backs enclosed a grassy area divided into greens by spiked railings, and each green had a midden. Gangs of midden-rakers from Blackhill crossed the canal to steal from the middens. He was told that Blackhill people were Catholics with beasts in their hair. One day two men came to the back greens with a machine that squirted blue flame and clouds of sparks. They cut the spikes from the railings with the flame, put them in a bag and took them away to use in the war. Mrs Gilchrist downstairs said angrily, 'Now even the youngest of these Blackhill kids will be able to rake our middens.' Other workmen build air-raid shelters in the back greens and a very big one in the school playground, and if Thaw heard the air-raid warning on the way to school he must run to the nearest shelter. Going up to school by the steep back lane one morning he heard the siren wailing in the blue sky. He was almost at school but turned and ran home to where his mother waited in the back-green shelter with the neighbours. At night dark green blinds were pulled down over the windows. Then Mr Thaw put on an armband and steel hat and went into the street to search for houses showing illegal chinks of light.

Someone told Mrs Thaw that the former tenants of her flat had killed themselves by putting their heads in the oven and turning the gas on. She wrote at once to the corporation asking that her gas cooker be changed for an electric one, but as Mr Thaw would still need food when he returned from work she baked him a shepherd's pie, but with her lips more tightly pursed than usual.

Her son always refused shepherd's pie or any other food whose appearance disgusted him: spongy white tripe; soft penis-like sausages, stuffed sheep's hearts with their valves and little arteries. When one of these came before him he poked it uncertainly with his fork and said, 'I don't want it.'
'Why not?'
'It looks queer.'
'But you havnae tasted it! Taste just a wee bit. For my sake.'
'No.'
'Children in china are starving for food like that.'
'Send it to them.'
After more discussion his mother would say in a high-pitched voice, 'You'll sit at this table till you eat every bit' or 'Just you wait till I tell your father about this, my dear.' Then he would put a piece of food in his mouth, gulp without tasting and vomit it back onto the plate. After that he would be shut in the back bedroom. Sometimes his mother came to the door and said, 'Will you not eat just a wee bit of it? For my sake?' then Thaw, feeling cruel, shouted 'No!' and went to the window and looked down into the back green. He would see friends playing there, or the midden-rakers, or neighbours hanging out washing, and feel so lonely and magnificent that he considered opening the window and jumping

out. It was a bitter glee to imagine his corpse thudding to the ground among them. At last, with terror, he would hear his father coming *clomp-clomp* upstairs, carrying his bicycle. Usually Thaw ran to meet him. Now he heard his mother open the door, the mutter of voices in conspiracy, then footsteps coming to the bedroom and his mother whispering, 'Don't hurt him too much.' Mr Thaw would enter with a grim look and say, 'Duncan! You've behaved badly to your mother again. She goes to the bother and expense of making a good dinner and ye won't eat it. Aren't ye ashamed of yourself?'

Thaw would hang his head.

'I want you to apologize to her.'

'Don't know what 'polgize means.'

'Tell her you're sorry and you'll eat what you're given.'

Then Thaw would snarl 'No, I won't!' and be thrashed.

During the thrashing he screamed a lot and afterward stamped, yelled, tore his hair and banged his head against the wall until his parents grew frightened and Mr Thaw shouted, 'Stop that or I'll draw my hand off yer jaw!'

Then Thaw beat his own face with his fists, screaming, 'Like this like this like *this*?'

It was hard to silence him without undoing the justice of the punishment. On the advice of a neighbour they one day undressed the furiously kicking boy, filled a bath with cold water and plunged him in. The sudden chilling scald destroyed all his protest, and this treatment was used on later occasions with equal success. Shivering slightly he would be dried with soft towels before the living-room fire, then put to bed with his doll. Before sleep came he lay stunned and emotionless while his mother tucked him in. Sometimes he considered withholding the goodnight kiss but could never quite manage it.

From *Lanark* (Canongate, 1981)

ALASDAIR GRAY (BORN 1934) IS A PAINTER, NOVELIST AND SHORT-STORY WRITER.

Ronald Eden

IN THE WILDERNESS

For anyone aged over fifty today, 1939 was one of life's turning points. I was eight years old when war broke out, and my early childhood had been no different from other offspring of well-to-do parents living in London. Life followed an ordered pattern. We were ruled by nanny or governess, and isolated from the parents in a nursery on the second floor of the house. Glimpses of the wider world were restricted to walks in Kensington Gardens and, once a year in the summer, a visit for a few weeks to the house in Hertfordshire.

How I yearned for those holidays in the country! I recall so clearly the joy of being able to run about in open spaces, gathering cowslips in the meadow beside the garden or, a little later, learning to use a gun and shooting rooks in the neighbouring farmer's trees.

War changed everything. A year or two earlier, my parents had rented Strathmashie, an 8000-acre sporting estate in Inverness-shire with excellent shooting, stalking and fishing. There my mother and I went to live while my father, who had fought in the First War, rejoined the army. The staff likewise, who moved North each autumn with the family to run the house, vanished, and my mother's sole support on the domestic front was an elderly housemaid called Grace.

Having hardly ever seen my parents up to that time, my only appearance with them being more or less restricted to a short daily audience in the evening before going to bed, I was suddenly thrust into my mother's company, sharing with her the daily household burdens. Life was not uncomfortable, and food was plentiful – game from the estate, vegetables from the garden, dairy produce from the farmers. But how on earth did one cook? My mother, in common with so many other women at that time, had never even boiled an egg. At her first attempt to do so, she did at least know that you put it in a pan of water, but after it had been boiling for twenty minutes she had to go and ask the gamekeeper if he thought it had had long enough. If practice never did make perfect, at least my mother learned to cope, even to the extent of baking scones.

Outside the house, my world was now extended from a few fields in England to a vast horizon of moor and mountain. Strathmashie, in common with many other Highland estates, has been 'improved', fragmented and spoiled in terms of sport. Forty years ago the variety of game was prodigious. I have not acquired many skills in life, but my ability to perform proficiently with both gun and rifle dates from that time.

I had little patience for indoor pursuits and the games which children usually played. My days were spent wandering over the land in pursuit of bird or beast, and by the age of nine I had killed my first stag and my first grouse. The stalking ground comprised part of the Monadhliadh range of hills. To reach the deer there was a ten-mile trek up a high glen, and as the youngest member of the party I was privileged to ride a Highland pony on the journey outwards and upwards. The steep path was overhung with blaeberry plants, and I would lean out of the saddle and pluck and eat the berries as we rode along. At the top of the glen was a hut where we could tether the ponies and begin the stalk. Then, if successful, the ponies would be loaded with the deer slung across the saddle and led home. Shotguns as well as rifles had been brought up on the saddles, and we walked back in line over the high ridges of the glen, bagging a brace or two of ptarmigan on our homeward way.

On the heather-clad slopes of the lower end of the glen, running down to the River Spey, grouse abounded, and we would shoot these in the time-honoured manner over pointers and setters. Conifers now coat these hillsides and the grouse have gone. The plantations that existed then were spacious, mature mixtures of conifers that provided exciting stalks after heavy woodland stags or roe deer. They also held big numbers of capercaillie, which were a menace to the stalker. So often a stalk would apparently be approaching a successful conclusion when one of these great birds clattered away and the deer would vanish. Caper were no mean quarry themselves, and I became adept at stalking them with my little 28-bore gun.

Down from the hills and woodlands, along the floor of the valley lay the farms and crofts on which the grey partridge thrived.

Remarkably, even in the rough pastures of the uncultivated uplands, a respectably large population was sustained. No doubt these farms are more productive nowadays in terms of farming output, for the snipe bogs along the banks of the river have been drained and lush pasture has replaced quaking bog. We would kill dozens of snipe each year on these Speyside marshes. Interspersed with areas of bog were shallow, open lagoons of water populated with pike. An uusual form of shooting was to creep up to the edge of the water and, as the startled fish streaked away from the bank, a shot aimed at the apex of the bow wave would stun them, and they could be lifted from the water.

As an angler, I never profited as I should have done from living by the river. I have always enjoyed fishing, but size of fish has never been important to me. My haunts were the burns and tributaries of the river, where I went with my worming rod and stewart tackle, dipping the line in the pools and runs and jerking the trout out of the water when the nibble came. They were much too small to 'play', but a dozen or more of these little fish, perhaps weighing no more than a couple of ounces apiece, commonly went home with me. I cannot recommend a greater delicacy than baby trout, rolled in oatmeal and fried in butter. Sometimes I would catch eels on nightlines similarly baited with worms, and these were skinned, cut into lengths and fried in the manner of the trout.

In 1943, when I was twelve years old, we left Strathmashie and moved to Perthshire. I remember that as I sat in the back of the car that bore us to the railway station I turned, looked back upon the hills and reflected on the four wonderful years of my short life that I had spent there. And I can look back now forty years to my boyhood with gratitude and pleasure, for in subsequent years I have never enjoyed such a rich tapestry of sport. In that particular paradise, now so changed, I do not suppose that anyone ever will again.

THE HON. RONALD EDEN (BORN 1931) IS AN ESTATE OWNER AND WRITER.

Donald John MacLennan

ISLAND CHILDHOOD

I was born on a small island called Scarp, off the west coast of Harris, in 1936. Like scores of other islands, Scarp had no roads, no motor vehicles, no bicycles, no telephone communication with the outside world, no mechanized implements to cultivate the little patches of arable ground. But unlike most other islands, it was splendidly isolated – wide open to the Atlantic Ocean from both north and south.

My home was a modern, detached, stone-built house, three rooms upstairs and three downstairs; the entrance porch of corrugated iron was a general workshop and store for cleaning materials, kitchen utensils and, most importantly, for fresh water carried in pails from the well about four hundred yards away. It follows, of course, that there was no bathroom or toilet. This was no great problem – just a slight inconvenience. One could still wash in the old zinc bath and, for toilet flushing devices, there cannot be anything more consistent and reliable than the Atlantic high tide.

Having no electricity or gas supplies meant that everyone relied on paraffin to fuel the wick lamps or the more sophisticated tilley. I still regard the tilley lamp as one of the great modern inventions. Lighting the lamp for the evening was a pleasurable experience, like sawing logs or chopping sticks for the fire. The peat burning range in the living-room provided the main heat and cooking facility for the house.

This, then, was part of the environment into which I was born. It seems strange to describe it as a community in more modern-day terms, but that was indeed what it was. Everyone relied on everyone else for very survival.

How did a child 'operate' in such an environment? After all, I was one of fewer than ten pupils in the school to which I was dragged by my older sister in the summer of 1941. I suppose the answer is that anyone adapts to the environment to which one is born. The first twelve years of my life included the Second World War and I still hold many happy memories of them.

The War was just a figment of the imagination to me. I had no idea what people around me were talking about. I imagined they were talking about a huge machine that churned on relentlessly every day; aeroplanes were shot down, battleships were sunk, soldiers and sailors performed incredible acts of heroism. My father talked to me about these feats of valour and to this day I remember the very names of the ships, the commanders, the events, the geography of the world long, long before I came across them in school textbooks. It was part of my education, although I still didn't understand what all this war business was about.

Whatever that war was about, I thoroughly enjoyed my childhood within its context. My contemporaries and I kept on 'playing' regardless. But there was this pleasant diversion of the War which added a bit of spice to life. For example, in my real war game, I used to go to school equipped with my gas mask for drill in the use thereof. I loved having to do this and thought it was fun trying to fit this strange-looking thing over my face. As I recall, the teacher herself did not actually demonstrate how to fit the appliance as all good NCOs should. She merely told one what to do; to be fair, in many other ways she behaved as a good drill sergeant should.

Unlike the gas mask fitting drill, there was an aspect of the War that still sticks in my throat, as it were. That was the daily ritual of drinking National Dried Milk. I swear that I can still taste it.

And then there was the fun of real beachcombing. It was a dangerous game (so we were told) in time of war. That made it even more exciting. Hardly a day passed without something interesting being washed ashore along the beaches and rocks of Scarp. Some of the objects were very ordinary and boring, such as pit-props, planks of wood, an assortment of bottles and tins, etc. Other objects, much more interesting, appeared in profusion – cartons of ready-salted Lucky Strike cigarettes, huge slabs of butter and lard, and, most prized of all, life rafts complete with survival packs of food, each consisting of a small tin of coffee, three biscuits and a couple of cubes of barley sugar. I particularly remember the coffee because I had never seen it before.

The most dangerous objects, to be avoided at all costs, were those thin, tubular, fish-like objects with fins sticking out of them. Equalling them in potential danger, and excitement, were those golf-ball shaped things with horns sticking out of them, bobbing up and down in the Sound of Scarp. They created marvellous tension and excitement because it was incumbent on the coast guard authorities to report the sightings of these objects to the police. Along would come a high-ranking naval officer to 'fix' these mines. This extraordinarily brave man would defuse the mine and then blow it up with a lesser charge. The result was the most beautiful bang a ten-year-old ever heard.

I am a native Gaelic speaker and I have often been asked when I became bilingual. I cannot remember. All I know and can recall is that I was aware of my environment in both Gaelic and English before I started the process of general education at the age of five. From then and onwards, everything (curriculum-wise) was taught in English. I suspect that outside the walls of the classroom of my early years, my simple ideas and views of the world were firmly based on my thinking in terms and concepts of my native language. That would be difficult to prove but, forty or so years later, I still dream in Gaelic.

The war ended and we celebrated with a bonfire because everyone kept saying 'We've won.' I wasn't sure what we had won, if anything. I can only imagine, but I must have been a little depressed and harboured feelings of anticlimax. And like all ten-year-olds, one follows the pack and the so-called process of education was to be embarked on in earnest. Between 1945 and 1948 I went through a period of formal indoctrination at school in order to be exported to the 'mainland' for my secondary education. I haven't been back to Scarp since, except for vacations. But it is still home.

DONALD JOHN MACLENNAN (BORN 1936) WAS LECTURER IN ENGLISH, CALLENDAR PARK COLLEGE OF EDUCATION 1968–82, AND HAS WRITTEN AND PRESENTED GAELIC PROGRAMMES FOR STV.

Eileen Dunlop

WARTIME – LIFE WITHOUT FATHER

I was three when my father went away 'to the War'. In fact, he was above the age for active service, and was to spend most of the four remaining War years as ground crew on an RAF station at Ballykelly, Northern Ireland, which, he assured my mother, was the safest place in Europe at that time. To me, it made no difference where he was, if he was not at home. The day of his departure was the first day of my life which I remember clearly; after he had gone, I went and stood behind the front door, and there, despite all my mother's attempts to divert me, I spent most of the day, peeping through the letter box, and tracing with my finger the grain of the dark brown, varnished wood.

Gradually, I suppose, it dawned on me that he was not coming back – at least, not yet, and so I settled down with my mother to a life of waiting, waiting for a letter, waiting for the next leave, waiting for the War to end.

More often than not, there was a letter, with a comic-strip-type enclosure for me; I would then sit up at the kitchen table, with a pencil and a piece of paper, to compose a reply. The only problem was that I could not write, so I drew, always a picture of myself. I had no body, only a large round head, with long, skinny legs dangling from my chin, and scarecrow arms sticking out where ears should have been. I was afraid that my father would forget what I looked like while he was away.

Looking back over forty years, one realizes how very strange and unnatural wartime childhood was. At the time, it did not seem strange in the least, since there was no other life with which to compare it. Talk of street lights and bananas was meaningless to those who had never seen a street light or tasted a banana. Everything was simple, because all actions were, or ought to be, directed to one end – winning the War, so that one's father could come home. There were no moral dilemmas. The Germans were bad. We were good. God was on our side. Not to eat all the food on one's plate was wicked, because children elsewhere were starving, and – more alarmingly – Lord Woolton would be cross when he found out. Lord Woolton, the Minister of Food, was the innocent bogey of my early life; whenever there was a knock at the door at night, panic seized me, for I was sure it was Lord Woolton come to enquire why I had not helped the War Effort by eating up my greens. I was more afraid of him than I ever was of Hitler.

I was also afraid of the dark. No one living, I think, who was not a child in those years, can recollect darkness as something infinite and overwhelming, a vast mantle or mystery which blotted out the familiar shapes of day, out of which danger might come, in which one might be lost, for ever. Usually we think of light as good, and darkness as evil, but in the topsy-turvy world of the early Forties, that notion had its limitations; to show a light in that great darkness was the most anti-social thing that anyone could do, and solemn was the tea-time ritual, in winter, of pulling down blinds and drawing heavy curtains across windows, before a single lamp could be switched on.

My mother and I were not often out after dark, but once a week, on Friday, we went to Alloa to do our shopping. Afterwards, we visited my mother's sister, and came home in the evening, creeping over inky country roads in a bus lit by a dim blue lamp, its windows blackened by oilskin blinds. We had a little way to walk when we got off the bus, and since my mother had to carry the shopping bag in one hand, and keep hold of me with the other, I had to carry the tiny torch which was supposed to provide a discreet puddle of light for us to step into. Of course, I could never resist the temptation to shine it heavenwards, which put my poor mother in a tizzy; I was given to understand that if the Germans dropped a bomb on top of us, the responsibility would be mine, and mine alone. So we would walk on, falling off the pavement at intervals. When we got to our house, we did sometimes manage to go in at the gate, but as often as not we went in through the hedge. I was not a great success with the torch.

It was all very well, however, being abroad in the dark with my mother's hand to hold on to. Nothing would ever have persuaded me to cross the doorstep alone, after nightfall, and I would not go to sleep without a night-light – although that probably had less to do with wartime fears than with the unwelcome intelligence, gathered at the Sunday School, that God could see me in the dark.

Every so often, my father came home on leave. These were usually nine-day visits, and were looked forward to through weeks of rising excitement, and crossing off days on the calendar beside the sitting room fireplace. I can remember only one of these homecomings specifically, but the memory has gathered into it the joy of every one.

It was a summer morning, of great heat. The house and the garden, with its rows of vegetables which would surely have delighted Lord Woolton, lay waiting under the sun. I had on a red silk frock with white spots, my best. I must have been restless – I think I was about five at the time – because my mother told me to go out into the little garden at the front of the house, where we still had flowers, and pick a bunch to put in a vase 'for Daddy'. I went out into a patch of cool shadow outside the kitchen window, and began to pick some orange mimulus which grew along the path. While I was there, with my back to the gate, I knew suddenly that if I turned round I would see my father – and so it was. He was coming up the street in his uniform, with his kitbag on his shoulder. Scattering the flowers to right and left, I ran out of the shadow into the white sunlight, through the gate and down the street; when I got to my father I didn't stop, but shinned right up the front of him. I can remember everything about that moment, with a clearness of pure happiness, the smell of the uniform jacket, the texture of my father's face, the burning of hot brass buttons on my bare legs, the last of the bright mimulus lying around the kitbag in the road.

Then there would begin a week of family life, with country walks, and visiting of friends, and modest feasting on delicacies which my father had brought from the NAAFI, or my mother had saved from the ration. A tin of peaches. Sardines.

But for every joyous coming, there was a bleak parting. Nobody complained; that was just the way things were. Once, in January, we all went to Glasgow in the train, to see a matinée performance of the pantomime, *Little Red Riding Hood*, at the Pavilion Theatre. Afterwards, we were to go to Central Station, from where my father would take a train to Stranraer, and the Irish ferry, and my mother and I would come home, alone. Not, it seems to me now, a recipe for a cheerful day. However, since I had never been to a pantomime before, I was distracted for a while from the fear and misery I always felt when I saw my father in his uniform again, at the end of a leave. I thought that the comedian Harry Gordon, as Red Riding Hood's Granny, was the funniest thing I had ever seen, and I sat between my parents, laughing uproariously. My father laughed to keep me company, my mother could scarcely summon a smile.

When we came out of the theatre, it had been snowing; already the whiteness had been sullied by the passing of city feet, and we had to pick our way through fawn slush to the edge of the pavement, where my father called a taxi to take us to the station. Now the nearness of our parting overwhelmed me; neither the memory of the pantomime, nor the novelty of a taxi ride could console me, and I wept all the way home.

In 1943, I went to school at Alloa Academy, where I was to remain until I was nearly eighteen. I had a new maroon blazer, a satchel, and a gas mask, which I had to take along with me every Friday morning. I sat in the classroom wearing it, along with thirty other small oddities, while the teacher read a story, and the little perspex window before my eyes misted over and my face sweated blindly in the damp, rubbery space. I had a navy Burberry too, and a photograph was taken of me wearing it, against a background of Brussels sprouts, to send to my father in Ireland. I remember that coat well. It had been bought with hoarded clothing coupons, and it was bought with growth in mind. Even with a vast hem, it reached down to the tops of my boots. Since this adjustment of length left the bottom of the pocket only an inch or so above the hem, whenever I wanted to take out my handkerchief, or my bus penny, I had to bend my knees, and grope somewhere near my ankle. It was not very convenient.

At school, I learned to read.

> By the shore of Gitche Gumee,
> By the shining Big-Sea-Water,
> Stood the wigwam of Nokomis,
> Daughter of the Moon, Nokomis.

I learned to write, which was useful in corresponding with my father; I noticed that people had bodies, and my drawing improved accordingly. One day, I drew a picture for my father. It began as me, but when it was completed, it occurred to me that it was really more like somebody else. To emphasize the resemblance, I drew on a hat, like an inverted chamber pot, then, to clear up any lingering uncertainty, I wrote underneath the name, 'Mooza Leeny'. But I was not allowed to send it, for reasons which may have had to do with national security.

On VE Night in 1945, everyone in our village danced at the Market Cross, because the War with Germany was over, and fathers would be coming home. But not all fathers. I can remember my mother telling me gently of the fathers and sons and brothers who would not come back, and how we must never forget that they had given everything they had, so that we might live in peace, and be free. It meant little to me then, but I have often thought of it since, in the long, uneasy peace which has been my lifetime, and for which they died.

Later that year, my mother gave away the pram, which had always stood in the recess under the stair, and a few weeks later, discovered that she was pregnant. In 1946, my father came home 'for good', and my little brother was born. Not long after that, we moved to a new house, and our real life as a family had begun.

EILEEN DUNLOP (BORN 1938) IS AN AUTHOR OF CHILDREN'S BOOKS AND HEAD OF THE PREPARATORY SCHOOL OF DOLLAR ACADEMY.

Malcolm Baird

LIFE WITH AN INVENTIVE FATHER

Early on an April morning in 1947, the through train from King's Cross steamed into Helensburgh Upper station. My mother, my sister Diana and I had come to live in Scotland. This was a great transition point in my life, because my first eleven years had been spent in England.

My father's work on television kept him in London and until 1939 the family had lived in Sydenham, near the Crystal Palace.

At the outbreak of war, we moved to Bude in North Cornwall and it was there that my really vivid memories begin. The family at that time included my maternal grandmother and we all crammed into a succession of rented terrace houses, each of which seemed to be a long walk from the school, the shops or the beach. My father continued with his research at Sydenham despite the bombing, and he would come down to Bude once or twice a month. I recall the excitement of standing on the Southern Railway platform, waiting for the 5.09 to appear. My father would emerge tired after the slow and crowded journey, but he usually had small presents for Diana and me. Sometimes there would be sweets, and sometimes a small gadget from his laboratory.

My father tried to instruct me in optics, and I recall the pleasure of discovering that a piece of paper could be set on fire by focussing the sun's rays on it with a lens. If the weather permitted, he would take Diana and me for a walk along the beach. He was a slow-moving figure, muffled in cap and greatcoat even in summer. From time to time he would stop and stare out to sea, deep in abstraction.

He may have been thinking of research in progress, such as the 600-line colour television system that he demonstrated in 1941; or the important consulting work he was doing for the government-owned company, Cable and Wireless. He may also have been thinking back over the turbulent history of television; his early breakthrough with the world's first television pictures in 1925, then the transatlantic transmission in 1928, and the long and bitter struggle of the Baird Company against its Marconi competitors and the sceptics in the BBC.

My mother was temperamentally quite different from my father. She was about twenty years younger, and had begun a promising career as a concert pianist in the late 1920s. She cheerfully admitted that she could not mend a fuse, let alone understand the technicalities of television. My father for his part was totally unmusical. My mother tells the story that late one evening they were listening to the radio, and my father said, 'Margaret, I think I recognize that tune.' It was the National Anthem.

Whereas my father was abstracted and absent-minded to a fault, my mother had an outgoing personality and took up most of the household responsibilities during the war years. She also found time to play in concerts for charities and for the troops, and to teach some pupils from Clifton College which had been evacuated to Bude from Bristol.

From my own selfish point of view, World War II was a happy time. I enjoyed school, and as I got older I explored more widely the superb beaches and cliffs of North Cornwall, which have been described so well in John Betjeman's poems. For my parents, however, the War was a struggle. My mother had been used to an affluent prewar life, but now she had to make do with wartime rationing and shortages. My father continued to carry a punishing workload in London, combining private research and secret government work amid the air raids.

At the end of the War, the family moved to Bexhill, in Sussex. My father's health had been weakened by his war work and he died in June 1946. Four months later, my grandmother died. My mother was left in a difficult position with Diana aged fourteen and me aged eleven, and with my father's estate greatly depleted by the expenses of his wartime research.

Thus it was that in April 1947 we all moved to Helensburgh to stay with my father's older sister Annie Baird, who lived with her housekeeper Margaret Scott in 'The Lodge'.

This house had been bought by my grandfather, the Rev. John Baird, shortly after his marriage in 1878. Annie and my father had both been born there, and the house had passed on to Annie on my grandfather's death in 1932. It stood (and still stands) four-square on the corner of Argyle Street and Suffolk Street, a solid grey stone villa in a large garden containing overgrown shrubs. The house had started life as a bungalow, but my grandfather had added an additional floor, the rooms of which had much lower ceilings than the ground-floor rooms.

Annie Baird was a formidable character, well known and respected in Helensburgh. She had been raised as a daughter of the manse, and then she qualified as a nurse and served throughout the 1914–18 War in casualty clearing stations. She was always reticent about her war service, but her notebooks, medals and citations tell a story of heroism. She served again in World War II, by this time in her late fifties, as Assistant Matron at Lennox Castle Hospital, near Glasgow.

On arrival in Helensburgh, I was enrolled as a day boy at Larchfield, the local preparatory school. Here again I was fortunate that it was a happy school, in great contrast to what it had been fifty years earlier when my father had been a pupil. The headmaster, William (Nobby) Clark was a true scholar and a gentleman. It was with his coaching and encouragement that I was able to win a scholarship to Fettes in 1949.

Outside school, my abiding early impressions of Helensburgh are of the lush greenery, the marvellously aromatic air, and persistent rainfall. The population consisted mainly of retired people and affluent businessmen, and there were few organized amusements for youth. In 'The Lodge' I discovered a wealth of Victorian books – Dickens, Stevenson, Conan Doyle, and in particular the early works of H. G. Wells. These books had belonged to my father and his name was still on the flyleaves. Wells' scientific stories influenced me as much as they had influenced my father, and led me along the lines of experimentation and gadgetry. To some extent my exploits in Helensburgh in 1947–57 were a parallel to my father's early exploits described in his memoirs. But whereas my father had been interested in cameras, telephones and early motoring, my interests centred on chemistry and radio transmission.

Chemical enthusiasm crept up on me insidiously. I started innocently enough with a bought chemistry set containing 'safe' and rather boring chemicals, but my interest soon extended to homemade fireworks . . . and explosives. With a few contemporaries I endangered life and limb and the peace of the back streets of Helensburgh. I must have given many grey hairs to my mother and my aunt, but the only accident was a burn to my hand from a badly behaved mixture containing red phosphorous.

Radio was a good hobby thirty years ago because of the abundance of cheap army surplus components. My other source of material was the occasional defunct radio set obtained from Mr Manderson's repair shop. In the course of building a badly adjusted receiver, I discovered the art of transmission and it was not long before I was in two-way radio contact with a friend about half-a-mile away. We carried out our experiments in dread of detection by the Post Office, as we had not attended to the small formality of obtaining an amateur radio licence.

157

Perhaps it was as well for all concerned that these activities were somewhat curtailed after I entered Fettes in September 1949. It had been a great coup to win the scholarship, for it covered all the fees and the family finances would not have allowed me to attend otherwise. However, Fettes proved to be a much less pleasant experience than my earlier schools. Like my Baird ancestors I was an individualist, and the pervasive discipline of an English-style public school did not suit my temperament at all.

Moreover, Fettes at this time laid a tremendous emphasis on sport, notably rugby football, at which I did not excel. School life thus became a continuous exercise in evasion, and only in my last two years when I got into the sixth form did I regain some self-respect. Academically, of course, I gravitated to the science side. Although the academic slant of the school in those days was decidedly to the classics, the mathematics and science teaching was excellent. I owe a particular debt to Dr Harland and Mr Naiff who were able to direct my enthusiasm into constructive channels which have led me away from explosions and into a career in chemical engineering research.

What would have happened if my father had not died in 1946? The family would have stayed on at Bexhill, the financial situation would undoubtedly have improved, and in all probability Diana and I would have received a completely English education. It is curious that my father's tragically early death was the factor that caused me to have a Scottish childhood, and to learn so much about him through living at his birthplace in Helensburgh for ten years.

MALCOLM BAIRD (BORN 1935), SON OF JOHN LOGIE BAIRD, NOW LIVES IN CANADA, WHERE HE IS CHAIRMAN OF THE CHEMICAL ENGINEERING DEPARTMENT, MCMASTER UNIVERSITY.

Phyllida Law

SOMEWHERE ALONG THE LINE

Station names are wonderfully evocative. The very sound of Eglinton Street, a soot-covered station at the edge of Glasgow, still brings me out in goose bumps. Just hereabouts one caught sight of the first black tenements, the first tramcar, the first green and orange bus of the boarding school holidays.

Stern Eglinton is now extinct. Not so Inverkip and Fort Mathilda, the best names in the short list of stations leading to the Clyde and, for my two small daughters and me, to the ferry for Blairmore, Grannie and the glories of Argyll. It's a weary way for the small and London-born, so we used to count lighted Christmas trees in the windows of the gaunt Clydeside terraces, and round about Inverkip I would tell them the story of my guilty secret.

Evacuated at very much their tender age to a school in Skelmorlie, I used to travel solo in the Ladies Only compartment on this very same line. One winter term, I was tucked in the corner of an empty Ladies Only with my luggage and my Christmas spoil to make my lonely journey to Wemyss Bay. Amongst my presents was a large box of chocolates from an aunt in Canada. It was of the kind made doubly interesting to a child by having drawers opened by tassels and a soft padded lid held upright by coloured ribbons. I would have been expected to hand this luscious prize into the sweetie cupboard at Miss Jenny McAra's for sharing out on the Sabbath. It would certainly have lasted the term.

I remember the journey was cold.

I remember it was dark.

I remember there was no corridor and thus no toilet.

I remember I became desperate somewhere after Port Glasgow.

Between there and Inverkip, I ate all the chocolates.

Between Inverkip and Fort Mathilda I peed in the box and threw it out of the window.

PHYLLIDA LAW IS A STAGE AND TV ACTRESS.

THE HERRING RUN

I was lucky to be part of a family of five, but unlucky in that my two elder brothers teased me unmercifully about my more imaginative pursuits, and about the fact that I preferred the company of girls to boys. I think that they thought I was a potential 'cissy', whereas I was really just an early developer!

My imaginative pursuits consisted mainly of shutting myself in an empty room and acting out dramas and adventures of all kinds, but mainly westerns. My horse was the arm of the sofa, and my gun was an old hockey stick which belonged to my elder sister. I created the scenarios out of my fertile little mind – fired by films and boys' papers – and played all the parts with suitable dialogue and accents. My nasty brothers used to delight in stationing themselves outside the window until I had reached the denouement, which was accompanied by wild gestures and shouts of battle, and then they would jump up and down, leering at me and taunting me with abuse. They would then come into the house, laugh themselves silly, and tell everyone what I had been up to. I would stand the jeers and jibes as long as I could, and then run away to a favourite tree and sit in its branches for hours, or go and visit the little girl next door. I grew up into a desperately shy recluse, with a yearning for the opposite sex.

My mother was, and is, a farmer's daughter, and all our holidays were spent on my grandfather's farm. My father was an accountant in the town of Ayr. He was something important in the Masons, played cricket for Ayr CC (which was later to produce an England captain in Mike Denness) and took us to watch Ayr United play football every second Saturday. He taught us not only the arts of cricket and football, but marbles, conkers, cards, and the luxuries of aniseed balls and hot mutton pies, and cruises on the *Duchess of Hamilton* in the summer, round the Firth of Clyde. He also taught us to swim, played the piano (self-taught) on Sunday mornings, and drove an old Singer motorcar with mud-guards, in the reflection of which I could see myself, in a world that was distorted by their curvature.

The highlight of the year was Hallowe'en – a licence to beg – although I was always the one that was pushed forward to recite, so it was really working for a living as far as I was concerned. The excitement of dressing up and blackening faces with burnt cork! The bonfires and the fireworks. The mashed potatoes with silver threepenny bits and trinkets wrapped in tissue paper. The dooking for apples and the treacle scone. The games of Murder. *You are the murderer!*

On the farm, I learned about the secrets of nature and the countryside, and when my sister became engaged to a fisherman, I learned some of the secrets of the sea too, by spending a week on a herring drifter during the summer holidays. That was the first time that I was treated as an adult, by these marvellous men of the sea with their horny hands and the consistent expletives. I was allowed to haul the corks and brew the tea. In my borrowed oilskins and seaboots, I was every inch a man, though I was only 62 inches tall. I even tolerated the stings of the jellyfish which hung in fronds from the corks, as I clutched at them with my soft little hands.

Oh the herring! The silver darlings!

Oh the relief to climb into the bunk at dawn!

At the end of the week, the relief to get back home, even if the ground kept on moving for a couple of days afterwards.

Then there was the joy of waking up at 11.30 in the tranquil sunshine of the Bay of Brodick on the island of Arran, after being tossed about on a stormy sea, with the rest of the crew still asleep. My hunger was raging. Would I dare to start cooking the breakfast? The pangs of hunger drove me to dare, and when they woke up to the smell of sizzling bacon and lace-edged eggs, they were kind enough to declare it to be the best breakfast they had ever tasted, and would I not think of giving up my studies at Ayr Academy and joining the crew as permanent cook? I was tempted, but the twinkling blue of their eyes told me they were just grateful not to have been burnt to death in their bunks.

After breakfast came the ritual of going up the burn for a wash, with great splashing about and soapsuds, and then lounging about in the sun, waiting for the gloaming, when the search for the shoals of herring and mackerel would begin again round the shores of Arran, with the sun behind Goat Fell and already a rise of sprats in the bay as we slipped our moorings.

The slow chug along the coast, with the man at the bow holding the leaded line in his fingers. If there was a shoal below, their sleek bodies could be felt brushing against the line. When it was dark, to watch the mackerel fan away from the bows of the boat, like arrows of phosphorescence. Then, the excitement when the net was shot, and the men worked in pairs, leaping from one boat to another as the end of the net was picked up by the neighbour, before the hauling began.

The contents of the net came slowly out of the shallow water. Weird and wonderful creatures were dumped on the deck. Once, a fisherman called my name and threw something at me. I looked down with horror at a squid – its tentacles spread tight across the front of my oversized oilskins. A friendly soul plucked it from me with a huge hand and threw it back into the sea, where it propelled itself swiftly below the glare of the lights.

What a life for a boy! What adventure! What an introduction to the harsh world of making a living! But one thing I never got used to was the 'honey bucket'. I was a fastidious youngster and was always nervously constipated for the whole week.

BILL SIMPSON (BORN 1931) WAS A TV NEWSCASTER BEFORE BECOMING KNOWN AS AN ACTOR FOR HIS ROLE IN THE TV SERIES *DR FINLAY'S CASEBOOK*.

Fiona Thyssen-Bornemisza
(Fiona Campbell-Walter)

ROOTS

Although my father was born in the shadows of the Himalayas, my mother in Sumatra, my sister in Malta, my brothers in America, and I in New Zealand, we are a Scottish family.

My first visit to Scotland at the age of thirteen was a revelation, and a confirmation of my roots. So much seemed familiar, the sheep-sheared grass, heather's misty mauve, silvered lochs, softly contoured hills, and everything bathed in opalescent light, but I had only dreamt it, or seen pictures. Now I could smell the reality, tread on the spongy grass, taste the sweet burn-water and breathe in the mist.

We came to stay with cousins who lived in a grey stone castle, looking like every foreigner's image of a Scottish home. The entrance hall was vast, with a massive staircase which wound upwards, linking the galleried floors, its walls hung with the hunting trophies of generations.

As I climbed the stairs that evening, clutching my paraffin lamp, the glass eyes of the dead beasts followed the flickering flame, and I felt as if they were watching my reluctant progress.

There was to be a ball the next day, and although I was too young to be allowed to go, I did my share of rolling up carpets, shifting furniture and preparing for it.

I was sitting next to my mother at her dressing-table, watching her get ready for the ball, when I was electrified by the sound of pipes. A keening, yearning, lilting sound, so beautiful I thought my heart would burst, and although I was laughing, tears were streaming down my face.

My mother was as astonished by this reaction as I was. It was impossible to explain that it was my music, the sounds of the past linking me firmly to the present. I had come home.

Although nominally still a child, my parents finally relented, and I went to the ball, where I learnt the reels as if by osmosis. My childhood dreams had become reality, and surrounded by my magnificent kinsmen, I was whirled through the dances. I loved the exuberance, and the wild beauty of the pipes.

It was the first time I was conscious of being happy, when after all those years of travelling, I finally knew where I belonged.

FIONA CAMPBELL-WALTER WAS, IN HER PROFESSION AS A MODEL, THE 'FACE OF THE FIFTIES'.

Netta Martin
(Lucy Ashton)

CLOSE ENCOUNTER OF THE ROYAL KIND

On the day it happened I woke with no special excitement stirring in my veins, no premonition that I was about to have an adventure which would imprint itself indelibly on my memory and years later would earn me thousands of pounds.

It was 1945, the War had ended, and my parents had taken the family to the island of Arran for a holiday. Arran has been called Scotland in miniature. There are heather-clad hills, rolling moorlands, glorious beaches, and mountains which shade from iridescent green in the blaze of the sun to shimmering purple under the panoply of dusk.

And there is something more: some indefinable magic which makes Arran Scotland's most popular holiday island and lures exiles back to it year after year from all over the world. Childhood holidays on Arran are part of the social history of the West of Scotland, and Glaswegians will maintain with a blatant disregard for bias that 'if you haven't been to Arran you haven't lived'.

In addition they are as fiercely partisan as football fans about the comparative merits of different parts of the island. Tell a

Lochranza man that Brodick is better and he is liable to push you off the pier.

I am not biased at all, but I confess that now I own a house on Blackwaterfoot I simply cannot understand what possessed my parents to holiday on 'the other side' of the island. Yet I must admit that my first holiday at Lamlash was idyllic. I suspect that the first holiday after the War for any Scottish child was idyllic, but that year Arran seemed to be a childhood paradise.

We children chased each other across the moorland, rowed in the bay, climbed Goat fell and transformed beaches at a stroke of our imagination into Indian reservations, cowboy ranches, or castles waiting to be defended. We fought and lost battles until we were streaked with dirt and exhaustion and then recharged with an invisible source of energy we would romp and swim in the water.

One evening the boys stole off on some secret expedition from which I as a mere girl was excluded. I was kicking disconsolately at some stones on the path outside our cottage when a neighbour noticed my dejection and took pity on me.

He was taking a relative over to Brodick to catch the late boat. I could go with him for the trip if my parents did not object. They were about to protest that it was long past my bedtime when the storm of tears gathering in my eyes made them relent.

I remember little of the drive to Brodick or the leave taking at the boat. For it was on the journey home that it happened. By then dusk was beginning to blur the edges of the landscape and make familiar shapes mysterious. My companion put on the lights of the car as he approached a sharp bend and almost at the same time, or so it seemed to me, he slammed his foot hard on the brakes.

I looked up and could hardly believe what I saw. Right in the middle of the road, illuminated by the car's headlights, was a monster. In that first panic-stricken moment I thought the devil himself had descended down to earth. His horns were tossing his eyes were flashing. He seemed consumed with fire and anger.

'It's a Royal Stag,' my companion breathed reverently. 'Look, six points on each beam and that antler span . . . it must be four foot in width. Strange. The deer don't usually come down so early.'

For a few minutes the stag seemed hypnotized by the glaring

lights. Then he vanished into the heather. My heart was pounding so hard I felt it would burst through my rib cage. Being confronted by a Royal Stag at night had been a truly terrifying experience.

'They don't attack humans, do they?' I asked, seeking reassurance.

'Very rarely,' my companion replied. 'Though I did hear a tale of a stag which had been brought up in captivity. Regarded his keeper as a friend but in October in the mating season the stag looked on him differently. As a rival. One day he turned on the keeper and nearly killed him. If a stag like that got loose it would be very dangerous.'

Seeing my look of alarm he laughed. 'Wheesht child, it's not October and yon stag was mebbe angry at being caught in the headlights. Put it out of your mind.'

I never did. In 1977 I picked up my pen and wrote the first page of my first novel: *Stag*.

'It was morning in October when the killer stag came to Abermady. After that the valley was never the same again. Later, when it was all over, people said the village had been marked down for vengeance.

'Was that really true? The villagers never tired of asking themselves that. Nor did they tire of picking up the shattered mosaic of that Autumn and trying to fit the fragments together in a different way. Yet they could never agree about anything except one sure fact. It all started the day the big stag came. . . .

'He stood silhouetted against the skyline: four foot three inches at the shoulder, twenty-four stone in weight and bearing an unusually massive head of antlers. He had cast his old ones in the Spring, eating them as many stags do to replace their calcium.

'His new ones had grown quickly and when eventually he had rubbed off all his protective velvet he boasted a new antler span four foot in width with six points on each beam: the mark of a Royal Stag. Now that the rutting season had started his shaggy mane and neck had swollen too and every day he added to his ferocious appearance by churning a peat hag into liquid and wallowing in it. Tufts of heather and black mud clung wetly to his coat as he roared his challenge from the mountain top. The mating instinct was firing his blood.

'And yet the glen looked so peaceful that hot Sunday morning. Here and there the scarlet of wild rowan flamed against the green and feathery birches draped their outlines over mountain burns, bent backwards like ballet dancers caught in camera. It seemed a world at peace.

'Motionless the stag surveyed the glen. His acute gaze took in not only the black shadow of a hawk and the white flurry of goosanders as they skimmed up the river, but the hundred minute movements of animal life.

'A gentle zephyr of a breeze blew up the mountain bringing human scent to the stag's nostrils. Man. Somewhere in his brain a primeval instinct urged flight. But that instinct had been overlaid by a more recent memory, a more recent conditioning.

'Down there was a rival he had to fight. He moved at a leisurely pace homing to the flash of movement in the heather.'

Between the first page of *Stag* and the last is a melodramatic tale of murder, rape, violence and a terrorist attack on a north sea oil rig. Small wonder that a reviewer in a national newspaper said with some surprise, 'this novel has an impact and an earthiness not usually associated with women writers'.

Although this book is now out of print, people still talk to me about it, and wonder how it came to be written.

'Did you yourself ever come face to face with an angry Royal Stag?' they ask.

'Only once when I was a child,' I reply. 'But I have never forgotten it.'

And I never will.

As Lucy Ashton, Netta Martin is the agony columnist of *The Sunday Express*. *Stag* was published by Panther in 1978.

Anna Neagle

'A REAL FILM STAR'

Shortly before World War II, Herbert and I had been invited to
visit a big exhibition at Hampden Park, Glasgow. It was winter, so
I felt a dark suit, fur coat and hat would be suitable attire.

In 1944, I was again invited to attend an exhibition at Hampden
Park – an army exhibition. What to wear? It was a blazing hot
August day, so I wore the only thin dress I had with me. To
complete the outfit, there was a hat with a large rose and
high-heeled shoes. As I teetered around the rough paths, having
tanks and guns explained to me by the CO, I felt a complete idiot.
Amongst the crowds, I spotted my cousins. I waved self-
consciously. I was to have tea at my aunt's house before going on
to the theatre, and when I arrived, I was greeted ecstatically by my
younger cousin who, with her charming Scottish burr, cried, 'Oh,
Cousin Marjorie, you look like a real film star. When you came
before, it was so disappointing – you looked just like an ordinary
person.'

From *Anna Neagle Says 'There's Always Tomorrow'* (W. H. Allen, 1974)

DAME ANNA NEAGLE IS A STAR OF STAGE AND SCREEN. THOUGH BORN IN ENGLAND,
HER FATHER'S FAMILY, THE ROBERTSONS, WERE OF CLAN DONNACHAIDH, WHO FOUGHT
ON THE RIGHT HAND OF BONNIE PRINCE CHARLIE AT CULLODEN.

Moira Anderson

MY AIN FOLK

Whenever I hear that Queen Elizabeth the Queen Mother is holidaying at her summer retreat, the Castle of Mey in Caithness, I am vividly reminded of my childhood, for it was to northern Scotland that I used to go with my family each summer to stay with relatives – with 'my ain folk'.

My parents, my two brothers, my sister and I spent our holidays with my Uncle Tom in Brora, Sutherland, and from there we explored Caithness to the north and Easter Ross to the south. The whole of the northern Highlands became our playground. Caithness and Sutherland are often called the 'big country' because they encompass 2400 square miles of rivers, lochs and mountains bounded by a rugged coastline. Along this coast, small fishing villages hug the headlands and sea birds plummet from high cliffs such as the ones at Dunnet Head. Inland lie heathered moors, strange rock formations and high mountains which are the haunt of the golden eagle.

To the south of Brora the old county of Ross stretches across the Highlands from coast to coast. The climate is mild, thanks to the Gulf Stream, and the scenery ranges from beautiful inland lochs to castles which stand beside humble crofts. The joy of Ross is its contrast: modesty and magnificence go hand in hand.

In our family the summer holiday excitement began at Easter. Soon after, we began counting the days till the day arrived. For weeks we would debate which clothes to take, and what we would do when we arrived there. Not surprisingly we rarely slept the night before we left. I used to lie in bed willing away the hours until morning.

Today, delays at airports and railway stations are a cause of frustration for everyone. But then, for us, the journey was half the fun – and it was quite a journey. We left Kirkintilloch in the early morning to travel to Glasgow's Buchanan Street Station where the north-bound train awaited us.

Since the railway carriage was to be 'home' for many hours, we devised various ploys for discouraging strangers from joining us.

The first small battle was to get a carriage to ourselves, then came the competition for the window seats. When I see children today setting off on long journeys armed with toys, books, puzzles and sweets, I cannot help smiling. My mother would have none of that. She took the view that we were lucky to be there and ought to sit back and enjoy what the journey itself had to offer. I am very grateful to her now because it made us appreciate that incredibly beautiful scenery.

One of the first high points of the journey was Stirling, the gateway to the Highlands. If it was going to be a good day, Stirling was often shrouded in heat haze, which added to the enchantment of the shadowy buildings surrounded by the Links of Forth. Yet it was not so much the town that fascinated us as the castle. From the train, we would gaze up at the 250-foot rock surmounted by Stirling Castle, dominating the landscape for miles around.

After Stirling the next eagerly awaited station was Perth because it was here that we could stretch our legs and buy mugs of railway tea to accompany our picnic. By that time nothing could have been more welcome.

From Perth the train sped northwards; Dunkeld, Pitlochry, Blair Atholl, Kingussie and Aviemore flashed past. In those days there was no Aviemore complex, no ski lifts, no hotels, and, since we journeyed north in summer, neither was there any snow.

Before too long we reached Inverness, the capital of the Highlands, with its silvery river and backdrop of woods and mountains. Here we changed trains for the last leg of our journey to Brora on the northeast coast.

We followed a circuitous route past the peninsulas formed by the Beauly, Cromarty and Dornoch Firths, and, since our destination lay to the east, we were filled with indignation when the train swung westward to the inland town of Lairg. By the time we arrived there we had been in the train a full six hours and were desperate to reach our journey's end.

From Lairg to Golspie seemed the longest part of the journey but our spirits rose on catching a glimpse of the statue of the first Duke of Sutherland which stands on the hill outside the town. Then came the spectacular Dunrobin Castle, seat of the Dukes of Sutherland, which resembles a French château and looks like something out of a fairy tale.

The next stop was Brora, at last, and when we finally tumbled out of our carriage we had been travelling for more than eight hours. But our tiredness was forgotten as we raced along the platform to meet Uncle Tom. By the time we had reached his house, unpacked and had a meal, exhaustion had usually caught up with us. That first night was one night in the year when there were no disputes when my mother announced it was bedtime.

The next morning we would wake early and run out into the garden to make sure nothing had changed. We were never disappointed. There was the beautiful sandy bay stretching for miles, and the sea sparkling in the morning light. Along the shore was the golf course and around us were hills and glens waiting to be explored.

Since my uncle's house was outside Brora, we children enjoyed our trips into the village every morning to collect milk, bread and other necessities. Even that was an adventure for us, and we would often linger at the small harbour from which the first settlers left for New Zealand after the Highland Clearances.

After the shopping, the day was ours and we always made full use of it. Sometimes we would bathe in one of the nearby sandy bays, and if we were not swimming, we would go looking for shells or exploring the pools left by the tide.

The boys were always wanting us to hunt for worms for their fishing (the River Brora teems with salmon). The most exciting time to walk along the river bank was at night, when we would sometimes see lights glowing in the dark, betraying the presence of poachers. We would stand and watch, then suddenly rush away in sheer fright in case we were discovered. The poachers were probably very angry because the noise we made would undoubtedly have frightened away any fish around.

One of the diversions we most enjoyed as children was to go to Winnie Sutherland's croft. Half of the people in the village were Sutherlands, and Winnie's croft had been handed down through many generations of the same family. No doubt she found running the place very hard work, but we loved feeding the hens and collecting the eggs. Best of all we liked helping with the hay, though I am quite sure we were more of a hindrance than a help.

Another magnet which drew us was Don (Sutherland, of course), the local weaver. His simple workshop had frames for weaving and wheels on which he spun his wool. We thought it magical to see his hands moving so swiftly and surely, for undoubtedly he was an expert at this craft and people came from far and wide to buy his tweeds and tartan rugs. Sometimes the Duke and Duchess of Sutherland would bring visitors to watch him working and to purchase something from him. The news would spread and we would race down and press our noses against the window to see the grand folk who lived in the fairy-tale castle. The minute they left, we would rush in and ask Don what the Duke and Duchess had said. Like most Highlanders, Don had that easy, nonchalant manner which made him treat everyone alike. He was surprised by our interest in the Duke and Duchess, but for our part we could not understand why he was not more impressed by his grand visitors.

Some people think it strange that the Queen Mother should have chosen such a wild, isolated spot for her holiday home, but they can only be those who have never seen the variety and rugged grandeur of Scotland's northern shorelines – the very coast I came to know and love through our summer holidays in Brora.

From *Moira Anderson's Scotland* (with Netta Martin) (Lutterworth, 1981)

MOIRA ANDERSON OBE IS AN INTERNATIONAL SINGING STAR.

Rita Davidson
(Darlinda)

PATTERNS IN THE FLAMES

I was the seventh child of a seventh daughter. I am psychic, and it was from my mother that I inherted this ability. Though she was forty-five when I was born, we were very close, even to the extent often of having the same dreams at night. Later on in her life, she never needed to phone me if she wanted any help. She used to will *me* to ring her.

We were often together on our own. Both of us loved collecting leaves. I would dry them and press them between the pages of a heavy book. When they were crisp, we would make pictures out of them and frame them. Once, some of the leaves got broken, so we crumbled them up and let the pieces settle on the table. Then we read each other's fortunes in the patterns they made. I still use this method sometimes today.

We would sit by the fire in winter, watching the patterns in the flames and the shapes that the soot made when it fell. My mother would tell me what they meant. If the flames were like a dancing lady, that usually meant that an invitation to a party or a wedding was on its way.

I remember one day sitting in front of the fire on my own, feeling absolutely miserable and weeping inconsolably. My brothers and sisters kept asking what was the matter. I couldn't tell them, because I did not know myself. Finally, to keep them quiet, I said I had toothache. But it wasn't that: I just felt a sense of doom, not in the room, but somewhere near. The next day, a neighbour's husband was killed in an accident. I think that was the first time that I really knew I was psychic. To 'sense' a tragedy before it occurs has happened to me many times since. However, on a family level, I was very useful. Answering the phone was no problem, even with so many of us in the house. I always knew who was on the line as soon as the phone started ringing.

At school, I got a reputation for being able to tell the future. One girl pestered me to tell her fortune. Finally, and reluctantly, I gave in. As I sat down beside her and took her hand in mine, I sensed, rather than saw, an image of a broken wedding-ring. I took a deep breath, and said: 'I think your parents are going to be divorced.'

The next day an irate mother invaded the school. Rita had told her daughter that her marriage had broken down. How did Rita know? No one knew! As this was the mid-1950s and the school was a convent school, I can see now her concern. My reward at the time from my friend was: 'I *know* I asked you to tell my future, but I didn't like it.'

My ambition in life at the time was, and still is, to sell flowers from a barrow at a Glasgow street corner, wearing a straw hat. My mother was horrified at the idea. But perhaps some day . . .

RITA DAVIDSON IS A PROFESSIONAL CLAIRVOYANT AND ASTROLOGER.

Bill McCue

FAMILY SONGS AND FOOTBALL

They say that distance lends enchantment, and, in my experience, the distance of years seems to colour my childhood with a glow of comfort. In August 1984, I reached the age of fifty years, and looking back to my childhood, I can remember detail that fills my present life with a confidence to succeed in the competitive life of a singer in the 1980s – not a simple task in these days of mass communication and commercial exploitation.

But let me tell you the story of a very fortunate childhood.

I was born on the 17th day of August 1934, the fifth child of Robert and Mary McCue, at 16, Houldsworth Crescent, Allanton, Shotts. My father was a miner with the National Coal Board, at Kingshill Colliery No 1, having worked previously with a private mining company, at Morningside, where the family began. My mother was a Denholm, from the Newmains district. Musically, the family interest was twofold – my father played the 'box', or accordion, and was involved in almost every local function, playing at dances, dinners and local gatherings of all kinds, either as a solo performer, or with his band, which was a trio, consisting of accordion, dulcimer and piano. On my mother's side was the great choral tradition – church choirs, and the Wishaw and District Choir, of local prominence in music.

My family recollection of music was in the home. We had a piano, and it was almost inevitable for every member of the family to be 'put to music'. My eldest sister, Ella, was taught piano by Cathy Lauder, a much respected piano teacher. My eldest brother, Bob, played the accordion. David (or Denny, as he is known), was a brass bandsman, playing euphonium at Newmains and Shotts. Agnes, my older sister by fourteen months, played the piano. By the time I got round to music, the singing side of the family made its presence felt, and I was to be the singer.

My earliest recollections were of singing in the house, in the weekly rehearsal sessions. My father, a self-taught musician, was very strict, not quite having the knowledge, but having a very keen ear, and a *passion* for his family to do well in music.

My mother was by far the greater influence on me. She was like many Scottish mothers – keen on education and enlightenment, always quick to point out, by example, the way to a fuller experience of life and music, by recommending that we worked to break out of the confining circle of working-class existence – not that she was ashamed of being working class, but always giving us advice on the alternative way of life that was to be had by those of ability and dedication.

Ours was a very happy family, and quite unique in the village in which we grew up. Our house was a 'talking shop', with discussions on many subjects – politics, naturally, but also things beyond the daily grind of work and rest; music and literature were the two things which influenced the path I was to follow. It was not an easy transition, but with the help of family, relatives and many friends, I made a career as a singer.

My first school was Allanton Primary School, and although we did not have a music teacher, our class teacher, Miss Amy Hutchinson, always gave us singing in class, and it was something that I enjoyed tremendously. I seem to remember that we mostly sang Scots songs.

When I went to Secondary School, at Calderhead (Shotts), my

interest in singing was encouraged by my English teacher – a true gentleman called John Louden, who sang in the local male voice choir. He helped me to prepare for the Annual Burns Federation competition for schools, in singing and recitation. My mother was a dedicated Burnsian, giving the Immortal Memory at Womens' Guilds throughout the county, and often replying to the Toast to 'the lassies', so I had great encouragement in the home, as well as at school.

In 1948, I won the premier award, and have my prize to this day – a bound volume of the works of Robert Burns, which has been *my* bible, and which my daughter is also using now in her studies of the poet. I was a boy soprano at that time – or rather, I had an unbroken boy's voice. I can still remember the final concert of the competition. The adjudicator earlier in the day was the eminent Scottish tenor, Robert Wilson, who also introduced the concert of award winners. I sang the beautiful 'Bonny Lass o' Ballochmyle', and all was going well, when nearing the end of the song, my voice cracked, and disappeared. A very compassionate Robert Wilson comforted me, and told the audience that they had been fortunate to hear my last performance as a boy soprano. Nature had taken its course, and it was to be four years before my voice returned, not as a tenor, but as a bass.

I would not like to give the impression that my childhood was only concerned with music and singing. I had a very full life, taking part in my other great love, sport, and football in particular. I played for the Lanarkshire schools' team, and also had a trial for the Scottish schools' team. I had a playing career at junior level, playing for Stoneyburn Juniors, then Muirkirk, and Shotts Bon Accord. I did not make senior grade, but did train at Motherwell, and played for Law Hearts, which was a superb team – I still have a few medals, and a barometer in daily use, won in the 1952–53 season, when we were Cup Winners. I also ran for Lanarkshire Schools, and was in the Shotts Miners Welfare Swimming Team, all of which contributed to an all-round happy and carefree childhood, which has been a great influence on my adult life, and which provides me with many varied and happy memories.

WILLIAM McCUE OBE (BORN 1934) IS AN INTERNATIONAL OPERA SINGER.

PENALTY!

It's a fairly well known fact that I am a loyal supporter of Clydebank Football Club – a somewhat solitary pursuit, I do admit, but one that is ideally suited to my equally well known shy and retiring disposition.

So, on those all-too-frequent occasions when the warmth and company of a 'Bankies' soul-mate is hard to find on the wind-swept terraces of Kilbowie Park, I allow myself the indulgence of a favourite daydream from my personal Big Match memory bank . . .

One of my earliest visits to Hampden was for the Rangers v Morton Scottish Cup Final of 1947–48, a match which split my allegiances in a most painful way. As a Greenockian, I obviously had a very soft spot for my home-town team, but as a pupil of Lenzie Academy, it was a more immediate and insistent demand that was put on my support, as the 'light blues' included in their line-up the school's PT teacher, a fresh-faced youth called Billy Williamson. The match ended in a disappointing 1–1 draw. The replay the following Wednesday evening also looked like petering out into an undistinguished 0–0 affair when suddenly, in the last minute and with the shades of night falling fast, a cross from the left found the ball at bustling Billy's feet and all he had to do was to pop it into the net – which he duly did.

A famous victory – which was cheered to the echo in the Assembly Hall of Lenzie Academy the following morning as our local hero displayed his Cup Winner's Medal. But my pride in Billy was eclipsed only by pride in myself a few days later when, in the annual Staff v Boys match, I was called upon to preserve the honour of the Boys' team when one of our defenders accidentally poleaxed the teachers' centre forward who, coincidentally, had only the previous day dealt out six-of-the-best to that same lad. A penalty kick. No doubt about it. And as the goalkeeper, it was all up to me. But who would take the vital kick? The answer soon became apparent as Billy Williamson placed the ball on the spot, took three or four short steps back, stepped forward, and blasted the ball towards my goal.

Instinctively, I hurled myself to the right – and to my intense surprise, found the ball wedged against my prostrate body. I had actually saved a penalty kick from the same boot that only days earlier had won the Scottish Cup!

Now, there aren't many fourteen-year-olds who can claim that, and I began to have wild fantasies of a glorious career leading me back to Hampden as the last line of defence in the Scottish team.

I have always thought it a cruel irony that the man who *did* keep goal for Scotland for the following three seasons was the man who had failed to stop Billy Williamson – Morton's Jimmy Cowan! Ah, well . . .

'Come on you Bankies!'

JIMMY MACK (BORN 1934) IS A FREELANCE JOURNALIST AND BROADCASTER. HE HAS PRESENTED HIS OWN DAILY RADIO PROGRAMME ON BBC SCOTLAND SINCE JANUARY 1979.

Bill Bryden

'MEMBER 'AT?

When they bombed the distillery, when my native streets flowed whisky for the only time, I was at the breast down in the air-raid shelter. Or so they told me.

'I fought the war for hooligans like you!' So they told me later.

The fever-van. Women at the closemouth in turbans, as they were called, with metal curlers underneath.

'Where is it?'

'Top flat.'

'It's terrible.'

I rushed upstairs to my house on the top flat. As I turned the corner . . . ' 'cuse me, son,' said the fever-man, in his Bovril-coloured uniform. There was my brother, happed in a red blanket, in the stretcher descending to the fever-van.

My mother crying. 'Dip-theria,' she whispered to Mrs Fox. 'Joey Fox! Joey Fox!' seemed to scream the budgie next door. 'Shut up, Joey. What are we gonnae tell 'im?'

I knew. The fever-van is the hearse for children. Sometimes. He didn't die. I still have a brother. Works for the IBM. Hardly see him now.

What you don't know then is that you travel. Carnegie, Graham Bell, doctors, lawyers, rivetters.

It was always called the Ranch. 'The Central Picture House'. Magic! Honest. Johnny Mack Brown (with Raymond Hatton), Hopalong Cassidy (with Andy Clyde), Lash Larue (with Smiley Burnette), The Durango Kid (my favourite), the heroes of Republic and Monogram. Sometimes it was better. Sometimes it was John Wayne. What you don't know then is that it's John Ford.

My Granny used to take me. 'Don't tell your mother.' And in short pants and 'sannies' we walked to the Ranch. There was a fire inside to keep the queue warm and Paddy and Albert chucked you out when you talked back to the film stars. I suppose some of you wanted to be bus-drivers and train-drivers when you grew up. No way. A cowboy for me. But you knew you couldn't. You knew that everybody worked in the shipyard.

Holidays in Campbeltown. Auntie Tina, Anna, Jamie, Bunty Paterson. The sea. Waves. Being sick on the boat. 1949. Three hundred Greenockians spewing their rings up beyond Lochranza. But, 'Arrived safely. Weather fine. Wish you were here'. The mystery tour.

'Is it Clachan or Carradale?'

'Cannae tell ye.'

'Is it Clachan or Carradale?'

'It's a mystery.'

'Look! I went on "the mystery" on Monday night and that was Clachan. I went on "the mystery" last night and that was Clachan as well. But, see Mrs Fielding! She went on "the mystery" on Tuesday and that was Carradale so I want tae know where "the mystery's" goin' the night?'

'It wouldnae be a mystery then, would it?'

'OK. Tell me it's no' goin' tae Clachan. I hate Clachan. Full o' midges.'

'Look, are you comin' or no?'

'Och, passes the night.'

The driver at that moment changed the solution to the mystery and took her to Clachan just for spite.

How can I go back to Campbeltown? I want to take my children. I probably won't. I'm sure it's too . . . changed.

The Coronation. One TV in Carwood Street. Jean Chambers. Number seven. The whole street for the whole day in a two room and kitchen. The fireworks at the end. A Duke of Norfolk production.

'It was like VE Night.'

'Aye. She was lovely.'

'We must get one.'

'Sixty poun's a lotta money.'

'You can rent it frae Clydesdale.'

'Can ye?'

'Sure.'

'Fourteen inch?'

'Aye. It's that cheery. And there's Muffin the Mule for the weans.'

The first night we got the television Leslie Mitchell exploded and no amount of banging brought him back to Alexandra Palace. My father who was rarely furious near did his nut.

'member 'at?

I still went to church then. We sang the Psalms. Crimond. The Auld Hundred. The minister made us famous. My first television was 'Songs of Praise'. Voice broken. A second tenor no less. You don't stammer when you sing. Sunday school prizes. *Coral Island*. You always got *Coral Island*. One day I'll read it. It's bound to be better than *Biggles Hunts Big Game*. English rubbish.

It's odd, though, how superstitious church-going Christians are.

'You don't live in number thirteen do you?'

'Green. You're always wearing green.' Of course, there's prejudice there too. I still don't walk under ladders. Not if I can help it. If I really have to I pray, briefly. Is that prayer? Yes it is. Eyes tight shut as we were as children in the hard, dark polished pew.

I still go to church sometimes. Weddings and funerals and to pray. It's not talking to myself, is it? It's strange that in churches from Buenos Aires to Connemara no matter how decorative, how beautiful, how different, real church is Cartsburn on the hill above the shipyard down the street from St Laurence's where the Catholics used to go.

My father was an Elder. He didn't hate Catholics. He didn't hate anybody except fanatics . . . Hitler, the Masons. He was a good man. When Paddy said his prayers, his rosary in his hand, in the upstairs room kneeling before my father's coffin, the Old Firm game at Ne'erday didn't make sense. I suppose Belfast's worse.

Church had the Sunday school picnic. That took place on the summer Saturday with the highest rainfall. We invented indoor sprinting on the station platform or under the covered bit of the pier.

The church had the Boys Brigade camp. That took place on the summer fortnight with the highest rainfall. Thunder stopped the tent building and by evening you're wondering why thirty boys are sleeping on straw in a cold church hall in Lamlash. You couldn't say you were homesick, of course, but Scutari's no fun.

I never joined the church. By that time I had discovered Sartre and Kerouac and Allen Ginsberg and Faulkner and it was fashionable to have doubts.

From *Jock Tamson's Bairns*, ed. Trevor Royle (Hamish Hamilton, 1977)

BILL BRYDEN IS A PLAYWRIGHT, AN ASSOCIATE DIRECTOR OF THE NATIONAL THEATRE, AND HEAD OF DRAMA, BBC SCOTLAND.

Arnold Kemp

OUT FOR A DUCK

Into every childhood, as into every life, a little rain must fall. When I was about ten, growing up near the Water of Leith in a district of north Edinburgh called Puddocky because of its riverside frogs, the summer rains gave me an early taste of guilt.

The gardens of our terrace ran down to the river and were separated from it by a wall. The Water of Leith, where we fished for minnows and dodged the leeches that lurked in its mud, was mostly an insignificant stream; but in spate it grew brown, swift and menacing.

Some neighbours, a most likeable English family one of whose daughters is now a well-known actress, acquired a duck to keep in the garden. Hens were more the thing in those days after the War; but in their eccentric way our friends preferred a duck.

They decided that it would prosper more if it could have access to the river and decided to make an opening for it in the wall, much in the way that a hatch may be let into a door for the nocturnal passage of cats.

A few of the local urchins, myself among them, were asked to help, and a merry little party we were. Armed with primitive tools like old bits of railing and iron bars, we spent a most agreeable summer's evening knocking a hole in the wall. We were very proud of that hole and felt the glow of achievement.

Some weeks later we went on holiday to the depths of Angus. Newspapers then did not penetrate to the head of Glen Clova until the day after publication, and the first we knew that anything was amiss was a telegram from my grandmother saying cheerfully: DON'T WORRY. FIREMEN PUMPING WATER OUT. My father's face went as black as the Angus skies and he departed rapidly to Edinburgh.

At home he found an appalling mess. The summer rains had produced an enormous spate. The swollen Water of Leith had poured through the wretched duck's hole in the garden. Its force knocked down the dividing wall, wrecking the Lord Provost's garden which he had primped and manicured in preparation for that year's festival. Then it flooded the houses, inundating the whole district.

When the waters fell and the silt was cleared from countless basements, our English friends encountered a certain froideur and found it necessary to move. My father's reflections were particularly rueful, since he and my mother had, shortly before our holiday, been at the dinner party where the duck had been on the menu. Eventually he came to see the funny side of the story. I was able to confess my part in the crime; and he dined out on that duck for the rest of his life.

ARNOLD KEMP (BORN 1939) IS EDITOR OF *THE GLASGOW HERALD*. HIS FATHER WAS THE PLAYWRIGHT AND NOVELIST, ROBERT KEMP.

Magnus Linklater

THE STRAP

———

Nigg School's a good school,
It's made o' stone and plaster;
The only thing that's wrong wi' it,
There's a bald-headed master . . .

It is not, however, Mr Miller's baldness that I remember. It is his temper. As we sat in the juniors, copying Miss Pirie's handwriting from the blackboard onto our squeaking slates, we could hear from the next-door room the occasional and disturbing sounds of it.

Mr Miller's temper took two forms. One was an oceanic storm of rage which rattled the thin partition between us and the senior class. The other, much more dreadful, was the strap. Its sound came through like a rifle shot, bracketed by silence, or, if we strained to hear it (and we did), by small stifled sobs.

We juniors next door knew intimately the details of Mr Miller's strap, though none of us had ever seen it. Unlike Miss Pirie's, which was a mere strip of leather, Mr Miller's was a weapon of vengeance, black with age and hardened by constant use. At one end it was sliced into three thongs. And each thong had been knotted twice.

The knots, we understood, had been placed in such a way that when the upturned hand was struck, the first row of knots whipped into the palm while the second row landed with centrifugal ferocity on the wrist. That, at least, is what we had been told.

So, when Eddie Robertson and I took up smoking in the woods, we knew perfectly well what the penalty was. Smoking was a crime which only the Head could deal with.

'Are you feared of the strap?' I asked Eddie.

'I'm no feared of the strap,' he answered. 'But I'm feared of the knots.'

The smoking itself was no fun at all. But neither Eddie nor I would have dreamt of admitting that. It was the thing to do, and we did it most days, in the bushes down by the burn, out of sight of the playground and Miss Pirie. As a matter of ritual, I slipped into my father's study before leaving home in the morning, and scooped a handful of cigarettes from his big blue box of Player's Navy Cut. Eddie and I puffed enthusiastically, turned a little green and covertly stubbed our fags out as soon as was decently possible.

All might have been well . . . No, our security was so bad, we were bound to be caught in the end. But we sealed our fate early on when we conducted a Viking raid on one of the lassies' 'homes' in the wood – a patch of earth, lovingly swept, then delicately furnished with piles of broken crockery.

I can't remember why we did it. It was probably as random in intention as most Viking raids; it was certainly every bit as damaging. By the time we had finished, the crockery was scattered and the earthen floor scuffed up by our tackety boots; Maisie Swanson's little domestic sanctuary had been reduced to a midden, and Maisie herself to tears. I think . . . I hope . . . that I can still feel the uncomfortable twinge of guilt as we completed our act of calculated vandalism.

Small wonder that Masie and her friends retaliated. Immediately after break, they cliped on us. Cliping was normally the school's one unforgivable sin, but in this case it may have been justified. They cliped on Eddie and me to Miss Pirie, and Miss Pirie cliped, officially, to Mr Miller.

That afternoon, the two of us were summoned from our desks and told to report to the senior classroom. It had been emptied, like a parade ground before an execution. Mr Miller stood, legs apart, wielding, not the famous strap, but a long black-painted bamboo cane, used normally to indicate his chalk scrawls on the blackboard, but on this occasion to emphasize his anger.

I remember nothing of what he said, only the roaring sound of it. I noticed, however, that he seemed to be less bald than the school song suggested; there were definite tufts of iron grey hair standing up, perhaps in fury, around his ears. Mesmerized, Eddie and I watched as he turned to his desk, pulled out a drawer and drew from it the strap.

We both saw it at the same time. And it had *no* knots. It was neither dark with use, nor was it hard. Indeed, it looked to us a little limp. It was certainly no more fearsome than the one Miss Pirie regularly used.

The pain from the six blows on our upturned palms, delivered alternately to each hand, was muffled by our surprise and overwhelming relief. We emerged from the senior classroom damp-eyed, but delighted.

'What happened to Mr Miller's strap?' I asked Garry Ross, who knew everything, as we recovered in the playground afterwards.

'Och, it was stolen,' he said in a matter of fact way. 'Someone took it during the tattie-picking.'

'And he never got it back?'

'Ay, but not the way he wanted. Whoever took it chopped it into wee pieces and then sent them back in an envelope. Miller was hopping mad.'

I believed it. I believed that the strap had been taken, and I believed that it had existed, knots and all. I still do – with all the conviction of a long and deeply-etched memory. But I wish I could have seen it for myself. Just to be absolutely sure.

There was no chance of asking the one person who could have told me. Shortly afterwards Mr Miller retired and Mr Nicholson arrived – a jolly man with a great thatch of red hair. Naturally, we had to change the school song:

Nigg School's a good school,
It's made o' stone and plaster,
The only thing that's wrong wi' it,
There's a hairy-headed master.

MAGNUS LINKLATER (BORN 1942) IS AN AUTHOR AND JOURNALIST. HIS FATHER WAS THE NOVELIST ERIC LINKLATER.

Jackie Stewart

UNWILLINGLY TO SCHOOL

—

When I think back to my childhood, I think of school, which sadly was the unhappiest period of my life. I hear parents constantly saying to their children and to young people in general, 'You'll never have it so good. You'll look back with fond memories. You'll realize in later years how lucky you were to have the camaraderie school provides.' For me none of those things is true.

When I was young, almost from the very beginning as I remember it, school hung over me like a thunder cloud. I simply was not a good student. In fact I was very poor in the learning process. In the end I was considered dumb, stupid and thick because I could not keep up with the rest of the children in whatever class I was in. It was therefore with great relief to all concerned when, at fifteen, I was able to part company with my formal education and go to work in a garage.

When I think back now I am only frustrated. Because I know a little more about what learning disabilities are and what dyslexia is, it perhaps annoys me a little more that people did not realize that maybe there was something in Jackie Stewart which would allow him to learn, if they used a different method of teaching. But in those days, it seems, people did not realize there was such a thing as a 'learning disability'. I was lucky, I was able to overcome my academic inabilities to work well with my hands, to get on with people, and in later life God blessed me by affording me the talent to drive racing cars.

The happiest time of my school life was every day at 4 o'clock when the bell went. I made my merry way by bicycle back to the village of Dumbuck – now called Milton – and more often than not worked on the farm next door to my father's garage, or in the garage itself. In both of those activities I was able to use my energy and my non-scholastic talents, and was rewarded with praise and appreciation for the effort I put into my small duties. I can assure you, it was most rewarding to be praised for something.

Around the time I left school, I started clay-pigeon shooting and I found I could be good at that, and for the first time in my life was told that I was really good at something. Not only was I told, but it was evident, in that I was actually beating other people doing exactly the same thing. I went on to shoot for Scotland and then for Britain and, when I think back, unquestionably I put much more into my shooting than I ever did to my motor racing because of course it was my first love. It was my first experience in life where I could stand up and be counted with pride.

Even having gone through all I did during my turbulent years at school, I did not identify the problem my sons were having, nor did the school they attended. It wasn't until they changed schools at the ages of twelve and fourteen that their new masters identified in both of them, to some extent, a learning disability. When they found out, it was an enormous relief to them to know that they were not thick, stupid or dumb – I know the feeling. They are both now overcoming the problem and experiencing stimulation and enjoyment from their school years.

So, unlike many children, my happiest years came after childhood.

JACKIE STEWART OBE (BORN 1939) WAS WORLD CHAMPION MOTOR RACING DRIVER IN 1969, 1971 AND 1973. IN ALL, HE WON 27 GRAND PRIX RACES.

Hamish Brown

THE PRICELESS GIFTS

The one thing we cannot choose in life is parents.

The longer I live the more I realize how lucky we three Broon boys were in our parents and how much their quiet enthusiasms were to influence me personally. Mother was born in Siam, daughter of a Scots engineer. Father, though born in Dunfermline, became a banker abroad after the First War (in which he was taken prisoner). Brothers and sisters scattered to Ireland, Cyprus and South Africa, and cousins even further afield. My big brother was born in Scotland, I was born in Colombo and my wee brother came on the scene in Japan, in 1939. We formed our own mini League of Nations.

Unlike many British in the waning of the Empire, we stayed a family unit. There was an *amah* certainly, and servants enough to cook and clean and drive, but we would go swimming together, rather than parents going off to the club and kids to *their* places. Father considered golf a rather ridiculous way of spoiling a good walk. We all walked. In Japan, they went up Fuji Yama and I peered forlornly from the window seat hoping to see them on the mountain forty miles away. Twenty years later they could squash their bumptious climbing offspring with sentences starting, 'When you have actually climbed as high as we have . . .' Eventually I did – and theirs is the blame!

We fled down the Malay peninsula as the war advanced and were lucky to escape before the fall of Singapore. Father disappeared. His ship was sunk and only after many adventures were we all reunited as refugees in South Africa. That wide and spacious landscape was my first mountain kingdom. The Valley of the Thousand Hills. Evocative name. I wandered off into it, even became blood-brother to the son of a Zulu chief, who was then booted out of our cottage when the proprietor found us there together playing with the Hornby trains. Asked what I wanted to be when I grew up I replied, 'A man who stops wars'. The wide-open spaces, freedom to roam, appreciation of all living things, these were the priceless gifts of my parents.

The rest of schooldays passed living in Dollar, one of the Hillfoot towns under the scarp of the Ochils. They were not the happiest days of my life and National Service in the RAF was a fantastic release from the false disciplines and standards of school. I received more beltings for asking WHY than for any other reason. Fortunately there were a few teachers who could reach me, and now, with hindsight, I see the role they played was vital. Art, English, Natural History, History and Geography were my joys, because they were made so, and now, years on, they are the basis of my livelihood. In South Africa, I had been top in Afrikaans but languages were hopeless thereafter, while maths and science were closed mysteries. I worked at what I liked and understood. Understanding and enthusiasm are teacher-pupil infections as much as original manifestations.

English came easily. I can remember vividly the day when I'd finished my set work and was beginning to be a nuisance. The teacher came over and quietly put an open book before me; 'Read that,' he said. I read the lines beginning, 'The isles of Greece, the isles of Greece!' – and life was never the same again.

My own enthusiasms received overmuch attention, no doubt. For years I was a fanatic genealogist (of kings and queens) and a whole wall of my bedroom was covered with a linked study of the world's rulers. Massive volumes of Strickland's *Queens of England* were devoured as if no more than lettuce. Reading before the fire, with classical records being played, is an abiding memory. We all read voraciously. I still do. We were all walkers and rambled extensively around and over the Ochils, we were all keen gardeners and many a plant found its way into the garden from the wilds. Youth has the time for enthusiasms. Lucky the person where many of them stick. As a teacher myself later on, a constant sorrow was seeing youthful enthusiasms evaporate into dull adulthood.

> Does wonder last but a single day?
> Does age tarnish? Green dragons slay?

The Ochils were my special kingdom and eventually a small gang of us came together. We roamed these grassy hills in all seasons and weathers, a valuable apprenticeship. We only ever met one adult regularly, W. K. Holmes, himself a mountain author, poet, and enthusiast for many things. He would smile as we nailed routes up the quarry (we had no pitons) or chopped an ice ascent up Kemp's Score to the castle with an axe borrowed from the woodshed. He *understood*. Cards in his spidery hand followed me about the world during National Service days; one would always come after the latest writing effort had appeared in the school magazine, or the old *Bulletin* (Tammy Troot and all that) or, great day, the *Scots Magazine*, where his own work was seen. Dear W.K.H. People like him, and my parents, taught by example. They were people of high ideals and honour, virtues sadly tarnished today. My book heroes were Robert the Bruce, Bonnie Prince Charlie, Claverhouse, Gino Watkins, Shipton and Tilman, later W. H. Murray. Cycling and walking took us into the Highlands and Islands every holiday. My first summit was Ben Nevis, alone, in mist, aged about fourteen. You put legs to your dreams then, rather than waiting for life to come on a plate.

Youth was still a world of open spaces (this fantastic Scotland), freedom to roam, appreciation of all living things, and of books, books and books. I am still unwrapping that priceless gift half a century later.

HAMISH BROWN (BORN 1934) IS A MOUNTAINEER, POET, PHOTOGRAPHER AND AUTHOR.

THE BURMA STAR

My father kept his medals in a cardboard Rolls Razor box in the top drawer of the tallboy. There were about a dozen of them; those from his father's war as well as his own. The medals were heavy and richly embossed, tied with brightly striped ribbons. My da didn't seem to think much of them. He reserved a particular contempt for the men who wore them pinned to the breast of their dark blue suits on Remembrance Sunday. 'The Pay Corps Heroes', he called such old soldiers in a derisive tone; I didn't know why. I wished he'd wear them himself.

Across the street from us was an old engineering works which now held a handful of lathes, and a handful of men to work them. In good weather the men would sometimes stand outside for their tea breaks. They drank out of tin cans, hot and tarnished, and rolled cigarettes as they talked. Sometimes they kicked a football about, keeping the ball up in the air with their feet, taking off their oily caps to head the ball to each other. They shouted and fought each other, and they laughed brashly and often. They were fascinating as all workmen are to small boys and to old women. I suppose that working men hold no glamour for young girls dreamily in love with dukes and fairy princes; those realities would dash the glass slipper of romance into a thousand shards. But to old women such men reminded them of their own time when their men had muscled backs and heavy arms to hold them. And to small boys workmen were a race of noble savages whose mothers had no powers over them at all.

Sometimes I tried to imagine my da at work. It was strange to think of him living somewhere else during the day, of him talking to other men like him, but men I didn't know. Strange to think that they would go home to small boys like me, to mothers like mine; would sit by the fire at night with their braces hanging and their collars lying on the sideboard, the tie coiled and shiny half inside. In the day they inhabited a different world, a world where they sweated and swore, where it was a grown-up and important world. I liked it when my da talked about his work, ignoring us children. I liked the names of people who were my father's workmates. I imagined faces for them. The workmen across the road were like that, like the faces I fitted to the ghosts my father brought home with him at night in his talk of work.

Sometimes my father had all day Saturday off. When that happened he would have a lengthy breakfast and then sit out on the steps of the close, smoking and reading his paper in the sun. He had a peculiar and inordinate interest in newspapers, I found, and no amount of interruption on my part could divert him. There was an endless supply of amiable and non-committal grunts instead of replies, and he could go on for hours without listening to you at all. It could drive you daft.

This Saturday he sat out on the steps reading the paper. I heard the factory whistle blow shrilly and strode across the street to watch the workmen streaming out. Some were already dressed in their Saturday suits. Most of the older men wore their overalls still, piece tins under their arm. One of them ruffled my hair as he passed. They were snapping on bicycle clips and rolling up their gear. Exciting as boys they were, noisy and cheerful. A young man called over to me. 'Sonny,' he said quietly. He was a youngish man, small and slightly built with dark hair and eyes. 'Here's a wee present fur ye, son,' he said as he pressed something hard and metallic in my hand. 'Ah've nae use for it.' I looked down at the object in my hand. It was of brownish metal, carved in the shape of a star. There was a design of some kind on it and some letters, and a pretty ribbon was tied to it. The small young man turned back to his mates.

I ran back to the close and to my father still reading on the steps. 'Look, Da!' I cried, 'Look what a man just gave me!' My father took the medal from my outstretched palm and looked intently at it. 'What is it, David?' I heard my mother ask from our doorway. 'Something a chap gave the boy,' my father answered. My mother appeared at his shoulder. Da turned the medal over in his hand. 'It's the Burma Star,' my father said softly, half to himself. 'That was a bad one,' he said. 'The Burma Star,' he repeated, 'poor bastard.'

He made me point out my benefactor; I began to think I had done something wrong. The thin dark man was walking slowly down the road, somehow quiet among all the whistling and cheerful shouts all around him. My father hurried across the street and started to talk to the young workman. I could not hear anything of their conversation. The other men walked on, leaving my father and their workmate talking together. I saw my father press the medal back on the man, and offer him a cigarette. Then they both walked down the street and turned into the public house at the corner.

My mother and I stood at the close mouth still; I didn't understand anything and I pulled at her apron. 'Does my da know that man?' I asked. 'No,' she said, and looked down at me. Suddenly she drew herself up, as though she had just come to a decision. 'Away you go and wash your hands, son,' she said. 'You'll get your dinner shortly.' I went along the dark walls of the close and into the house. But my mother stayed where she was, looking into the distance, as though she was waiting for my father to come back, as once she had done before.

JACK MCLEAN, A COLUMNIST ORIGINALLY ON *THE SCOTSMAN*, NOW HAS HIS OWN REGULAR COLUMN IN *THE GLASGOW HERALD*.

Trevor Royle

AN ENGLISHMAN ABROAD

By the time I got to secondary school – Madras College in St Andrews – I had learned enough to get by and to survive and, more importantly from a child's point of view, to merge into the background. I remained on the outside, keen to get on but not willing to involve myself too deeply. I could never (and this *was* a test) feel the intense dismay and dislike of the English that my friends felt. And why should I have, being one myself? No matter how hard I tried, my innate (to my fellows soft) southern background betrayed me. I even felt my too obvious name to be some sort of treason and longed for the simplicity of a more usual name. I knew when it was necessary to hold my tongue and surely that is the supreme English vice?

Not that as schoolchildren there was any deep understanding of Scotland, her past, her traditions and her possibilities. North Sea Oil was still in the future and loyalties to Scotland owed more to Jimmy Shand and to the White Heather Club than to any social or political reality. That that should have been the case was partly due to the education system which was then rooted in the idea that a complete education based on the classics with a grounding in the sciences was the key that opened all doors. In their approach our teachers were more like the old village dominies who turned out lads o'pairts, pupils who had a solid factual grounding in the arts and sciences. Men like Thomas Chalmers, Duncan Mac-Laren or Thomas Guthrie, the great social reformers of the nineteenth century. In case any of my old teachers read this, let me say that I make this comparison not out of criticism, but out of an understanding of what they were trying to do. It was we, their pupils, who were out of sympathy and growing away too quickly from a kind of Scotland that was gradually fading into memory.

But of Scotland's real past we knew little. Culloden was the necessary and probably deserved putting down of a rebellion against authority. Gaelic was a dead language spoken by the people killed at Culloden. The Clearances were part of the world movement of peoples. Bagpipe music was the school band. The Industrial Revolution was a good thing that gave work to all those Highlanders who had gone down to Glasgow. Maclean and Maxton? Didn't they play for Third Lanark? There was no essential grounding in the political facts of Scotland's past, no intellectual debate or analysis about what had happened, why it had happened and what might be done to prevent it from happening again. We knew more about the Risorgimento than we did about the Land League resistance on Skye.

Sport gave the best clue to patriotic feelings for Scotland and provided a national focus, especially when Scotland played England at football or at rugby. Madras was a rugby-playing school albeit not a very distinguished one. The idea that football should be played as well had been discussed in the twenties but had been dismissed as a silly season aberration. Nevertheless it was the game that dominated most of our childhoods in one way or another. We supported teams which to us were only names, played twenty-a-side football on the damp corporation park on

Saturday afternoons, headers against walls, kicking tennis balls along pavements and endless games of keepie-uppie and three and in. As far as I can remember there was no social differentiation about playing football or rugby and most of us played both, rugby for a school team in the morning and football for our enjoyment in the afternoon.

The greatest test though was at rugby and it came every second year at Murrayfield when Scotland played England (Wales and Ireland one year, France and England the next). Although it was expected of all of us to support Scotland with an undying devotion I cannot remember ever going to a match wholeheartedly expecting Scotland to win. Neither did many of my friends and we would sit gloomily in the train to Edinburgh forecasting yet another miserable defeat. Except against England. Then it was all bravado with myself keeping a wary silence or sporting a cocky indifference. It didn't matter who had won – on the return journey either I had to stifle my joy or I joined in the general despondency. Scotland never seemed to win in the fifties.

Looking back, I am sure that those were the heights of nationalism for me to climb and yet they were such gentle foothills that it would be wrong to give a bleak picture of a childhood spent in isolation because I had been, so to speak, born on the wrong side of the blanket. It would be convenient and perhaps half truthful to say that there was a sense of duality in my childhood. Living in Scotland, English but half Scottish and yet orphaned from the country to the south. Every year when my brother and I were dispatched to England to spend summer holidays with relatives a curious transformation took place. When we were in Scotland we were inescapably English, but in the south the mantle of the Scot was thrust upon us. Despite our surnames we were 'Scotties' or 'Jocks' and people smiled at the way we rolled our 'r's (how I tired of that sly joke). After a week or two we became more Scottish than the Scots and in the absence of critical countrymen arrogantly boasted about our adopted country's superiority. I was constantly aware that Scotland was a different place and my links with both countries only served to make the disparities more clearly and sharply defined. I grew to understand my friends' gut reactions to England and their feelings of inadequacy when they looked back at the two centuries of political partnership between the two countries. The Union of 1707 had been an awkward way of doing things and many Scots still smarted with shame at the nature of the joining together of the two very different peoples.

My English relatives certainly didn't see it in that light and it was here that the Scotch comic had made such a mark on the British imagination. Scotland for the rest of my family was a country of quaint, hairy-kneed and parsimonious old men who went about muttering into their whisky: 'It's a braw bricht moonlicht nicht the nicht, ye ken.' Such smiling small talk was calculated to bring out in me feelings of intense moral indignation which never failed to amuse my uncles and aunts.

I always rose to the bait, too.

From *Jock Tamson's Bairns* (Hamish Hamilton, 1977)

TREVOR ROYLE (BORN 1945) IS A FULL-TIME WRITER AND REGULAR BROADCASTER, AND AUTHOR OF *THE MACMILLAN COMPANION TO SCOTTISH LITERATURE*. HE WAS LITERATURE DIRECTOR OF THE SCOTTISH ARTS COUNCIL 1971–79.

Malcolm Rifkind

ALL THOSE IN FAVOUR . . .

My schooldays were a period of very modest academic achievement and minimal sporting accomplishment. As a result I was both happy and content.

In one vital respect, however, my future life was influenced, if not determined, by an unexpected initiative on the part of my English master. At the age of thirteen, I was asked by him to be one of the two opening speakers in a junior debating society he was establishing at my school. Why he asked me I am not very clear. Apart from having acted the title role in a class play about Christopher Columbus, I had shown, so far as I am aware, no theatrical or exhibitionist tendencies.

My debating debut was not very auspicious. I had been given

the task of leading the opposition to a motion that condemned television as a harmful influence on the young. As the audience consisted entirely of schoolboys one might have expected my task to be easy. I failed. Despite (or because of) my oratorical prowess, these modern schoolboys rejected television as if it was the devil incarnate, and did so by a healthy majority.

Undaunted by this humiliation, I found that I had discovered an activity that I enjoyed and which has kept me enslaved ever since. School debates had their own particular charm. They were boisterous, funny, no-holds-barred occasions with no quarter asked for or given. I still have an old school notebook with the notes I prepared at that time for many of these debates. I spoke strongly in favour of the Press in a motion that declared, 'That Newspapers had done more for Education than the History Books'. It appears that I excluded the popular press from this praise, a view which I would still strongly endorse. I concluded that my school colleagues' education had benefited more from reading newspapers than from reading about the Peloponnesian War. I doubt whether Mr Enoch Powell would agree.

I am relieved to see that I was a great defender of Mr Macmillan's government, at that time managing to quote in support Disraeli, Shaftesbury and the Duke of Wellington. Not only had we never had it so good, but I also challenged my opponents to identify another time when you could not have told margarine from butter!

These youthful flights of rhetoric also included the occasional mock elections which were a great feature of school debating, and gave rise to the birth of many new and short-lived political parties. I recall 'Ilikeme' (which turned out to be I like Me) and 3D (Doom Death and Destruction). I even founded my own one-man party, which actually won with a ragbag of policies I do not care to remember.

University provided new opportunities for these youthful follies. On one occasion I had to represent Edinburgh at an inter-university debate in Dublin. My unhappy task was to propose the motion, 'That the Republic of Ireland should rejoin the Commonwealth'. We did not win. On another evening I travelled to Newcastle to propose, 'That a Regional Accent is not a Social Handicap.' Any inherent prejudices of my Geordie hosts must have been magnified when I turned up wearing a kilt borrowed for the occasion from my fellow student, James Douglas-Hamilton.

My favourite recollection of these days is presiding at a meeting addressed by Lord Hailsham before an audience of at least a thousand Edinburgh students. As he launched into spontaneous oratory a long-haired lout in the gallery kept shouting, 'Hogg, you're a fascist.' After the third such interruption, Hailsham stopped in full flood, pointed an accusing finger at his tormentor and declared, 'Young man, I have the wounds of fascism upon my body – which is more than can be said for you!' Not another peep was heard.

Public speaking had its heyday many years ago. Today that same television that I unsuccessfully defended in my youth has made politics an armchair ordeal or entertainment, depending on your preference. No great public meetings take place even during general elections and the speeches of the great often seem less inspiring than telephone directories and just as long.

But, for me, there is no substitute for a packed House of Commons chamber or even a draughty, heckler-infested village hall. Politics in a democratic society means communication, and only the spoken word can both inspire and educate in a natural and unaffected manner.

I would insist that every school needs a debating society far more than it needs a computer. For a free society, it is essential.

MALCOLM RIFKIND (BORN 1946) IS MINISTER OF STATE AT THE FOREIGN OFFICE.

Andy Irvine

FOOTBALL CRAZY

My earliest memories are not of Scotland, but of Africa. I was the youngest of the family by a long way – my two elder brothers had left home by the time I was born. My father was in 1955 appointed to an engineering post in northern Nigeria, and my mother took me out to visit him.

I remember the heat and the sun and the unspoilt bush, where I played all day, with a dog and the son of the cook for company. He and I got on famously. He didn't have much English, but I reckon at the age of four I wasn't much of a conversationalist either.

My brothers had left school when they were sixteen. My father, who had had no higher education, was determined that I should go to University, for he said that if you did that, you were set up for life. It was always drummed into me that I needed to pass my examinations. So I had to become reasonably conscientious at school work, even if my first instinct was to go out and kick a football around.

As the first step on the educational ladder, I was sent to James Gillespie's junior school. It was two bus journeys away from where we lived in Liberton. I felt odd at first, putting on a uniform and going away to school, when all the boys I knew went to local schools. The first thing I did when I got home every day was to strip off my school uniform and go out and play football, from 3.30 until it was time for supper at 5 – even if it was raining or snowing.

My father was to die when I was sixteen. Up till then we used to see him twice a year, when my mother took me to Nigeria for the summer holidays, and when he came home on leave, which usually coincided with Christmas. Because I had never known any other kind of life, this did not seem strange to me until I was in my teens. Especially I missed him when all the other dads used to come and watch their sons play rugby on Saturdays. He could only be there for the two or three matches while he was on leave. He never played rugby himself, but he was interested in anything I did. My mother could never understand the game at all. In fact, she has only been to one match in her life – Scotland v England, a few years back. Her first question after a match was always, and still is, 'Are you all right?' Today, she is satisfied on this count if she manages to see my name on the score-line in the paper.

I played my first game of rugby at thirteen, when I went to George Heriot's School. I think I had only watched one game before that. I was taken to Murrayfield, but I was so small that all I could see were the heads of the crowd in front of me and occasionally the ball sailing up into the sky.

At Heriot's we were given a choice of rugby or cross-country. I opted to run the shorter distances, and found myself in the trial for the first-year fifth and sixth teams. After ten minutes, during which I had scored quite a few tries, I was promoted to the senior trial. Here the boys knew a bit about the game, and I couldn't run riot! However, I was a reasonably fast runner, and I was put into the first XV of my year that same afternoon.

It was not an easy season, though. There was the match against Dollar Academy – away. To go on a bus for that distance was for me like going to Tokyo. The journey must have taken two hours or more. Dollar had one player of gigantic size. Every time he got the ball, he simply ran straight through us. We were all very upset about it afterwards and reckoned it was unfair. We then beat Edinburgh Academy 6–3. I was twice tackled very hard by a thoroughly aggressive, as I thought at the time, lad with striking blond hair. He was Norman Morrison, and we played against each other right the way through our respective schools, and then together for Scottish Schoolboys. Later, he was in the Scotland B squad.

That is one of the things about playing rugby in Scotland. After one of my tours with the British Lions, I went to Merchiston to talk to some of the younger boys. A bright, perky young teenager asked most of the questions. I thought he deserved encouragement, and I explained that if he really got 'stuck in' and trained hard, he might make the grade at top level. He did, and he is still perky. His name is Roger Baird, and a few years after that incident, he and I were playing alongside each other for Scotland.

ANDY IRVINE (BORN 1951) HAS PLAYED RUGBY FOR SCOTLAND 51 TIMES, 15 OF THEM AS CAPTAIN, AND HOLDS THE WORLD RECORD FOR POINTS SCORED IN INTERNATIONAL MATCHES. HE IS A PARTNER IN AN EDINBURGH FIRM OF CHARTERED SURVEYORS.

Helen Joseph

AFRICAN CHILDHOOD

My 'Scottish' childhood was spent in the middle of Central Africa, but in a country so marked by Scotland that a link is natural. I look back now on what seemed then – through the eyes of a child – to be normal. I compare the climate, language, flora and fauna, smells, colours, architecture, music and dress of sub-tropical Malawi with palaearctic Aberdeenshire. And if I try to isolate the essential detail that makes a childhood memory 'Scottish' it is almost always to compare it with Africa. But was it the picture of Scotland established in Scotland, or was it Scotland seen from Africa? Both existed.

Any expatriate Scot knew the clichés of tourist-guide, picture-book Scotland – Burns' suppers, Bannockburn, national pride, pioneer spirit, glossy pictures of fine buildings and majestic scenery. My childhood Malawi was this, and much more, for the late-Victorian spirit of David Livingstone and the Scottish missions was still very present. The emphasis on a certain strictness of behaviour, the importance of education, the need for standards and a rejection of the purely material were not out of date, against the poverty and pride of developing Africa. The President of Malawi was living proof of this – an elder of the Kirk with a Scottish medical training, he exemplified the link between the two countries. However, I always had difficulty in reconciling the austere granite churches of windswept Peterhead with the more edifying red-brick and thatched roofs of sunny Blantyre – the presence and purpose of the latter seemed so much more real.

I grew up amongst the MacDonalds, the Campbells, the McIntoshes and the McDougalls of the north and west, and the Bruces, Buchans, Strachans and Duthies of my parents' east coast, not to mention names of the early settlers like Moir, Buchanan, Scott and Young.

That names were important was made clear to me the day that we visited a tea planter, who had been born on my great-grandfather's farm in Aberdeenshire the day my grandfather went off to the war in 1918. The child had been named after the departing soldier – I was there when they met again in 1961! After that war, my grandfather studied medicine in Aberdeen. The adjoining tea estate in Malawi was owned by a female fellow-student of his, who went to Nyasaland – as it then was – as a medical missionary, and there married a tea planter also from her home town of Peterhead. Such coincidences illustrated from afar the closeness and fraternity of the Scottish community when it is at home.

When the elder daughter of that contemporary of my grandfather married an Edinburgh doctor, we celebrated in beautiful dresses sent from Jenners specially for the occasion. Never have kilts, lace and jabots looked so colourful, against flame trees, bougainvillaea and fragrant frangipani; nor the sound of the pipes been so glorious as in chorus with humming-birds!

Night falls quickly in Africa, and because of this we had perhaps more time to talk – and listen – in those long evenings when the moths gathered round the Tilly lamps and the noises from the undergrowth started up after the heat of the day. There was no television to provide instant entertainment, and it was at moments like these that I felt a hint of nostalgia and sadness as friends came round to reminisce. We often listened to crackling gramophone records, and although we knew 'Geordie's Byre' and the 'Black Bear', we also knew the laments, and the vanished glory of 'Row, bonnie boat . . .' A young uncle sent out 'A Scottish Soldier' when Andy Stewart reached Top of the Pops in Britain. How we paraded back and forth, loving the stirring beat of the pipes and drums, but already aware of the intensity of '. . . those hills are not Highland hills . . . nor island hills . . . but are far land hills . . .'

Coming home, or perhaps more exactly 'going home' was the moment of truth. We left Blantyre Airport, and after stops in Rome, Paris and London, landed at Dyce, Aberdeen. Dyce, a small county airport, with two flights to London a day! If it was winter, we arrived to rich dark soil and the sound of seagulls wheeling round the tractors as they ploughed the colour back into the land. The cattle were fat and sleek compared with those bony African animals, covered with red dust, and the sheep almost unrecognizable. The cold was so novel that it hardly mattered.

It was not until I was eight that I watched – mesmerized – snow falling in soft, silent flakes which slowly transformed a dark and bleak afternoon into a scene of cotton wool and icing sugar. That was unforgettable, as were the words of my school teacher – 'Sit down, children. You've all seen snow before.'

HELEN JOSEPH (NÉE ROBERTSON, 1956) NOW LIVES IN FRANCE, WHERE SHE IS MARRIED TO A BANKER, AND HAS TWO YOUNG CHILDREN.

Cathie Panton

FAMILY FOURSOME

Home, until I was eighteen, was a flat above the club house of a golf course – Glenbervie, by Larbert. It was, I suppose, an unusual place in which to be brought up, but I never thought of it as out-of-the-ordinary or that I was any different from other kids in school by having a father who was often away, playing in golf tournaments – I remember his presence most, in that in my teens I had to be home every night at 11 o'clock.

To get anywhere was a bus ride, so it was a kind of isolated life, and because my sister was four years older, I often had to find ways of amusing myself: hitting a tennis ball endlessly against a wall ('That'll ruin your golf swing,' members of the club would offer as they passed by), climbing trees, knocking down conkers and hardening them in vinegar to use in games at school, anything, in fact, that called for some energy – at primary school I played football with the boys in the playground. I went on bicycle rides with a girl who lived not so far away, and climbed up the ruined broch on the hill behind Glenbervie, and with my sister explored all the woods around, looking for the first primroses of spring. Then there were games of badminton with her and my mother on the lawn in front of the club house, and golf too, though my mother usually had time only to join us for the last four holes, and my sister tended to lose interest at about the fifth. This may have had something to do with the fact that she swears that on

203

one occasion I hit her over the head with my club while practising an over-ambitious back-swing.

I had winter pursuits, too. When I was about ten, something of my father's interest in horse racing must have rubbed off on me. For two years or so, I studied form in the newspapers, picked winners, and rushed home from school to listen to the results on the radio. If I was late, my mother had to take them down for me. I got quite good at it, which has sometimes stood me in good stead since.

Every summer, my mother took us to stay in a guest house wherever the Open Golf Championship was being played – St Andrews, Troon, Carnoustie, Lytham. We were never allowed actually to watch my father play, in case we put him off, but we saw (and occasionally met) many of the other great players – my mother was a habitual follower of Arnold Palmer. When not watching the golf, we'd go paddling or walk along the beach.

To me, school was mainly a means to get to university, and university a way of getting a good job, which is what I wanted to do rather than just to get married. I always used to see myself as some kind of top business executive, but though I did quite well both at school and university, it was my sister who made the grade. She is an accountant.

Golf was an ever-present pastime, rather than a preoccupation. My father taught me, and I am told that I was hitting balls up from the pro's shop to the club house and back when I was three or four. I started going in for competitions when I was ten, and later managed to win the Stirlingshire girls' championship six times in a row.

My first appearance, however, was not so promising. At one of the nine holes of the under-12s competition, my putt hung on the lip of the hole. So I got down on my hands and knees, and blew it in. A horrified woman official rushed over and fined me innumerable penalty strokes. Even so, I ended up in second place, I think, though needless to say I have never holed out like that since!

A later appearance in the Scottish Girls' Championship, at Edzell, Angus, was rather more successful. I was fourteen, and a no-hoper, playing mainly against girls who were much older, and better, than I was. But on the day, for several days, everything went just right for me, and I found myself in the final, against yet another eighteen-year-old, Alison Coutts, who would, if we had been playing under handicap, have had to give me about six strokes. As it was, we were playing off scratch, and on the 18th green I had an 8-foot putt to square the match. I holed it. At the first extra hole I holed one of 25 feet, and we were level again. I left myself equally long ones, each time to square the match, at the 20th, 21st and 22nd, and they all went in, bang! I wish I could still putt with the deadly abandon of that fourteen-year-old, but it doesn't work that way any more. Anyway, at the 23rd, the fifth extra hole, I played the hole normally, and got a par. Alison could only manage a bogey, and that was the match, and the championship, to me. True to family tradition, my father and mother, who had driven over simply to take me home, stayed in the hotel, unable to bring themselves to watch.

It would be nice to say that that was the first of several titles in that championship. But though I reached the final or semi-final most times, I never won it again. I guess I got more interested in boys than in practising golf . . .

CATHIE PANTON (BORN 1955) WON THE BRITISH LADIES GOLF CHAMPIONSHIP IN 1976. SHE BECAME A PROFESSIONAL GOLFER IN 1979 AND WAS EUROPEAN LADIES CHAMPION IN 1981.

Kirsty Reith

HAPPINESS

I love to see hills in the sun, flowerbeds in bloom, little babies surprises, exciting things, and I love to see the return of my Mu and Dad from their work at the end of the day. The chirping bird in spring, the constant 'tick-tock, tick-tock' of a clock, pe laughing, the pitter-patter of the rain on a window, the nois kettle boiling; I like these sounds.

My favourite tastes are those of blackcurrant cheeseca blackcurrant jam, for I think blackcurrants have a lovely ta I love the crumble and cream on a cheesecake. I beefburgers, sausages, chops and chicken. My reason for this is that beefburgers, sausages and chops have a nice meaty taste. Chicken is tender. I often like having the famous 'Meaux Mustard' with these kinds of meat and poultry. As a Sunday dinner, we might get beef.

Salad is another thing I like, especially if it's made up from Marks and Spencers' things, for they have some super ideas! Crumpets, rolls and hot buttered toast are really tasty according to my tongue.

A wafting smell of a lovely dinner attacks my nose. Smells of toast, the air on a frosty morning, for it is so crisp and fresh. One of my favourite smells is of my toy rabbit. He possesses his own smell, and I cannot fit anything as a description to it. Another smell I like is of wood, burning in our stove.

Doing things. Doing things I like, such as whizzing through the crispy air on a pair of skis. Diving off a high rock into the swimming pool. Playing. Playing with my brother Alistair. Reading, for this can be a varied kind of pastime, depending on what kind of subject the book's based.

Picnics are fun. I love them, especially if I'm with all my family. Soaring into the air in a plane. The take-off is lovely. All these things please me. Each in its own way.

I like to visit places. Sometimes I want to visit the same place again and again, but sometimes I want to explore a new place. It's nice to see beautiful sights, while perhaps having a picnic, or ¹aying. Holidays are probably my favourite type of visiting, for can stay overnight, and wake up to it again in the morning.

` my greatest overall happiness is when my whole family are ⸜nd enjoying themselves as much as I am.

ᴼRN 1973) LIVES IN BRIDGE OF ALLAN. SHE WROTE THIS PIECE WHEN AN EXERCISE IN SCHOOL.